THIS SPECIAL EDITION OF

COMMON SENSE

AND

RIGHTS OF MAN

by Thomas Paine

HAS BEEN PRIVATELY PRINTED
FOR THE MEMBERS OF
THE AMERICAN HERITAGE LIBRARY

THE AMERICAN HERITAGE LIBRARY

PUBLISHED BY PALLADIUM PRESS

Special Contents Copyright © 2000
PALLADIUM PRESS
Post Office Box 530065
Birmingham, Alabama 35253
Printed in the United States of America

INTRODUCTION

By Wayne LaPierre

MOST AMERICANS will probably recall only one quotation of Thomas Paine's: "These are the times that try men's souls." These words were first set forth as the lead sentence of Paine's pamphlet *The American Crisis*.

Paine published *The American Crisis* on December 23, 1776, while he was serving in General George Washington's Continental army at its winter headquarters in Morristown, New Jersey. Several days later, Washington was to achieve two great strategic victories over General Howe's British forces: first, the capture of a Hessian brigade at Trenton on December 26, 1776, after his famous crossing of the Delaware river; and second, the January 3, 1777 victory over Howe's subordinate, General Lord Cornwallis, at Princeton. In a campaign lasting only three weeks, in the dead of winter when traditionally gentlemen-soldiers were not supposed to fight, the military genius of America's greatest gentleman, combined with the fortitude of his five thousand men, had driven the British from New Jersey and saved the American cause.

However, even with these victories, Washington's army was by no means in a comfortable situation. Cornwallis' forces were still on his trail, and his men were cold, malnourished, and dog-tired, frequently falling asleep on the march. In an effort to boost the morale of his troops, Washington, who had been particularly impressed by Paine's pamphlet, ordered that it be read to his troops.

Not only the celebrated first sentence but the entire pamphlet remains worthy of our attention. Here is the stirring first paragraph:

> These are the times that try men's souls. The summer soldier and the sunshine patriot will, in this crisis, shrink from the service of their country; but he that stands it *now* deserves the love and thanks of man and woman. Tyranny, like hell, is not easily conquered; yet we have this consolation with us, that

> the harder the conflict, the more glorious the triumph. What
> we obtain too cheap, we esteem too lightly; it is dearness only
> that gives everything its value. Heaven knows how to put a
> proper price upon its goods; and it would be strange indeed if
> so celestial an article as *Freedom* should not be highly rated.

As felicitous a statement on the value of patriotism as this is, the impact of *The American Crisis* is overshadowed by that of two of Paine's other writings, one written just as hostilities were beginning in the American Revolution, one written long after its conclusion. I am referring, of course, to Paine's two classic writings that are contained in the current volume, *Common Sense* and *Rights of Man*. You will also find at the back of this edition two of Paine's shorter writings: "Letter to Mr. Secretary Dundas," in which he elaborates on his condemnation of the hereditary system of British government; and "Address to the Addressers of the Proclamation" in which Paine rails against the British parliament for bringing a prosecution for seditious libel against him.

When Paine wrote *Common Sense* in late 1775, he had yet to gain a reputation as a political essayist. Indeed, he had yet to gain a reputation for doing anything of distinction or merit whatsoever. The first thirty-seven years of his life, since his birth in Thetford, England on January 29, 1737, were particularly undistinguished.

The son of Joseph Paine, a Quaker corset maker, and Frances Cocke Paine, an Anglican, Paine quit grammar school after seven years to begin an apprenticeship in his father's corset shop in Thetford. After seven years at the corset trade, he became a sailor, serving for six months on the privateer *King of Prussia*. Then he was back to making corsets, opening his own shop in Sandwich, England in 1759. He married Mary Lambert, an orphan employed as a domestic servant, that same year. Mary died while giving birth to their first child, who also died, in 1760.

After his first wife's death, Paine returned to Thetford, where he became an excise officer, or tax collector. However, he was fired from his job for filing a report without having examined the goods. He then returned to corset making, taught school in London, and eventually won reinstatement in the excise service in Lewes, England in 1768. Three years later, he married his second wife, Elizabeth Olive, daughter of a local shopkeeper. They had no children.

It was during this period that Paine began engaging in political debates and writing political pamphlets. Paine later wrote that in his second stint as a revenue officer, he was in a unique position "to see into numerous and various distresses" of ordinary people. However, he was again fired from the revenue service, this time for being absent from his post without leave. He and his second wife separated, and to pay his debts, he was forced to sell his household possessions at public auction.

Soon thereafter, Paine was fortunate to make the acquaintance of a man who knew Benjamin Franklin. Armed with a letter of introduction from his new friend to Franklin, he left England to pursue a new life in the American colonies. There, with Franklin's assistance, he was appointed editor of the *Pennsylvania Magazine*. In 1775, at age thirty-eight, he began writing political essays and poems condemning slavery and supporting abolition.

As the struggle between the American colonies and Great Britain accelerated and war broke out at Lexington and Concord, Paine, then living in Philadelphia, joined a group of advocates of the American cause, including two individuals who would come to be recognized as Founding Fathers of our republic, John Adams and Benjamin Rush.

By the end of 1775, this group had concluded that American independence was inevitable. Recognizing his writing talent, Rush suggested to Paine that he write a pamphlet supporting the idea, cautioning him not to use the word *independence* so as to avoid alarming those who believed that an open avowal of independence would unleash a movement for democratic change within the colonies. *Common Sense* first appeared in print in January, 1776. It quickly became one of the most successful and influential pamphlets in the history of political writing, selling, by Paine's estimate, some 150,000 copies. (Paine directed that his share of the profits be used to buy supplies for the Continental army.)

Common Sense presents a powerful argument for American independence. It is also a vigorous attack on the British Constitution and the principle of hereditary rule. Paine later wrote that the aim of his work was "to bring forward and establish the representative system of government."

The language of *Common Sense* is powerful stuff. "Of more worth is one honest man to society, and in the sight of God," Paine wrote, "than all the crowned ruffians that ever lived."

George III is "the royal brute of England." On the issue of independence, he wrote, "There is something absurd in supposing a continent to be perpetually governed by an island." Towards the end of the pamphlet, he offered an awesome view of the significance of the American Revolution. "We have it in our power to begin the world over again." In a world "overrun with oppression," America alone would be the home of freedom, "an asylum for mankind."

However, *Common Sense* was important to its readers in the colonies (and survived as one of the most important documents in American history) not because of the ideas that Paine advocated — they were the common currency among a number of American patriots — but the way in which he presented them. Here was a new style of political writing directed not merely to the educated elite. Paine assumed knowledge of no authority but the Bible, with which all citizens were familiar, and avoided the florid language common to political pamphlets of the era. His style was the equal of his argument: anyone could grasp the nature of politics and government; all that is required is common sense.

Paine's other writings during this time included *The Crisis Extraordinary* (1780), which urged state governments to levy new taxes to support the war effort; *Public Good* (1780), which argued against Virginia's western land claims, insisting that all such territory belonged to the federal government; and *Dissertations on Government: the Affairs of the Bank; and Paper Money* (1786), which supported the rechartering of the Bank of North America.

Part I of his second most celebrated writing, *Rights of Man,* was published in early 1791. At that time, Paine was living in France, having traveled there in April 1787 in pursuit of one of his scientific interests, the design and construction of a wrought-iron bridge. He was to reside in France until 1802, traveling back and forth between France and England promoting his plan for an iron bridge.

During the same time period the influential Whig Member of Parliament and noted British statesman Edmund Burke published *Reflections on the Revolution in France* in 1790. Burke's work was a bitter criticism of the French Revolution of 1789, particularly its excesses, in Burke's view, in the areas of injustice to individuals, attacks on religion, and its attempts to build a completely new social order. So enraged by the book was Paine that he immediately began writing *Rights of Man,*

Part I. Paines book, dedicated to George Washington, bears the subtitle *An Answer to Mr. Burke's Attack on the French Revolution*. Part vindication of the events in France, part elaboration of the principles of republican government that Paine had earlier supported in the United States, the book was a scathing denunciation of Burke.

But even more radical was Part II, published in 1792. In Chapter Five of Part II, for example, Paine advocated a number of extreme social proposals that surely must have alarmed the Whig politicians in London. Among these proposals was a rudimentary welfare state financed by progressive taxation on property, in which each poor family would receive direct grants from the government to educate its children, workers would receive retirement benefits after age sixty, and public employment would be provided for the "casual poor."

Part II was widely circulated in England. By the end of 1792 it had sold over 200,000 copies. The pamphlet was to inspire an upsurge of radical politics among the "lower and middling" classes of British society. The British government's predictable response was to unleash a wave of political repression against its radical citizens and to indict Paine, in absentia, for the crime of seditious libel.

Paine reinforced his reputation as a radical in later writings, principally *The Age of Reason* (1794), an attack on organized Christianity and the idea that the Bible was divinely inspired; and *Agrarian Justice* (1796), an argument that the ownership of private property in America deprived millions of citizens of their natural right to a portion of the land.

Paine never returned to England and therefore was never brought to trial for his alleged crime of libelous sedition. In 1802, at the invitation of Thomas Jefferson, who was then president, he returned to the United States, where he died in 1809 in Greenwich Village, New York.

Today, Thomas Paine might be called "a piece of work." A fearless propagandist, he aimed in his writings (as well as his personal relationships with colleagues) to be candid rather than tactful. When Ben Franklin once remarked to Paine "Where liberty is, there is my country," Paine replied, "When liberty is not, there is my country."

He consciously determined to be bold and shock his readers into attention. He discredited reactionary ideas with merciless satire. He framed his language so as to "bring out a clear conclusion that [should] hit the point in question and nothing else." He insisted on unrestricted debate, believing that "when opinions are free, either in matters of government or religion, truth will finally prevail."

And as we now know, although some of the ideas he came to champion in his later years were quite radical, many of Thomas Paine's truths did prevail. No less a personage than John Adams observed in 1806: "I know not whether any man in the world has had more influence on its inhabitants or affairs in the last thirty years than Thomas Paine."

Wayne LaPierre

FAIRFAX, VIRGINIA
MARCH 10, 2000

CONTENTS

Common Sense

COMMON SENSE:

———

Man knows no master save creating heaven,
Or those whom choice and common good ordain.
Thomson.

INTRODUCTION.

PERHAPS the sentiments contained in the following pages, are not *yet* sufficiently fashionable to procure them general favor; a long habit of not thinking a thing *wrong*, gives it a superficial appearance of being *right*, and raises at first a formidable outcry in defence of custom. But the tumult soon subsides. Time makes more converts than reason.

As a long and violent abuse of power is generally the means of calling the right of it in question, (and in matters too which might never have been thought of, had not the sufferers been aggravated into the inquiry) and as the king of England hath undertaken in his *own right*, to support the parliament in what he calls *theirs*, and as the good people of this country are grievously oppressed by the combination, they have an undoubted privilege to inquire into the pretensions of both, and equally to reject the usurpations of either.

In the following sheets, the author hath studiously avoided every thing which is personal among ourselves. Compliments as well as censure to individuals make no part thereof. The wise and the worthy need not the triumph of a pamphlet; and those whose sentiments are injudicious or unfriendly, will cease of themselves, unless too much pains is bestowed upon their conversion.

The cause of America is, in a great measure, the cause of all mankind. Many circumstances have, and will arise, which are not local, but universal, and through which the principles of all lovers of mankind are affected, and in the event of which, their affections are interested. The laying a country desolate with fire and sword, declaring war against the natural rights of all mankind, and extirpating the defenders thereof from the face of the earth, is the concern of every man to whom nature hath given the power of feeling; of which class, regardless of party censure, is

THE AUTHOR.

PHILADELPHIA, *Feb.* 14, 1776.

COMMON SENSE.

———

SOME writers have so confounded society with government, as to leave little or no distinction between them; whereas they are not only different, but have different origins. Society is produced by our wants, and government by our wickedness; the former promotes our happiness *positively*, by uniting our affections, the latter *negatively*, by restraining our vices. The one encourages intercourse, the other creates distinctions. The first is a patron, the last is a punisher.

Society in every state is a blessing, but government even in its best state is but a necessary evil; in its worst state an intolerable one; for when we suffer, or are exposed to the same miseries by *a government*, which we might expect in a country *without government*, our calamity is heightened by reflecting that we furnish the means by which we suffer. Government, like dress, is the badge of lost innocence; the palaces of kings are built upon the ruins of the bowers of paradise. For were the impulses of conscience clear, uniform and and irresistibly obeyed, man would need no other lawgiver; but that not being the case, he finds it necessary to surrender up a part of his property to furnish means for the protection of the rest; and this he is induced to do by the same prudence which in every other case advises him out of two evils to choose the least. *Wherefore*, security being the true design and end of government, it unanswerably follows, that whatever *form* thereof appears most likely to insure it to us, with the least expense and greatest benefit, is preferable to all others.

In order to gain a clear and just idea of the design and end of government, let us suppose a small number of persons settled in some sequestered part of the earth, unconnected with the rest, they will then represent the first peopling of any country, or of the world. In this state of natural liberty, society will be their first thought. A thousand motives will excite them thereto; the strength of one man is so unequal to his wants, and his mind so unfitted for perpetual solitude, that he is soon obliged to seek assistance and relief of another, who in his turn requires the same. Four or five united would be able to raise a tolerable dwelling in the midst of a wilderness, but *one* man might labor out the common period of life without accomplishing any thing; when he had felled his timber he could not remove it, nor erect it after it was removed; hunger in the mean time would urge him from his work, and every different want would call him a different way. Disease, nay, even misfortune, would be death, for though neither might be mortal, yet either would disable him from living, and reduce him to a state in which he might rather be said to perish than to die.

Thus necessity, like a gravitating power, would soon form our newly arrived emigrants into society, the reciprocal blessings of which would supersede, and render the obligations of law and government unnecessary while they remained perfectly just to each another; but as nothing but heaven is impregnable to vice, it will unavoidably happen, that in proportion as they surmount the first difficulties of emigration, which bound them together in a common cause, they will begin to relax in their duty and attachment to each other; and this remissness will point out the necessity of establishing some form of government, to supply the defect of moral virtue.

Some convenient tree will afford them a state-house, under the branches of which the whole colony may assemble to deliberate on public matters. It is more than probable that their first laws will have the title only of *Regulations*, and be enforced by no other penalty than public disesteem. In this first parliament, every man, by natural right, will have a seat.

But as the colony increases, the public concerns will increase likewise, and the distance at which the members may be separated, will render it too inconvenient for all of them to meet on every occasion as at first, when their number was small, their habitations near, and the public concerns trifling. This will point out the convenience of their consenting to leave the legislative part to be managed by a select number chosen from the whole body, who are supposed to have the same concerns at stake which those have who appointed them, and who will act in the same manner as the whole body would were they present. If the colony continue increasing, it will become necessary to augment the number of the representatives, and that the interest of every part of the colony may be attended to, it will be found best to divide the whole into convenient parts, each part sending its proper number; and that the *elected* might never form to themselves an interest separate from the *electors*, prudence will point out the propriety of having elections often; because as the *elected* might by that means return and mix again with the general body of the *electors* in a few months, their fidelity to the public will be secured by the prudent reflection of not making a rod for themselves. And as this frequent interchange will establish a common interest with every part of the community, they will mutually and naturally support each other, and on this (not on the unmeaning name of King) depends the *strength of government, and the happiness of the governed.*

Here then is the origin and rise of government; namely, a mode rendered necessary by the inability of moral virtue to govern the world; here too, is the design and end of government, *viz.* freedom and security. And however our eyes may be dazzled with show, or our ears deceived by sound; however prejudice may warp our wills, or interest darken our understanding, the simple voice of nature and reason will say, it is right.

I draw my idea of the form of government from a principle in nature, which no art can overturn, *viz.* that the more simple any thing is, the less liable it is to be disordered, and the easier repaired when disordered; and with this maxim in view, I offer a few remarks on the so much boasted constitution of England. That it was noble for the dark and slavish times in which it was erected, is granted. When the world was overrun with tyranny, the least remove therefrom was a glorious rescue. But that it is imperfect, subject to convulsions, and incapable of producing what it seems to promise, is easily demonstrated.

Absolute governments, (though the disgrace of human nature) have this advantage with them, that they are simple; if the people suffer, they know the head from which their suffering springs, know likewise the remedy, and are not bewildered by a variety of causes and cures. But the constitution of England is so exceedingly complex, that the nation may suffer for years together without being able to discover in which part the fault lies; some will say in one and some in another, and every political physician will advise a different medicine,

I know it is difficult to get over local or long standing prejudices, yet if we will suffer ourselves to examine the component parts of the English constitution, we shall find them to be the base remains of two ancient tyrannies, compounded with some new republican materials.

1st, The remains of monarchical tyranny in the person of the king.

2d, The remains of aristocratical tyranny in the persons of the peers.

3d, The new republican materials, in the persons of the commons, on whose virtue depends the freedom of England.

The two first, by being hereditary, are independent of the people; wherefore in a *constitutional sense* they contribute nothing towards the freedom of the state.

To say that the constitution of England is a union of three powers, reciprocally checking each other, is farcical; either the words have no meaning, or they are flat contradictions.

To say that the commons is a check upon the king, presupposes two things:

1st, That the king is not to be trusted without being looked after; or in other words, that a thirst for absolute power is the natural disease of monarchy.

2d, That the commons, by being appointed for that purpose, are either wiser or more worthy of confidence than the crown.

But as the same constitution which gives the commons a power to check the king by withholding the supplies, gives afterwards the king a power to check the commons, by empowering him to reject their other bills; it again supposes that the king is wiser than those whom it has already supposed to be wiser than him. A mere absurdity!

There is something exceedingly ridiculous in the composition of monarchy; it first excludes a man from the means of information, yet empowers him to act in cases where the highest judgment is required. The state of a king shuts him from the world, yet the business of a king requires him to know it thoroughly; wherefore the different parts, by unnaturally opposing and destroying each other, prove the whole character to be absurd and useless.

Some writers have explained the English constitution thus; the king, say they, is one, the people another; the peers are an house in behalf of the king: the commons in behalf of the people; but this hath all the distinctions of an house divided against itself: and though the expressions be pleasantly arranged, yet when examined they appear idle and ambiguous; and it will always happen, that the nicest construction that words are capable of, when applied to the description of something which either cannot exist, or is too incomprehensible to be within the compass of description, will be words of sound only, and though they may amuse the ear, they cannot inform the mind, for this explanation includes a previous question, *viz. How came the king by a power which the people are afraid to trust, and always obliged to check?* Such a power could not be the gift of a wise people, neither can any power *which needs checking*, be from God; yet the provision, which the constitution makes, supposes such a power to exist.

But the provision is unequal to the task; the means either cannot or will not accomplish the end, and the whole affair is a *felo de se;* for as the greater weight will always carry up the less, and as all the wheels of a machine are put in motion by one, it only remains to know which power in the constitution has the most weight, for that will govern; and though the others, or a part of them, may clog, or as the phrase is, check the rapidity of its motion, yet so long as they cannot stop it, their endeavors will be ineffectual; the first moving power will at last have its way, and what it wants in speed is supplied by time.

That the crown is this overbearing part in the Englisn constitution needs not be mentioned, and that it derives its whole consequence merely from being the giver of places and pensions is self-evident; wherefore, though we have been wise enough to shut and lock a door against absolute monarchy, we at the same time have been foolish enough to put the crown in possession of the key.

The prejudice of Englishmen, in favor of their own government by king, lords, and commons, arises as much or more from national pride than reason. Individuals are undoubtedly safer in England than in some other countries, but the *will* of the king is as much the *law* of the land in Britain as in France, with this difference, that instead of proceeding directly from his mouth, it is handed to the people under the formidable shape of an act of parliament. For the fate of Charles I. hath only made kings more subtle—not more just.

Wherefore, laying aside all national pride and prejudice in favor of modes and forms, the plain truth is, that *it is wholly owing to the constitution of the people, and not the constitution of the government*, that the crown is not as oppressive in England as in Turkey.

An inquiry into the *constitutional errors* in the English form of government is at this time highly necessary; for as we are never in a proper condition of doing justice to others, while we continue under the influence of some leading partiality, so neither are we capable of doing it to ourselves while we remain fettered by an obstinate prejudice. And as a man who is attached to a prostitute is unfitted to choose or judge of a wife, so any prepossession in favor of a rotten constitution of government will disable us from discerning a good one.

OF MONARCHY AND HEREDITARY SUCCESSION.

MANKIND being originally equals in the order of creation, the equality could only be destroyed by some subsequent circumstance; the distinctions of rich and poor, may in a great measure be accounted for, and that without having recourse to the harsh, ill-sounding names of avarice and oppression. Oppression is often the *consequence*, but seldom or never the *means* of riches; and though avarice will preserve a man from being necessitously poor, it generally makes him too timorous to be wealthy.

But there is another and greater distinction, for which no truly natural or religious reason can be assigned, and that is, the distinction of men into *kings* and *subjects*. Male and female are the distinctions of nature; good and bad the distinctions of heaven; but how a race of men came into the world so exalted above the rest, and distinguished like some new species, is worth inquiring into, and whether they are the means of happiness or of misery to mankind.

In the early ages of the world, according to the scripture chronology, there were no kings; the consequence of which was there were no wars; it is the pride of kings which throws mankind into confusion. Holland without a king hath enjoyed more peace for this last century than any of the monarchical governments of Europe. Antiquity favors the same remark; for the quiet and rural lives of the first patriarchs hath a happy something in them, which vanishes when we come to the history of Jewish royalty.

Government by kings was first introduced into the world by the heathen, from whom the children of Israel copied the custom. It was the most prosperous invention that ever was set on foot for the promotion of idolatry. The heathen paid divine honors to their deceased kings, and the Christian world hath improved on the plan by doing the same to their living ones. How impious is the title of *sacred majesty*, applied to a worm, who in the midst of his splendor is crumbling into dust!

As the exalting one man so greatly above the rest, cannot be justified on the equal rights of nature, so neither can it be defended on the authority of scripture; for the will of the Almighty, as declared by Gideon and the prophet Samuel, expressly disapproves of government by kings. All anti-monarchical parts of scripture have been very smoothly glossed over in monarchical governments, but they undoubtedly merit the attention of countries, which have their governments yet to form. "Render unto Cæsar the things which are Cæsar's," is the scripture doctrine of courts, yet it is no support of monarchical government, for the Jews at that time were without a king, and in a state of vassalage to the Romans.

Near three thousand years passed away, from the Mosaic account of the creation, till the Jews, under a national delusion, requested a king. Till then, their form of government (except in extraordinary cases, where the Almighty interposed) was a kind of republic, administered by a judge and the elders of the tribes. Kings they had none, and it was held sinful to acknowledge any being under that title but the Lord of Hosts. And when a man seriously reflects on the idolatrous homage which is paid to the persons of kings, he need not wonder that the Almighty, ever jealous of his honor, should disapprove of a form of government which so impiously invades the prerogative of heaven.

Monarchy is ranked in scripture as one of the sins of the Jews, for which a curse in reserve is denounced against them. The history of that transaction is worth attending to.

The children of Israel being oppressed by the Midianites, Gideon marched against them with a small army, and victory, through the divine interposition, decided in his favor. The Jews, elate with success, and attributing it to the generalship of Gideon, proposed making him a king, saying, " rule thou over us, thou and thy son, and thy son's son." Here was temptation in its fullest extent; not a kingdom only, but an hereditary one; but Gideon in the piety of his soul replied, " I will not rule over you, neither shall my son rule over you. *The Lord shall rule over you.*" Words need not be more explicit; Gideon doth not *decline* the honor, but denieth their right to give it; neither doth he compliment them with invented declarations of his thanks, but in the positive style of a prophet charges them with disaffection to their proper sovereign, the king of heaven.

About one hundred and thirty years after this, they fell again into the same error. The hankering which the Jews had for the idolatrous customs of the heathen, is something exceedingly unaccountable; but so it was, that laying hold of the misconduct of Samuel's two sons, who were entrusted with some secular concerns, they came in an abrupt and clamorous manner to Samuel, saying, " Behold thou art old, and thy sons walk not in thy ways, now make us a king to judge us like all the other nations." And here we cannot but observe that their motives were bad, *viz.* that they might be *like* unto other nations, *i.e.* the hea-

then, whereas their true glory lay in being as much *unlike*
them as possible. "But the thing displeased Samuel when
they said, give us a king to judge us; and Samuel prayed
unto the Lord, and the Lord said unto Samuel, hearken
unto the voice of the people in all that they say unto thee,
for they have not rejected thee, but they have rejected
me, *that I should not reign over them*. According to all the
works which they have done since the day that I brought
them out of Egypt, even unto this day; wherewith they
have forsaken me and served other gods; so do they also
unto thee. Now therefore hearken unto their voice, how-
beit, protest solemnly unto them and show them the manner of the king that shall reign over them," (*i.e.* not of
any particular king, but the general manner of the kings
of the earth, whom Israel was so eagerly copying after.
And notwithstanding the great distance of time and difference of manners, the character is still in fashion.) "And
Samuel told all the words of the Lord unto the people, that
asked of him a king. And he said, this shall be the manner of the king that shall reign over you; he will take
your sons and appoint them for himself, for his chariots,
and to be his horsemen, and some shall run before his
chariots," (this description agrees with the present mode
of impressing men) "and he will appoint him captains
over thousands, and captains over fifties, and will set them
to ear his ground and to reap his harvest, and to make his
instruments of war, and instruments of his chariots; and
he will take your daughters to be confectionaries, and to
be cooks, and to be bakers," (this describes the expense
and luxury as well as the oppression of kings) "and he
will take your fields and your olive yards, even the best of
them, and give them to his servants; and he will take the
tenth of your seed, and of your vineyards, and give them to
his officers and to his servants," (by which we see that bribery, corruption and favoritism are the standing vices of
kings) "and he will take the tenth of your men servants,
and your maid servants, and your goodliest young men,
and your asses, and put them to his work; and he will
take the tenth of your sheep, and ye shall be his servants,
and ye shall cry out in that day because of your king
which ye shall have chosen, *and the Lord will not hear you
in that day*." This accounts for the continuation of monarchy; neither do the characters of the few good kings
which have lived since, either sanctify the title, or blot out

the sinfulness of the origin; the high encomium given of David takes no notice of him *officially as a king*, but only as a *man* after God's own heart. "Nevertheless the people refused to obey the voice of Samuel, and they said, nay, but we will have a king over us, that we may be like all the nations, and that our king may judge us, and go out before us, and fight our battles." Samuel continued to reason with them but to no purpose; he set before them their ingratitude, but all would not avail; and seeing them fully bent on their folly, he cried out, "I will call unto the Lord, and he shall send thunder and rain" (which was then a punishment, being in the time of wheat harvest) "that ye may perceive and see that your wickedness is great which ye have done in the sight of the Lord, *in asking you a king.* So Samuel called unto the Lord, and the Lord sent thunder and rain that day, and all the people greatly feared the Lord and Samuel. And all the people said unto Samuel, pray for thy servants unto the Lord thy God that we die not, for *we have added unto our sins this evil, to ask a king.*" These portions of scripture are direct and positive. They admit of no equivocal construction. That the Almighty hath here entered his protest against monarchical government is true, or the scripture is false. And a man hath good reason to believe, that there is as much of kingcraft, as priestcraft in withholding the scripture from the public in popish countries. For monarchy in every instance is the popery of government.

To the evil of monarchy we have added that of hereditary succession; and as the first is a degradation and lessening of ourselves, so the second, claimed as a matter of right, is an insult and imposition on posterity. For all men being originally equals, no one by *birth*, could have a right to set up his own family, in perpetual preference to all others for ever, and though himself might deserve *some* degree of honors of his contemporaries, yet his descendants might be far too unworthy to inherit them. One of the strongest *natural* proofs of the folly of hereditary right in kings, is, that nature disapproves it, otherwise she would not so frequently turn it into ridicule, by giving mankind an *ass* for a *lion.*

Secondly, as no man at first could possess more public honors than were bestowed upon him, so the givers of those honors could have no power to give away the right of posterity and though they might say, "We choose you for *our* head," they could not without manifest injustice to their children, say, that " your children and your children's children shall reign over *ours* for ever." Because such an unwise, unjust, unnatural compact might (perhaps) in the next succession put them under the government of a rogue or a fool. Most wise men in their private sentiments, have ever treated hereditary right with contempt ; yet it is one of those evils, which when once established is not easily removed ; many submit from fear, others from superstition, and the more powerful part shares with the king, the plunder of the rest.

This is supposing the present race of kings in the world to have had an honorable origin ; whereas it is more than probable, that, could we take off the dark covering of antiquity, and trace them to their first rise, we should find the first of them nothing better than the principal ruffian of some restless gang, whose savage manners, or pre-eminence in subtlety obtained him the title of chief among plunderers ; and who by increasing in power, and extending his depredations, overawed the quiet and defenceless to purchase their safety by frequent contributions. Yet his electors could have no idea of giving hereditary right to his descendants, because such a perpetual exclusion of themselves was incompatible with the free and unrestrained principles they professed to live by. Wherefore, hereditary succession in the early ages of monarchy could not take place as a matter of claim, but as something casual or complimental ; but as few or no records were extant in those days, and traditionary history stuffed with fables, it was very easy, after the lapse of a few generations, to trump up some superstitious tale, conveniently timed, Mahomet-like, to cram hereditary right down the throats of the vulgar. Perhaps the disorders which threatened, or seemed to threaten, on the decease of a leader and the choice of a new one (for elections among ruffians could not be very orderly) induced many at first to favor hereditary pretensions ; by which means it happened, as it hath happened since, that what at first was submitted to as a convenience, was afterwards claimed as a right.

England, since the conquest, hath known some few good monarchs, but groaned beneath a much larger number of bad ones ; yet no man in his senses can say that their claim under William the Conqueror is a very honorable one. A French bastard, landing with an armed banditti,

and establishing himself king of England against the consent of the natives, is, in plain terms, a very paltry, ras-
cally original.—It certainly hath no divinity in it. However, it is needless to spend much time in exposing the folly
of hereditary right; if there are any so weak as to believe
it, let them promiscuously worship the ass and the lion,
and welcome. I shall neither copy their humility, nor
disturb their devotion.

Yet I should be glad to ask, how they suppose kings
came at first? The question admits but of three answers,
viz. either by lot, by election, or by usurpation. If the
first king was taken by lot, it establishes a precedent for
the next, which excludes hereditary succession. Saul was
by lot, yet the succession was not hereditary, neither does
it appear from that transaction that there was any intention it ever should. If the first king of any country was
by election, that likewise establishes a precedent for the
next; for to say, that the right of all future generations is
taken away, by the act of the first electors, in their choice
not only of a king, but of a family of kings for ever, hath
no parallel in or out of scripture but the doctrine of original sin, which supposes the free will of all men lost in
Adam ; and from such comparison, and it will admit of no
other, hereditary succession can derive no glory. For as
in Adam all sinned, and as in the first electors all men
obeyed ; as in the one all mankind were subjected to sa-
tan, and in the other to sovereignty; as our innocence was
lost in the first, and our authority in the last ; and as both
disable us from re-assuming some former state and privilege, it unanswerably follows, that original sin and hereditary succession are parallels. Dishonorable rank ! Inglo-
rious connexion ! Yet the most subtile sophist cannot produce a juster simile.

As to usurpation, no man will be so hardy as to defend
it; and that William the Conqueror was an usurper is a
fact not to be contradicted. The plain truth is, that the
antiquity of English monarchy will not bear looking into.

But it is not so much the absurdity as the evil of hereditary succession which concerns mankind. Did it ensure a
race of good and wise men, it would have the seal of divine authority, but as it opens a door to the *foolish*, the
wicked, and the *improper*, it hath in it the nature of oppression. Men who look upon themselves born to reign, and
others to obey, soon grow insolent ; selected from the rest

of mankind, their minds are early poisoned by importance; and the world they act in differs so materially from the world at large, that they have but little opportunity of knowing its true interests, and when they succeed to the government, are frequently the most ignorant and unfit of any throughout the dominions.

Another evil which attends hereditary succession is, that the throne is subject to be possessed by a minor at any age; all which time the regency, acting under the cover of a king, have every opportunity and inducement to betray their trust. The same national misfortune happens, when a king, worn out with age and infirmity, enters the last stage of human weakness. In both these cases the public becomes the prey to every miscreant, who can tamper successfully with the follies either of age or infancy.

The most plausible plea, which hath ever been offered in favor of hereditary succession, is, that it preserves a nation from civil wars; and were this true, it would be weighty: whereas, it is the most barefaced falsity ever imposed upon mankind, The whole history of England disowns the fact. Thirty kings and two minors have reigned in that distracted kingdom since the conquest; in which time there have been (including the revolution) no less than eight civil wars and nineteen rebellions. Wherefore, instead of making for peace, it makes against it, and destroys the very foundation it seems to stand upon.

The contest for monarchy and succession, between the houses of York and Lancaster, laid England in a scene of blood for many years. Twelve pitched battles, besides skirmishes and sieges, were fought between Henry and Edward; twice was Henry prisoner to Edward, who in his turn was prisoner to Henry. And so uncertain is the fate of war and the temper of a nation, when nothing but personal matters are the ground of a quarrel, that Henry was taken in triumph from a prison to a palace, and Edward obliged to fly from a palace to a foreign land; yet, as sudden transitions of temper are seldom lasting, Henry in his turn was driven from the throne, and Edward recalled to succeed him. The parliament always following the strongest side.

This contest began in the reign of Henry VI. and was not entirely extinguished till Henry VII. in whom the families were united: including a period of 67 years, *viz.* from 1422 to 1489.

In short, monarchy and succession have laid (not this or that kingdom only, but) the world in blood and ashes. 'Tis a form of government which the word of God bears testimony against, and blood will attend it.

If we inquire into the business of a king, we shall find (and in some countries they have none) that after sauntering away their lives without pleasure to themselves or advantage to the nation, they withdraw from the scene, and leave their successors to tread the same useless and idle round. In absolute monarchies the whole weight of business, civil and military, lies on the king; the children of Israel in their request for a king urged this plea, "that he may judge us, and go out before us and fight our battles." But in countries where he is neither a judge nor a general, as in England, a man would be puzzled to know what *is* his business.

The nearer any government approaches to a republic, the less business there is for a king. It is somewhat difficult to find a proper name for the government of England. Sir William Meredith calls it a republic; but in its present state it is unworthy of the name, because the corrupt influence of the crown, by having all the places in its disposal, hath so effectually swallowed up the power, and eaten out the virtue of the house of commons (the republican part in the constitution) that the government of England is nearly as monarchical as that of France or Spain. Men fall out with names without understanding them. For it is the republican and not the monarchical part of the constitution of England which Englishmen glory in, *viz.* the liberty of choosing an house of commons from out of their own body: and it is easy to see that when republican virtue fails, slavery ensues. Why is the constitution of England sickly, but because monarchy hath poisoned the republic; the crown hath engrossed the commons?

In England the king hath little more to do than to make war and give away places; which, in plain terms, is to impoverish the nation and set it together by the ears. A pretty business indeed for a man to be allowed eight hundred thousand sterling a year for, and worshipped into the bargain! Of more worth is one honest man to society, and in the sight of God, than all the crowned ruffians that ever lived.

THOUGHTS ON THE PRESENT STATE OF AMERICAN AFFAIRS.

In the following pages I offer nothing more than simple facts, plain arguments, and common sense; and have no other preliminaries to settle with the reader, than that he will divest himself of prejudice and prepossession, and suffer his reason and his feelings to determine for themselves; that he will put *on*, or rather that he will not put *off*, the true character of a man, and generously enlarge his views beyond the present day.

Volumes have been written on the subject of the struggle between England and America. Men of all ranks have embarked in the controversy, from different motives, and with various designs : but all have been ineffectual, and the period of debate is closed. Arms, as the last resource, must decide the contest; the appeal was the choice of the king, and the continent hath accepted the challenge.

It has been reported of the late Mr. Pelham (who, though an able minister was not without his faults) that on his being attacked in the house of commons, on the score, that his measures were only of a temporary kind, replied, "*they will last my time.*" · Should a thought so fatal and unmanly possess the colonies in the present contest, the name of ancestors will be remembered by future generations with detestation.

The sun never shined on a cause of greater worth. 'Tis not the affair of a city, a county, a province, or a kingdom, but of a continent—of at least one eighth part of the habitable globe. 'Tis not the concern of a day, a year, or an age; posterity are virtually involved in the contest, and will be more or less affected, even to the end of time, by the proceedings now. Now is the seed time of continental union, faith, and honor. The least fracture now will be like a name engraved with the point of a pin on the tender rind of a young oak; the wound will enlarge with the tree, and posterity read it in full grown characters.

By referring the matter from argument to arms, a new era for politics is struck; a new method of thinking hath arisen. All plans, proposals, &c. prior to the nineteenth of April, *i.e.* to the commencement of hostilities, are like the almanacks of last year; which, though proper then, are superseded and useless now. Whatever was advanced

by the advocates on either side of the question then, terminated in one and the same point, *viz.* a union with Great
Britain; the only difference between the parties was the
method of effecting it; the one proposing force, the other
friendship; but it hath so far happened that the first has
failed, and the second has withdrawn her influence.

As much hath been said of the advantages of reconciliation, which, like an agreeable dream, hath passed away
and left us as we were, it is but right, that we should examine the contrary side of the argument, and inquire into
some of the many material injuries which these colonies
sustain, and always will sustain, by being connected with
and dependant on Great Britain. To examine that connexion and dependance, on the principles of nature and common sense; to see what we have to trust to, if separated,
and what we are to expect, if dependant.

I have heard it asserted by some, that as America hath
flourished under her former connexion with Great Britain,
the same connexion is necessary towards her future happiness, and will always have the same effect. Nothing
can be more fallacious than this kind of argument. We
may as well assert that because a child has thrived upon
milk, that it is never to have meat, or that the first twenty
years of our lives is to become a precedent for the next
twenty. But even this is admitting more than is true, for
I answer roundly, that America would have flourished as
much, and probably much more, had no European power
had any thing to do with her. The articles of commerce,
by which she hath enriched herself, are the necessaries of
life, and will always have a market while eating is the
custom of Europe.

But she has protected us, say some. That she hath engrossed us is true, and defended the continent at our expense as well as her own, is admitted, and she would have
defended Turkey from the same motives, *viz.* for the sake
of trade and dominion.

Alas! we have been long led away by ancient prejudices, and made large sacrifices to superstition. We have
boasted the protection of Great Britain, without considering, that her motive was *interest* not *attachment;* and that
she did not protect us from *our enemies* on *our account,* but
from *her enemies* on *her own account,* from those who had no
quarrel with us on any *other account,* and who will always
be our enemies on the *same account.* Let Britain waive her

pretensions to the continent, or the continent throw off the
dependance, and we should be at peace with France and
Spain, were they at war with Britain. The miseries of
Hanover last war ought to warn us against connexions.

It hath lately been asserted in parliament, that the colonies have no relation to each other but through the parent
country, *i.e.* that Pennsylvania and the Jerseys, and so on
for the rest, are sister colonies by the way of England;
this is certainly a very round-about way of proving relationship, but it is the nearest and only true way of proving
enemyship, if I may so call it. France and Spain never
were, nor perhaps ever will be, our enemies as *Americans,*
but as our being the *subjects of Great Britain.*

But Britain is the parent country, say some. Then the
more shame upon her conduct. Even brutes do not de-
vour their young, nor savages make war upon their families; wherefore, the assertion, if true, turns to her reproach; but it happens not to be true, or only partly so,
and the phrase *parent* or *mother country* hath been jesuiti-
cally adopted by the king and his parasites, with a low
papistical design of gaining an unfair bias on the credulous
weakness of our minds. Europe, and not England, is the
parent country of America. This new world hath been
the asylum for the persecuted lovers of civil and religious liberty from *every part* of Europe. Hither have they
fled, not from the tender embraces of the mother, but from
the cruelty of the monster; and it is so far true of England,
that the same tyranny which drove the first emigrants from
home, pursues their descendants still.

In this extensive quarter of the globe, we forget the narrow limits of three hundred and sixty miles (the extent of
England) and carry our friendship on a larger scale; we
claim brotherhood with every European Christian, and
triumph in the generosity of the sentiment.

It is pleasant to observe by what regular gradations we
surmount local prejudices, as we enlarge our acquaintance
with the world. A man born in any town in England divided into parishes, will naturally associate most with his
fellow parishioners (because their interests in many cases
will be common) and distinguish him by the name of *neighbor;* if he meet him but a few miles from home, he drops
the narrow idea of a street, and salutes him by the name
of *townsman;* if he travel out of the county, and meets him
in any other, he forgets the minor divisions of street and

town, and calls him *countryman, i.e. county-man;* but if in their foreign excursions they should associate in France or any other part of *Europe,* their local remembrance would be enlarged into that of *Englishmen.* And by a just parity of reasoning, all Europeans meeting in America, or any other quarter of the globe, are *countrymen;* for England, Holland, Germany, or Sweden, when compared with the whole, stand in the same places on the larger scale, which the divisions of street, town, and county do on the smaller one; distinctions too limited for continental minds. Not one third of the inhabitants, even of this province, are of English descent. Wherefore, I reprobate the phrase of parent or mother country applied to England only, as being false, selfish, narrow and ungenerous.

But, admitting that we were all of English descent, what does it amount to? Nothing. Britain, being now an open enemy, extinguishes every other name and title: and to say that reconciliation is our duty, is truly farcical. The first king of England, of the present line (William the Conqueror) was a Frenchman, and half the peers of England are descendants from the same country; wherefore, by the same method of reasoning, England ought to be governed by France.

Much hath been said of the united strength of Britain and the colonies, that in conjunction they might bid defiance to the world. But this is mere presumption; the fate of war is uncertain, neither do the expressions mean any thing; for this continent would never suffer itself to be drained of inhabitants, to support the British arms in either Asia, Africa, or Europe.

Besides, what have we to do with setting the world at defiance? Our plan is commerce, and that, well attended to, will secure us the peace and friendship of all Europe; because it is the interest of all Europe to have America a *free port.* Her trade will always be a protection, and her barrenness of gold and silver secure her from invaders.

I challenge the warmest advocate for reconciliation, to show a single advantage that this continent can reap, by being connected with Great Britain. I repeat the challenge; not a single advantage is derived. Our corn will fetch its price in any market in Europe, and our imported goods must be paid for, buy them where we will.

But the injuries and disadvantages which we sustain by that connexion, are without number; and our duty to mankind at large, as well as to ourselves, instructs us to renounce the alliance; because, any submission to or dependance on Great Britain, tends directly to involve this continent in European wars and quarrels; and sets us at variance with nations, who would otherwise seek our friendship, and against whom, we have neither anger nor complaint. As Europe is our market for trade, we ought to form no partial connexion with any part of it. It is the true interest of America to steer clear of European contentions, which she never can do, while, by her dependance on Britain, she is made the make-weight in the scale of British politics.

Europe is too thickly planted with kingdoms to be long at peace, and whenever a war breaks out between England and any foreign power, the trade of America goes to ruin, *because of her connexion with Britain.* The next war may not turn out like the last, and should it not, the advocates for reconciliation now will be wishing for separation then, because, neutrality in that case, would be a safer convoy than a man of war. Every thing that is right or natural pleads for separation. The blood of the slain, the weeping voice of nature cries, *'tis time to part.* Even the distance at which the Almighty hath placed England and America, is a strong and natural proof, that the authority of the one over the other, was never the design of heaven. The time likewise at which the continent was discovered, adds weight to the argument, and the manner in which it was peopled increases the force of it. The Reformation was preceded by the discovery of America, as if the Almighty graciously meant to open a sanctuary to the persecuted in future years, when home should afford neither friendship nor safety.

The authority of Great Britain over this continent, is a form of government, which sooner or later must have an end: and a serious mind can draw no true pleasure by looking forward, under the painful and positive conviction, that what he calls "the present constitution" is merely temporary. As parents, we can have no joy, knowing that *this government* is not sufficiently lasting to ensure any thing which we may bequeath to posterity: and by a plain method of argument, as we are running the next generation into debt, we ought to do the work of it, otherwise we use them meanly and pitifully. In order to discover the line of our duty rightly, we should take our children in

our hand, and fix our station a few years farther into life ;
that eminence will present a prospect, which a few present
fears and prejudices conceal from our sight.

Though I would carefully avoid giving unnecessary offence, yet I am inclined to believe, that all those who espouse the doctrine of reconciliation, may be included within the following descriptions.

Interested men, who are not to be trusted ; weak men,
who *cannot* see ; prejudiced men, who *will not* see ; and a
certain set of moderate men, who think better of the European world than it deserves : and this last class, by an
ill-judged deliberation, will be the cause of more.calami-
ties to this continent than all the other three.

It is the good fortune of many to live distant from the
scene of sorrow ; the evil is not sufficiently brought to *their*
doors to make *them* feel the precariousness with which all
American property is possessed. But let our imaginations
transport us a few moments to Boston ; that seat of wretchedness will teach us wisdom, and instruct us forever to renounce a power in whom we can have no trust. The inhabitants of that unfortunate city, who but a few months
ago were in ease and affluence, have now no other alternative than to stay and starve, or turn out to beg. Endangered by the fire of their friends if they continue within the city, and plundered by the soldiery if they leave it.
In their present situation they are prisoners without the
hope of redemption, and in a general attack for their relief, they would be exposed to the fury of both armies.

Men of passive tempers look somewhat lightly over the
offences of Britain, and, still hoping for the best, are apt
to call out, " *come, come, we shall be friends again, for all
this.*" But examine the passions and feelings of mankind,
bring the doctrine of reconciliation to the touchstone of
nature, and then tell me, whether you can hereafter love,
honor, and faithfully serve the power that hath carried
fire and sword into your land ? If you cannot do all these,
then are you only deceiving yourselves, and by your delay bringing ruin upon your posterity. Your future connexion with Britain, whom you can neither love nor hon-
or, will be forced and unnatural, and being formed only on
the plan of present convenience, will in a little time fall
into a relapse more wretched than the first. But if you
say, you can still pass the violations over, then I ask, hath
your house been burnt ? Hath your property been de-

stroyed before your face? Are your wife and children destitute of a bed to lie on, or bread to live on? Have you
lost a parent or a child by their hands, and yourself the
ruined and wretched survivor? If you have not, then are
you not a judge of those who have. But if you have, and
can still shake hands with the murderers, then are you unworthy the name of husband, father, friend, or lover, and
whatever may be your rank or title in life, you have the
heart of a coward, and the spirit of a sycophant.

This is not inflaming or exaggerating matters, but trying
them by those feelings and affections which nature justifies,
and without which, we should be incapable of discharging
the social duties of life, or enjoying the felicities of it. I
mean not to exhibit horror for the purpose of provoking
revenge, but to awaken us from fatal and unmanly slum-
bers, that we may pursue determinately some fixed object.
It is not in the power of Britain or of Europe to conquer
America, if she does not conquer herself by *delay* and *tim-
idity*. The present winter is worth an age if rightly employed, but if lost or neglected, the whole continent will
partake of the misfortune; and there is no punishment
which that man will not deserve, be he who, or what, or
where he will, that may be the means of sacrificing a season
so precious and useful.

It is repugnant to reason, and the universal order of
things, to all examples from former ages, to suppose, that
this continent can longer remain subject to any external
power. The most sanguine in Britain do not think so.
The utmost stretch of human wisdom cannot, at this time,
compass a plan short of separation, which can promise
the continent even a year's security. Reconciliation is
now a fallacious dream. Nature hath deserted the connexion, and art cannot supply her place. For, as Milton
wisely expresses, "never can true reconcilement grow,
where wounds of deadly hate have pierced so deep."

Every quiet method for peace hath been ineffectual.
Our prayers have been rejected with disdain; and only
tended to convince us, that nothing flatters vanity, or con-
firms obstinacy in kings more than repeated petitioning—
nothing hath contributed more than this very measure to
make the kings of Europe absolute: witness Denmark and
Sweden. Wherefore, since nothing but blows will do, for
God's sake, let us come to a final separation, and not leave

the next generation to be cutting throats, under the violated unmeaning names of parent and child.

To say, they will never attempt it again, is idle and visionary; we thought so at the repeal of the stamp-act, yet a year or two undeceived us: as well may we suppose that nations, which have been once defeated, will never renew the quarrel.

As to government matters, it is not in the power of Britain to do this continent justice: the business of it will soon be too weighty and intricate to be managed with any tolerable degree of convenience, by a power so distant from us, and so very ignorant of us; for if they cannot conquer us, they cannot govern us. To be always running three or four thousand miles with a tale or a petition, waiting four or five months for an answer, which, when obtained, requires five or six more to explain it in, will in a few years be looked upon as folly and childishness—there was a time when it was proper, and there is a proper time for it to cease.

Small islands not capable of protecting themselves, are the proper objects for kingdoms to take under their care; but there is something absurd, in supposing a continent to be perpetually governed by an island. In no instance hath nature made the satellite larger than its primary planet; and as England and America, with respect to each other, reverses the common order of nature, it is evident that they belong to different systems: England to Europe—America to itself.

I am not induced by motives of pride, party, or resentment, to espouse the doctrine of separation and independence; I am clearly, positively, and conscientiously persuaded that it is the true interest of this continent to be so; that every thing short of *that* is mere patchwork; that it can afford no lasting felicity,—that it is leaving the sword to our children, and shrinking back at a time, when, going a little further, would have rendered this continent the glory of the earth.

As Britain hath not manifested the least inclination towards a compromise, we may be assured that no terms can be obtained worthy the acceptance of the continent, or any ways equal to the expense of blood and treasure we have been already put to.

The object contended for, ought always to bear some just proportion to the expense. The removal of North, or the whole detestable junto, is a matter unworthy the millions we have expended. A temporary stoppage of trade, was an inconvenience, which would have sufficiently balanced the repeal of all the acts complained of, had such repeals been obtained; but if the whole continent must take up arms, if every man must be a soldier, it is scarcely worth our while to fight against a contemptible ministry only. Dearly, dearly do we pay for the repeal of the acts if that is all we fight for; for in a. just estimation, it is as great a folly to pay a Bunker-hill price for law as for land. I have always considered the independency of this continent, as an event which, sooner or later must take place, and from the late rapid progress of the continent to maturity, the event cannot be far off. Wherefore, on the breaking out of hostilities, it was not worth the while to have disputed a matter which time would have finally redressed, unless we meant to be in earnest; otherwise, it is like wasting an estate on a suit at law, to regulate the trespasses of a tenant, whose lease is just expiring. No man was a warmer wisher for a reconciliation than myself, before the fatal nineteenth of April, 1775,* but the moment the event of that day was made known, I rejected the hardened, sullen-tempered Pharaoh of England for ever; and disdain the wretch, that with the pretended title of *Father of his people*, can unfeelingly hear of their slaughter, and composedly sleep with their blood upon his soul.

But admitting that matters were now made up, what would be the event? I answer, the ruin of the continent. And that for several reasons.

1st, The powers of governing still remaining in the hands of the king, he will have a negative over the whole legislation of this continent. And as he hath shown himself such an inveterate enemy to liberty, and discovered such a thirst for arbitrary power; is he, or is he not, a proper person to say to these colonies, "*you shall make no laws but what I please!*" And is there any inhabitant of America so ignorant as not to know, that according to what is called the *present constitution*, this continent can make no laws but what the king gives leave to? and is there any man so unwise as not to see, that (considering what has happened) he will suffer no law to be made here, but such as suits *his* purpose? We may be as effectually enslaved by the

* Massacre at Lexington.

want of laws in America, as by submitting to laws made for
us in England. After matters are made up (as it is called)
can there be any doubt, but the whole power of the crown
will be exerted, to keep this continent as low and humble
as possible? Instead of going forward we shall go backward, or be perpetually quarrelling, or ridiculously petitioning.—We are already greater than the king wishes us
to be, and will he not hereafter endeavor to make us less?
To bring the matter to one point, Is the power who is jealous of our prosperity, a proper power to govern us? Whoever says *No*, to this question, is an *independent*, for independency means no more than this, whether we shall make
our own laws, or, whether the king, the greatest enemy
which this continent hath, or can have, shall tell us " *there
shall be no laws but such as I like.*"

But the king, you will say, has a negative in England;
the people there can make no laws without his consent.
In point of right and good order, it is something very
ridiculous, that a youth of twenty-one (which hath often
happened) shall say to several millions of people, older
and wiser than himself, I forbid this or that act of yours to
be law. But in this place I decline this sort of reply,
though I will never cease to expose the absurdity of it;
and only answer, that England being the king's residence,
and America not, makes quite another case. The king's
negative *here* is ten times more dangerous and fatal than it
can be in England; for *there* he will scarcely refuse his
consent to a bill for putting England into as strong a state
of defence as possible, and in America he would never suffer such a bill to be passed.

America is only a secondary object in the system of
British politics—England consults the good of *this* country
no further than it answers her *own* purpose. Wherefore,
her own interest leads her to suppress the growth of *ours*
in every case which doth not promote her advantage, or in
the least interferes with it. A pretty state we should soon
be in under such a second-hand government, considering
what has happened! Men do not change from enemies to
friends by the alteration of a name: and in order to show
that reconciliation *now* is a dangerous doctrine, I affirm,
*that it would be policy in the king at this time, to repeal the acts,
for the sake of reinstating himself in the government of the
provinces;* in order that *he may accomplish by craft and*

subtlety, in the long run, what he cannot do by force in the short one. Reconciliation and ruin are nearly related.

2dly, That as even the best terms, which we can expect to obtain, can amount to no more than a temporary expedient, or a kind of government by guardianship, which can last no longer than till the colonies come of age, so the general face and state of things, in the interim, will be unsettled and unpromising. Emigrants of property will not choose to come to a country whose form of government hangs but by a thread, and which is every day tottering on the brink of commotion and disturbance; and numbers of the present inhabitants would lay hold of the interval, to dispose of their effects, and quit the continent.

But the most powerful of all arguments, is, that nothing but independence, *i.e.* a continental form of government, can keep the peace of the continent and preserve it inviolate from civil wars. I dread the event of a reconciliation with Britain now, as it is more than probable that it will be followed by a revolt somewhere or other, the consequences of which may be far more fatal than all the malice of Britain.

Thousands are already ruined by British barbarity. (Thousands more will probably suffer the same fate.) Those men have other feelings than us who have nothing suffered. All they *now* possess is liberty, what they before enjoyed is sacrificed to its service, and having nothing more to lose, they disdain submission. Besides, the general temper of the colonies, towards a British government, will be like that of a youth, who is nearly out of his time; they will care very little about her. And a government which cannot preserve the peace, is no government at all, and in that case we pay our money for nothing; and pray what is it that Britain can do, whose power will be wholly on paper, should a civil tumult break out the very day after reconciliation? I have heard some men say, many of whom I believe spoke without thinking, that they dreaded an independence, fearing that it would produce civil wars. It is but seldom that our first thoughts are truly correct, and that is the case here; for there is ten times more to dread from a patched-up connexion than from independence. I make the sufferer's case my own, and I protest, that were I driven from house and home, my property destroyed, and my circumstances ruined, that as a man,

sensible of injuries, I could never relish the doctrine of reconciliation, or consider myself bound thereby.

The colonies have manifested such a spirit of good order
and obedience to continental government, as is sufficient to
make every reasonable person easy and happy on that
head. No man can assign the least pretence for his fears,
on any other grounds, than such as are truly childish and
ridiculous, *viz.* that one colony will be striving for supe-
riority over another.

Where there are no distinctions there can be no superi-
ority ; perfect equality affords no temptation. The republics of Europe are all (and we may say always) in peace.
Holland and Switzerland are without wars, foreign or domestic : monarchical governments, it is true, are never
long at rest : the crown itself is a temptation to enterpris-
ing ruffians at home ; and that degree of pride and insolence ever attendant on regal authority, swells into a rupture with foreign powers, in instances where a republican
government, by being formed on more natural principles,
would negociate the mistake.

If there is any true cause of fear respecting independence, it is because no plan is yet laid down. Men do not
see their way out, wherefore, as an opening into that business, I offer the following hints ; at the same time modestly
affirming, that I have no other opinion of them myself, than
that they may be the means of giving rise to something better. Could the straggling thoughts of individuals be collected, they would frequently form materials for wise and
able men to improve into useful matter.

Let the assemblies be annual, with a president only.
The representation more equal. Their business wholly
domestic, and subject, to the authority of a continental congress.

Let each colony be divided into six, eight, or ten, convenient districts, each district to send a proper number of
delegates to congress, so that each colony send at least
thirty. The whole number in congress will be at least
three hundred and ninety. Each congress to sit..............
and to choose a president by the following method. When
the delegates are met, let a colony be taken from the
whole thirteen colonies by lot, after which, let the congress choose (by ballot) a president from out of the delegates of that province. In the next congress, let a colony
be taken by lot from twelve only, omitting that colony

from which the president was taken in the former congress, and so proceeding on till the whole thirteen shall
have had their proper rotation. And in order that nothing may pass into a law but what is satisfactorily just, not
less than three-fifths of the congress to be called a majority. He that will promote discord, under a government
so equally formed as this, would have joined Lucifer in
his revolt.

But as there is a peculiar delicacy, from whom, or in
what manner, this business must first arise, and as it seems
most agreeable and consistent, that it should come from
some intermediate body between the governed and the
governors, that is, between the congress and the people,
let a *Continental Conference* be held, in the following manner, and for the following purpose.

A committee of twenty-six members of congress, *viz.*
two for each colony. Two members from each house of
assembly, or provincial convention; and five representatives of the people at large, to be chosen in the capital
city or town of each province, for, and in behalf of the
whole province, by as many qualified voters as shall think
proper to attend from all parts of the province for that
purpose; or, if more convenient, the representatives may
be chosen in two or three of the most populous parts thereof. In this conference, thus assembled, will be united, the
two grand principles of business, *knowledge* and *power*.
The members of congress, assemblies, or conventions, by
having had experience in national concerns, will be able
and useful counsellors, and the whole, being empowered
by the people, will have a truly legal authority.

The conferring members being met, let their business be
to frame a *Continental Charter*, or Charter of the United
Colonies; (answering to what is called the Magna Charta
of England) fixing the number and manner of choosing
members of congress, and members of assembly, with their
date of sitting, and drawing the line of business and juris-
diction between them: (always remembering, that our
strength is continental, not provincial) securing freedom
and property to all men, and above all things, the free exercise of religion, according to the dictates of conscience;
with such other matter as it is necessary for a charter to
contain. Immediately after which, the said conference to
dissolve, and the bodies which shall be chosen conform-
able to the said charter, to be the legislators and governors

of this continent for the time being : whose peace and happiness, may God preserve, Amen.

Should any body of men be hereafter delegated for this or some similar purpose, I offer them the following extracts from that wise observer on governments, Dragonetti. "The science" says he "of the politician consists in fixing the true point of happiness and freedom. Those men would deserve the gratitude of ages, who should discover a mode of government that contained the greatest sum of individual happiness, with the least national expense."

But where, say some, is the king of America? I'll tell you, friend, he reigns above, and doth not make havoc of mankind like the royal brute of Britain. Yet that we may not appear to be defective even in earthly honors, let a day be solemnly set apart for proclaiming the charter; let it be brought forth placed on the divine law, the word of God; let a crown be placed thereon, by which the world may know, that so far as we approve of monarchy, that in America *the law is king*. For as in absolute governments the king is law, so in free countries the law ought to be king; and there ought to be no other. But lest any ill use should afterwards arise, let the crown at the conclusion of the ceremony be demolished, and scattered among the people whose right it is.

A government of our own is our natural right: and when a man seriously reflects on the precariousness of human affairs, he will become convinced, that it is infinitely wiser and safer, to form a constitution of our own in a cool deliberate manner, while we have it in our power, than to trust such an interesting event to time and chance. If we omit it now, some Massanello* may hereafter arise, who, laying hold of popular disquietudes, may collect together the desperate and the discontented, and by assuming to themselves the powers of government, finally sweep away the liberties of the continent like a deluge. Should the government of America return again into the hands of Britain, the tottering situation of things, will be a temptation for some desperate adventurer to try his fortune; and in such a case, what relief can Britain give? Ere she

---

* Thomas Anello, otherwise Massanello, a fisherman of Naples, who after spiriting up his countrymen in the public market place, against the oppression of the Spaniards, to whom the place was then subject, prompted them to revolt, and in the space of a day became king.

could hear the news, the fatal business might be done; and ourselves suffering like the wretched Britons under the oppression of the Conqueror. Ye that oppose independence now, ye know not what ye do; ye are opening a door to eternal tyranny, by keeping vacant the seat of government. There are thousands and tens of thousands, who would think it glorious to expel from the continent, that barbarous and hellish power, which hath stirred up the Indians and negroes to destroy us—the cruelty hath a double guilt, it is dealing brutally by us, and treacherously by them.

To talk of friendship with those in whom our reason forbids us to have faith, and our affections, wounded through a thousand pores, instruct us to detest, is madness and folly. Every day wears out the little remains of kindred between us and them; and can there be any reason to hope, that as the relationship expires, the affection will increase, or that we shall agree better, when we have ten times more and greater concerns to quarrel over than ever?

Ye that tell us of harmony and reconciliation, can ye restore to us the time that is past? Can ye give to prostitution its former innocence? Neither can ye reconcile Britain and America. The last cord now is broken, the people of England are presenting addresses against us. There are injuries which nature cannot forgive; she would cease to be nature if she did. As well can the lover forgive the ravisher of his mistress, as the continent forgive the murders of Britain. The Almighty hath implanted in us these unextinguishable feelings, for good and wise purposes. They are the guardians of his image in our hearts, and distinguish us from the herd of common animals. The social compact would dissolve, and justice be extirpated from the earth, or have only a casual existence were we callous to the touches of affection. The robber, and the murderer, would often escape unpunished, did not the injuries which our tempers sustain, provoke us into justice.

O! ye that love mankind! Ye that dare oppose, not only the tyranny, but the tyrant, stand forth! Every spot of the old world is overrun with oppression. Freedom hath been haunted round the globe. Asia, and Africa, have long expelled her. Europe regards her like a stranger, and England hath given her warning to depart. O! receive the fugitive, and prepare in time an asylum for mankind.

OF THE PRESENT ABILITY OF AMERICA: WITH SOME MISCELLA-
NEOUS REFLECTIONS.

I HAVE never met with a man, either in England or America, who hath not confessed his opinion, that a separation between the countries would take place one time or other: and there is no instance, in which we have shown less judgment, than in endeavoring to describe, what we call, the ripeness or fitness of the continent for independence.

As all men allow the measure, and vary only in their opinion of the time, let us, in order to remove mistakes, take a general survey of things, and endeavor, if possible, to find out the *very* time. But we need not go far, the inquiry ceases at once, for, the *time hath found us.* The general concurrence, the glorious union of all things proves the fact.

It is not in numbers, but in unity, that our great strength lies; yet our present numbers are sufficient to repel the force of all the world. The continent hath, at this time, the largest body of armed and disciplined men of any power under heaven; and is just arrived at that pitch of strength, in which, no single colony is able to support itself, and the whole, when united, can accomplish the matter, and either more, or less than this, might be fatal in its effects. Our land force is already sufficient, and as to naval affairs, we cannot be insensible, that Britain would never suffer an American man of war to be built, while the continent remained in her hands. Wherefore, we should be no forwarder an hundred years hence in that branch, than we are now; but the truth is, we should be less so, because the timber of the country is every day diminishing, and that which will remain at last, will be far off or difficult to procure.

Were the continent crowded with inhabitants, her sufferings under the present circumstances would be intolerable. The more seaport-towns we had, the more should we have both to defend and to lose. Our present numbers are so happily proportioned to our wants, that no man need be idle. The diminution of trade affords an army, and the necessities of an army create a new trade.

Debts we have none; and whatever we may contract on this account will serve as a glorious memento of our virtue. Can we but leave posterity with a settled form of government, an independent constitution of its own, the purchase at any price will be cheap. But to expend millions for the sake of getting a few vile acts repealed, and routing the present ministry only, is unworthy the charge, and is using posterity with the utmost cruelty; because it is leaving them the great work to do, and a debt upon their backs, from which they derive no advantage. Such a thought is unworthy a man of honor, and is the true characteristic of a narrow heart and a pedling politician.

The debt we may contract doth not deserve our regard, if the work be but accomplished. No nation ought to be without a debt. A national debt is a national bond; and when it bears no interest, is in no case a grievance. Britain is oppressed with a debt of upwards of one hundred and forty millions sterling, for which she pays upwards of four millions interest. And as a compensation for her debt, she has a large navy; America is without a debt, and without a navy; yet for the twentieth part of the English national debt, could have a navy as large again. The navy of England is not worth, at this time, more than three millions and a half sterling.

The following calculations are given as a proof that the above estimation of the navy is a just one. [*See Entick's Naval History, Intro.* p. 56.]

The charge of building a ship of each rate, and furnishing her with masts, yards, sails, and rigging, together with a proportion of eight months boatswain's and carpenter's sea-stores, as calculated by Mr. Burchett, secretary to the navy.

For a ship of 100 guns			35,553*l.*
90	-	-	29,886
80	-	-	23,638
70	-	-	17,785
60	-	-	14,197
50	-	-	10,606
40	-	-	7,558
30	-	-	5,846
20	-	-	3,710

And hence it is easy to sum up the value, or cost, rather, of the whole British navy, which, in the year 1757, when it was at its greatest glory, consisted of the following ships and guns.

Ships.		Guns.		Cost of one.		Cost of all.
6	-	100	-	55,553l.	-	213,318l.
12	-	90	-	29,886	-	358,632
12	-	80	-	23,638	-	283,656
43	-	70	-	17,785	-	764,755
35	-	60	-	14,197	-	496,895
40	-	50	-	10,605	-	424,240
45	-	40	-	7,558	-	340,110
58	-	20	-	3,710	-	215,180
85 Sloops, bombs, and fireships, one with another, at				2,000		170,000

	Cost,	3,266,786l.
	Remains for guns,	233,214
	Total,	3,500,000l.

No country on the globe is so happily situated, or so internally capable of raising a fleet as America. Tar, timber, iron, and cordage are her natural produce. We need go abroad for nothing. Whereas the Dutch, who make large profits by hiring out their ships of war to the Spaniards and Portuguese, are obliged to import most of the materials they use. We ought to view the building a fleet as an article of commerce, it being the natural manufacture of this country. It is the best money we can lay out. A navy when finished is worth more than it cost: and is that nice point in national policy, in which commerce and protection are united. Let us build; if we want them not, we can sell; and by that means replace our paper currency with ready gold and silver.

In point of manning a fleet, people in general run into great errors; it is not necessary that one fourth part should be sailors. The privateer Terrible, captain Death, stood the hottest engagement of any ship last war, yet had not twenty sailors on board, though her complement of men was upwards of two hundred. A few able and social sailors will soon instruct a sufficient number of active landsmen in the common work of a ship. Wherefore, we never can be more capable of beginning on maritime matters than now, while our timber is standing, our fisheries blocked up, and our sailors and shipwrights out of employ. Men of war, of seventy and eighty guns, were built forty years ago in New-England, and why not the same now? Ship building is America's greatest pride, and in which, she will in time, excel the whole world. The great empires of the east are mostly inland, and consequently excluded from the possibility of rivalling her. Africa is in a state of barbarism; and no power in Europe, hath either such an extent of coast, or such an internal supply of materials. Where nature hath given the one, she hath withheld the other; to America only hath she been liberal of both. The vast empire of Russia is almost shut out from the sea; wherefore, her boundless forests, her tar, iron, and cordage are only articles of commerce.

In point of safety, ought we to be without a fleet? We are not the little people now, which we were sixty years ago; at that time we might have trusted our property in the streets, or fields rather; and slept securely without locks or bolts to our doors or windows. The case is now altered, and our methods of defence, ought to improve, with our increase of property. A common pirate, twelve months ago, might have come up the Delaware, and laid this city under contribution, for what sum he pleased; and the same might have happened to other places. Nay, any daring fellow, in a brig of fourteen or sixteen guns, might have robbed the whole continent, and carried off half a million of money. These are circumstances which demand our attention, and point out the necessity of naval protection.

Some, perhaps, will say, that after we have made it up with Britain, she will protect us. Can they be so unwise as to mean, that she will keep a navy in our harbors for that purpose? Common sense will tell us, that the power which hath endeavored to subdue us, is of all others, the most improper to defend us. Conquest may be effected under the pretence of friendship; and ourselves, after a long and brave resistance, be at last cheated into slavery. And if her ships are not to be admitted into our harbors, I would ask, how is she to protect us? A navy three or four thousand miles off can be of little use, and on sudden emergencies, none at all. Wherefore, if we must hereafter protect ourselves, why not do it for ourselves? Why do it for another?

The English list of ships of war, is long and formidable, but not a tenth part of them are at any one time fit for service, numbers of them not in being; yet their names are pompously continued in the list, if only a plank be left of the ship; and not a fifth part of such as are fit for service, can be spared on any one station at one time. The East and West Indies, Mediterranean, Africa, and other parts of the world, over which Britain extends her claim, make large demands upon her navy. From a mixture of preju-

dice and inattention, we have contracted a false notion respecting the navy of England, and have talked as if we
should have the whole of it to encounter at once, and for
that reason, supposed, that we must have one as large;
which not being instantly practicable, has been made use
of by a set of disguised tories to discourage our beginning
thereon. Nothing can be further from truth than this; for
if America had only a twentieth part of the naval force of
Britain, she would be by far an over match for her; because, as we neither have, nor claim, any foreign dominion, our whole force would be employed on our own coast,
where we should, in the long run, have two to one the advantage of those who had three or four thousand miles to
sail over, before they could attack us, and the same distance to return in order to refit and recruit. And although
Britain, by her fleet, hath a check over our trade to Europe, we have as large a one over her trade to the West
Indies, which, by laying in the neighborhood of the continent, is entirely at its mercy.

Some method might be fallen on to keep up a naval force
in time of peace, if we should not judge it necessary to support a constant navy. If premiums were to be given to
merchants, to build and employ in their service, ships
mounted with twenty, thirty, forty, or fifty guns (the premiums to be in proportion to the loss of bulk to the merchants), fifty or sixty of those ships, with a few guard-
ships on constant duty, would keep up a sufficient navy,
and that without burdening ourselves with the evil so
loudly complained of in England, of suffering their fleet, in
time of peace, to lie rotting in the docks. To unite the
sinews of commerce and defence is sound policy; for when
our strength and our riches play into each other's hand,
we need fear no external enemy.

In almost every article of defence we abound. Hemp
flourishes even to rankness, so that we need not want cordage. Our iron is superior to that of other countries. Our
small arms equal to any in the world. Cannon we can
cast at pleasure. Saltpetre and gunpowder we are every
day producing. Our knowledge is hourly improving.
Resolution is our inherent character, and courage hath
never yet forsaken us. Wherefore, what is it that we
want? Why is it that we hesitate? From Britain we can
expect nothing but ruin. If she is once admitted to the
government of America again, this continent will not be

worth living in. Jealousies will be always arising, insurrections will be constantly happening; and who will go forth to quell them? Who will venture his life to reduce his own countrymen to a foreign obedience? The difference between Pennsylvania and Connecticut, respecting some unlocated lands, shows the insignificance of a British government, and fully proves, that nothing but continental authority can regulate continental matters.

Another reason why the present time is preferable to all others, is, that the fewer our numbers are, the more land there is yet unoccupied, which instead of being lavished by the king on his worthless dependants, may be hereafter applied, not only to the discharge of the present debt, but to the constant support of government. No nation under heaven hath such an advantage as this.

The infant state of the colonies, as it is called, so far from being against, is an argument in favor of independence. We are sufficiently numerous, and were we more so, we might be less united. It is a matter worthy of observation, that the more a country is peopled, the smaller their armies are. In military numbers, the ancients far exceeded the moderns: and the reason is evident, for trade being the consequence of population, men became too much absorbed thereby to attend to any thing else. Commerce diminishes the spirit, both of patriotism and military defence. And history sufficiently informs us, that the bravest achievements were always accomplished in the non-age of a nation. With the increase of commerce, Engggland hath lost its spirit. The city of London, notwithstanding its numbers, submits to continued insults with the patience of a coward. The more men have to lose, the less willing are they to venture. The rich are in general slaves to fear, and submit to courtly power with the trembling duplicity of a spaniel.

Youth is the seed-time of good habits, as well in nations as in individuals. It might be difficult if not impossible, to form the continent into one government half a century hence. The vast variety of interests, occasioned by an increase of trade and population, would create confusion. Colony would be against colony. Each being able, might scorn each other's assistance: and while the proud and foolish gloried in their little distinctions, the wise would lament, that the union had not been formed before. Wherefore, the *present time* is the *true time* for establishing it. The

intimacy which is contracted in infancy, and the friendship which is formed in misfortune, are, of all others, the
most lasting and unalterable. Our present union is marked with both these characters: we are young, and we have
been distressed; but our concord hath withstood our
troubles, and fixes a memorable era for posterity to
glory in.

The present time, likewise, is that peculiar time, which
never happens to a nation but once, *viz.* the time of forming itself into a government. Most nations have let slip
the opportunity, and by that means have been compelled
to receive laws from their conquerors, instead of making
laws for themselves. First, they had a king, and then a
form of government; whereas the articles or charter of
government, should be formed first, and men delegated to
execute them afterwards: but from the errors of other nations, let us learn wisdom, and lay hold of the present opportunity—*to begin government at the right end.*

When William the Conqueror subdued England, he gave
them law at the point of the sword; and until we consent
that the seat of government, in America, be legally and
authoritatively occupied, we shall be in danger of having
it filled by some fortunate ruffian, who may treat us in the
same manner, and then, where will be our freedom? where
our property?

As to religion, I hold it to be the indispensable duty of
all governments, to protect all conscientious professors
thereof, and I know of no other business which government hath to do therewith. Let a man throw aside that
narrowness of soul, that selfishness of principle, which the
niggards of all professions are so unwilling to part with,
and he will be at once delivered of his fears on that head.
Suspicion is the companion of mean souls, and the bane of
all good society. For myself, I fully and conscientiously
believe, that it is the will of the Almighty, that there
should be a diversity of religious opinions among us: it
affords a larger field for our Christian kindness. Were
we all of one way of thinking, our religious dispositions
would want matter for probation; and on this liberal principle, I look on the various denominations among us, to be
like children of the same family, differing only in what is
called their Christian names.

In a former page, I threw out a few thoughts on the propriety of a Continental Charter (for I only presume to offer

hints, not plans) and in this place, I take the liberty of re-mentioning the subject, by observing, that a charter is to be understood as a bond of solemn obligation, which the whole enters into, to support the right of every separate part, whether of religion, personal freedom, or property. A firm bargain and a right reckoning make long friends.

I have heretofore likewise mentioned the necessity of a large and equal representation; and there is no political matter which more deserves our attention. A small number of electors or a small number of representatives, are equally dangerous. But if the number of the representatives be not only small, but unequal, the danger is increased. As an instance of this, I mention the following; when the associators' petition was before the house of assembly of Pennsylvania, twenty-eight members only were present; all the Bucks county members, being eight, voted against it, and had seven of the Chester members done the same, this whole province had been governed by two counties only; and this danger it is always exposed to. The unwarrantable stretch likewise, which that house made in their last sitting, to gain an undue authority over the delegates of this province, ought to warn the people at large, how they trust power out of their own hands. A set of instructions for their delegates were put together, which in point of sense and business would have dishonored a school-boy, and after being approved by a *few*, a *very few*, without doors, were carried into the house, and there passed *in behalf of the whole colony;* whereas, did the whole colony know, with what ill will that house had entered on some necessary public measures, they would not hesitate a moment to think them unworthy of such a trust.

Immediate necessity makes many things convenient, which if continued would grow into oppressions. Expedience and right are different things. When the calamities of America required a consultation, there was no method so ready, or at that time so proper, as to appoint persons from the several houses of assembly for that purpose; and the wisdom with which they have proceeded hath preserved this continent from ruin. But as it is more than probable that we shall never be without a *Congress*, every well-wisher to good order must own, that the mode for choosing members of that body, deserves consideration. And I put it as a question to those, who make a study of mankind, whether *representation and election* is not too great a power for one and the same body of men to possess? Whenever we are planning for posterity, we ought to remember that virtue is not hereditary.

It is from our enemies that we often gain excellent maxims, and are frequently surprised into reason by their mistakes. Mr. Cornwall (one of the lords of the treasury) treated the petition of the New-York assembly with contempt, because *that* house, he said, consisted but of twenty-six members, which trifling number, he argued, could not with decency be put for the whole. We thank him for his involuntary honesty.*

To conclude. However strange it may appear to some, or however unwilling they may be to think so, matters not, but many strong and striking reasons may be given, to show, that nothing can settle our affairs so expeditiously as an open and determined declaration for independence. Some of which are,

1st, It is the custom of nations, when any two are at war, for some other powers, not engaged in the quarrel, to step in as mediators, and bring about the preliminaries of a peace; but while America calls herself the subject of Britain, no power, however well disposed she may be, can offer her mediation. Wherefore, in our present state, we may quarrel on for ever.

2d, It is unreasonable to suppose, that France or Spain will give us any kind of assistance, if we mean only, to make use of that assistance for the purpose of repairing the breach, and strengthening the connexion between Britain and America; because, those powers would be sufferers by the consequences.

3d, While we profess ourselves the subjects of Britain, we must, in the eyes of foreign nations, be considered as rebels. The precedent is somewhat dangerous to *their peace*, for men to be in arms under the name of subjects; we, on the spot, can solve the paradox: but to unite resistance and subjection, requires an idea much too refined for common understanding.

4th, Should a manifesto be published, and despatched to foreign courts, setting forth the miseries we have endured, and the peaceful methods which we have ineffectually used for redress; declaring, at the same time, that not being

* Those who would fully understand of what great consequence a large and equal representation is to a state, should read Burgh's Political Disquisitions.

able, any longer, to live happily or safely under the cruel disposition of the British court, we had been driven to the necessity of breaking off all connexion with her; at the same time, assuring all such courts of our peaceable disposition towards them, and of our desire of entering into trade with them. Such a memorial would produce more good effects to this continent, than if a ship were freighted with petitions to Britain.

Under our present denomination of British subjects, we can neither be received nor heard abroad : the custom of all courts is against us, and will be so, until, by an independence, we take rank with other nations.

These proceedings may at first appear strange and difficult; but like all other steps, which we have already passed over, will in a little time become familiar and agreeable; and, until an independence is declared, the continent will feel itself like a man who continues putting off some unpleasant business from day to day, yet knows it must be done, hates to set about it, wishes it over, and is continually haunted with the thoughts of its necessity.

APPENDIX,

SINCE the publication of the first edition of this pamphlet, or rather, on the same day on which it came out, the king's speech made its appearance in this city. Had the spirit of prophesy directed the birth of this production, it could not have brought it forth at a more seasonable juncture, or at a more necessary time. The bloody-mindedness of the one, shows the necessity of pursuing the doctrine of the other. Men read by way of revenge :—and the speech, instead of terrifying, prepared a way for the manly principles of independence.

Ceremony, and even silence, from whatever motives they may arise, have a hurtful tendency, when they give the least degree of countenance to base and wicked performances; wherefore, if this maxim be admitted, it naturally follows, that the king's speech, as being a piece of finished villainy, deserved, and still deserves, a general execration, both by the congress and the people. Yet, as the domestic tranquillity of a nation, depends greatly on the *chastity* of what may properly be called *national manners*, it is often better to pass some things over in silent disdain, than to make use of such new methods of dislike, as might introduce the least innovation on that guardian of our peace and safety. And, perhaps, it is chiefly owing to this prudent delicacy, that the king's speech hath not before now suffered a public execution. The speech, if it may be called one, is nothing better than a wilful, audacious libel against the truth, the common good and the existence of mankind; and is a formal and pompous method of offering up human sacrifices to the pride of tyrants. But this general massacre of mankind, is one of the privileges and the certain consequences of kings; for as nature knows them *not*, they know *not her*, and although they are beings of our *own* creating, they know not *us*, and are become the gods of their creators. The speech hath one good quality, which is, that it is not calculated to deceive, neither can we, if we would, be deceived by it. Brutality and tyranny appear on the face of it. It leaves us at no loss; and every line convinces, even in the moment of reading, that he, who hunts the woods for prey, the naked and untutored Indian, is less savage than the king of Britain.

Sir John Dalrymple, the putative father of a whining jesuitical piece, fallaciously called, " *The address of the people of* England *to the inhabitants of* America," hath, perhaps, from a vain supposition that the people *here* were to be frightened at the pomp and description of a king, given (though very unwisely on his part) the real character of the present one: " But," says this writer, " if you are inclined to pay compliments to an administration, which we do not complain of" (meaning the Marquis of Rockingham's at the repeal of the Stamp Act) " it is very unfair in you to withhold them from that prince, *by whose* NOD ALONE *they were permitted to do any thing.*" This is toryism with a witness! Here is idolatry even without a mask: and he who can calmly hear and digest such doctrine, hath forfeited his claim to rationality; is an apostate from the order of manhood, and ought to be considered—as one, who hath not only given up the proper dignity of man, but sunk himself beneath the rank of animals, and contemptibly crawls through the world like a worm.

However, it matters very little now, what the king of England either says or does; he hath wickedly broken through every moral and human obligation, trampled nature and conscience beneath his feet ; and by a steady and constitutional spirit of insolence and cruelty, procured for himself an universal hatred. It is *now* the interest of America to provide for herself. She hath already a large and young family, whom it is more her duty to take care of, than to be granting away her property to support a power which is become a reproach to the names of men and Christians—*Ye*, whose office it is to watch over the morals of a nation, of whatsoever sect or denomination ye are of, as well as ye, who are more immediately the guardians of the public liberty, if you wish to preserve your native country uncontaminated by European corruption, ye must in secret wish a separation—but leaving the moral part to private reflection, I shall chiefly confine my further remarks to the following heads :

1st, That it is the interest of America to be separated from Britain.

2d, Which is the easiest and most practicable plan, *reconciliation* or *independence?* with some occasional remarks.

In support of the first, I could, if I judged it proper, produce the opinion of some of the ablest and most experienced men on this continent ; and whose sentiments, on that head, are not yet publicly known. It is in reality a self-evident position : for no nation, in a state of foreign dependance, limited in its commerce, and cramped and fettered in its legislative powers, can ever arrive at any material eminence. America doth not yet know what opulence is ; and although the progress which she hath made stands unparalleled in the history of other nations, it is but childhood, compared with what she would be capable of arriving at, had she, as she ought to have, the legislative powers in her own hands. England is, at this time, proudly coveting what would do her no good were she to accomplish it ; and the continent hesitating on a matter which will be her final ruin if neglected. It is the commerce and not the conquest of America by which England is to be benefited, and that would in a great measure continue, were the countries as independent of each other as France and Spain ; because in many articles neither can go to a better market. But it is the independence of this country of Britain, or any other, which is now the main and only object worthy of contention; and which, like all other truths discovered by necessity, will appear clearer and stronger every day.

1st, Because it will come to that one time or other.

2d, Because the longer it is delayed, the harder it will be to accomplish.

I have frequently amused myself both in public and private companies, with silently remarking the specious errors of those who speak without reflecting. And among the many which I have heard, the following seems the most general, *viz.* that if this rupture should happen forty or fifty years hence, instead of *now*, the continent would be more able to shake off the dependance. To which I reply, that our military ability, *at this time*, arises from the experience gained in the last war, and which in forty or fifty years time, would be totally extinct. The continent would not, by that time, have a general, or even a military officer left; and we, or those who may succeed us, would be as ignorant of martial matters as the ancient Indians : and this single position, closely attended to, will unanswerably prove that the present time is preferable to all others. The argument turns thus—at the conclusion of the last war, we had experience, but wanted numbers ; and forty or fifty years hence, we shall have numbers, without experience; wherefore, the proper point of time, must be some particular point between the two extremes, in which a sufficiency of the former remains, and a proper increase of the latter is obtained : and that point of time is the present time.

The reader will pardon this digression, as it does not properly come under the head I first set out with, and to which I again return by the following position, *viz.*

Should affairs be patched up with Britain, and she remain the governing and sovereign power of America, (which, as matters are now circumstanced, is giving up the point entirely) we shall deprive ourselves of the very means of sinking the debt we have, or may contract. The value of the back lands which some of the provinces are clandestinely deprived of, by the unjust extension of the limits of Canada, valued only at five pounds sterling per hundred acres, amount to upwards of twenty-five millions, Pennsylvania currency; and the quit-rents at one penny sterling per acre, to two millions yearly.

It is by the sale of those lands that the debt may be sunk, without burden to any, and the quit-rent reserved thereon, will always lessen, and in time, will wholly support the yearly expense of government. It matters not how long the debt is in paying, so that the lands when sold be applied to the discharge of it, and for the execution of which, the congress for the time being, will be the continental trustees.

I proceed now to the second head, *viz.* Which is the easiest and most practicable plan, *reconciliation* or *independence?* with some occasional remarks.

He who takes nature for his guide is not easily beaten out of his argument, and on that ground, I answer generally—*That* INDEPENDENCE *being a* SINGLE SIMPLE LINE, *contained within ourselves ; and reconciliation, a matter exceedingly perplexed and complicated, and in which a treacherous, capricious court is to interfere, gives the answer without a doubt.*

The present state of America is truly alarming to every man who is capable of reflection. Without law, without government, without any other mode of power than what is founded on, and granted by, courtesy. Held together by an unexampled concurrence of sentiment, which is nevertheless subject to change, and which every secret enemy is endeavoring to dissolve. Our present condition is, legislation without law ; wisdom without a plan ; a constitution without a name; and, what is strangely astonishing, perfect independence contending for dependance. The instance is without a precedent; the case never existed before ; and who can tell what may be the event? The property of no man is secure in the present unbraced system of things. The mind of the multitude is left at random, and seeing no fixed object before them, they pursue such as fancy or opinion presents. Nothing is criminal ; there is no such thing as treason; wherefore, every one thinks himself at liberty to act as he pleases. The tories dared not have assembled offensively, had they known that their lives, by that act, were forfeited to the laws of the state. A line of distinction should be drawn between English soldiers taken in battle, and inhabitants of America taken in arms. The first are prisoners, but the latter traitors. The one forfeits his liberty, the other his head.

Notwithstanding our wisdom, there is a visible feebleness in some of our proceedings which gives encouragement to dissentions. The Continental Belt is too loosely buckled. And if something is not done in time, it will be too late to do any thing, and we shall fall into a state, in which neither *Reconciliation* nor *Independence* will be practicable. The king and his worthless adherents are got at their old game of dividing the continent, and there are not wanting among us, printers, who will be busy in spreading specious falsehoods. The artful and hypocritical letter which appeared a few months ago in two of the New-York papers, and likewise in others, is an evidence that there are men who want both judgment and honesty.

It is easy getting into holes and corners and talking of reconciliation : but do such men seriously consider how difficult the task is, and how dangerous it may prove should the continent divide thereon. Do they take within their view, all the various orders of men whose situation and circumstances, as well as their own, are to be considered therein. Do they put themselves in the place of the sufferer whose *all* is *already* gone, and of the soldier, who hath quitted *all* for the defence of his country ? If their ill-judged moderation be suited to their own private situations *only*, regardless of others, the event will convince them that " they are reckoning without their host."

Put us, say some, on the footing we were in the year 1763 : to which I answer, the request is not *now* in the power of Britan to comply with, neither will she propose it ; but if it were, and even should it be granted, I ask, as a reasonable question, by what means is such a corrupt and faithless court to be kept to its engagements ? Another parliament, nay, even the present, may hereafter repeal the obligation, on the pretence of its being violently obtained, or unwisely granted ; and in that case, where is our redress ? No going to law with nations ; cannon are the barristers of crowns ; and the sword, not of justice, but of war, decides the suit. To be on the footing of 1763, it is not sufficient, that the laws only be put in the same state, but, that our circumstances, likewise, be put in the same state ; our burnt and destroyed towns repaired or built up, our private losses made good, our public debts (contracted for defence) discharged ; otherwise, we shall be millions worse than we were at that enviable period. Such a request, had it been complied with a year ago, would have won the heart and soul of the continent—but now it is too late : " The Rubicon is passed."

Besides, the taking up arms, merely to enfore the repeal of a pecuniary law, seems as unwarrantable by the divine law, and as repugnant to human feelings, as the taking up arms to enforce obedience thereto. The object, on either side, doth not justify the means ; for the lives of men are too valuable to be cast away on such trifles. It is the violence which is done and threatened to our persons; the destruction of our property by an armed force; the invasion of our country by fire and sword, which conscientiously qualifies the use of arms : and the instant in which such mode of defence became necessary, all subjection to Britain ought to have ceased; and the independence of America should have been considered as dating its era from, and published by, *the first musket that was fired against her.* This line is a line of consistency; neither drawn by caprice, nor extended by ambition; but produced by a chain of events, of which the colonies were not the authors.

I shall conclude these remarks, with the following timely and well-intended hints. We ought to reflect, that there are three different ways by which an independency may hereafter be effected; and that *one* of those *three*, will, one day or other, be the fate of America, *viz.* By the legal voice of the people in congress; by a military power; or by a mob : it may not always happen that our soldiers are citizens, and the multitude a body of reasonable men; virtue, as I have already remarked, is not hereditary, neither is it perpetual. Should an independency be brought about by the first of those means, we have every opportunity and every encouragement before us, to form the noblest, purest constitution on the face of the earth. We have it in our power to begin the world over again. A situation, similar to the present, hath not happened since the days of Noah until now. The birth-day of a new world is at hand, and a race of men, perhaps as numerous as all Europe contains, are to receive their portion of freedom from the events of a few months. The reflection is awful—and in this point of view, how trifling, how ridiculous, do the little paltry cavilings, of a few weak or interested men appear, when weighed against the business of a world.

Should we neglect the present favorable and inviting period, and independence be hereafter effected by any other means, we must charge the consequence to ourselves, or to those rather, whose narrow and prejudiced souls, are habitually opposing the measure, without either inquiring or reflecting. There are reasons to be given in support of independence, which men should rather privately think of, than be publicly told of. We ought not now to be debating whether we shall be independent or not, but anxious to accomplish it on a firm, secure, and honorable basis, and uneasy rather, that it is not yet began upon. Every day convinces us of its necessity. Even the tories (if such beings yet remain among us) should, of all men, be the most solicitous to promote it; for, as the appointment of committees at first, protected them from popular rage, so, a wise and well established form of government, will be the only certain means of continuing it securely to them. Wherefore, if they have not virtue enough to be *Whigs*, they ought to have prudence enough to wish for independence.

In short, independence is the only *bond* that can tie and keep us together. We shall then see our object, and our ears will be legally shut against the schemes of an intriguing, as well as cruel, enemy. We shall then, too, be on a proper footing to treat with Britain; for there is reason to conclude, that the pride of that court, will be less hurt by treating with the American states for terms of peace, than with those, whom she denominates "rebellious subjects," for terms of accommodation. It is our delaying it that encourages her to hope for conquest, and our backwardness tends only to prolong the war. As we have, without any good effect therefrom, withheld our trade to obtain a redress of our grievances, let us *now* try the alternative, by independently redressing them ourselves, and then offering to open the trade. The mercantile and reasonable part of England, will be still with us; because, peace, *with* trade, is preferable to war, *without* it. And if this offer be not accepted, other courts may be applied to.

On these grounds I rest the matter. And as no offer hath yet been made to refute the doctrine contained in the former editions of this pamphlet, it is a negative proof, that either the doctrine cannot be refuted, or, that the party in favor of it are too numerous to be opposed. *Wherefore*, instead of gazing at each other, with suspicious or doubtful curiosity, let each of us, hold out to his neighbor the hearty hand of friendship, and unite in drawing a line, which, like an act of oblivion, shall bury in forgetfulness every former dissention. Let the names of whig and tory be extinct; and let none other be heard among us, than those of *a good citizen; an open and resolute friend;* and *a virtuous supporter of the* RIGHTS *of* MANKIND, *and of the* FREE AND INDEPENDENT STATES OF AMERICA.

END OF COMMON SENSE.

Rights of Man

RIGHTS OF MAN.

BEING

AN ANSWER

TO MR. BURKE'S ATTACK ON THE FRENCH REVOLUTION.

—

PART I.

6

TO

GEORGE WASHINGTON,

PRESIDENT OF THE UNITED STATES OF AMERICA.

SIR,

I PRESENT you a small treatise in defence of those principles of freedom which your exemplary virtue hath so
eminently contributed to establish.   That the rights of
man may become as universal as your benevolence can
wish, and that you may enjoy the happiness of seeing the
new world regenerate the old, is the prayer of

Sir,

Your much obliged, and

Obedient humble servant,

THOMAS PAINE.

RIGHTS OF MAN.

Among the incivilities by which nations or individuals provoke and irritate each other, Mr. Burke's pamphlet on the French revolution is an extraordinary instance. Neither the people of France, nor the national assembly, were troubling themselves about the affairs of England, or the English parliament; and why Mr. Burke should commence an unprovoked attack upon them, both in parliament and in public, is a conduct that cannot be pardoned on the score of manners, nor justified on that of policy.

There is scarcely an epithet of abuse to be found in the English language, with which Mr. Burke has not loaded the French nation and the national assembly. Every thing which rancor, prejudice, ignorance or knowledge could suggest, are poured forth in the copious fury of near four hundred pages. In the strain and on the plan Mr. Burke was writing, he might have wrote on to as many thousand. When the tongue or the pen is let loose in a phrenzy of passion, it is the man, and not the subject that becomes exhausted.

Hitherto Mr. Burke has been mistaken and disappointed in the opinions he had formed on the affairs of France; but such is the ingenuity of his hope, or the malignancy of his despair, that it furnishes him with new pretences to go on. There was a time when it was impossible to make Mr. Burke believe there would be any revolution in

France: His opinion then was, that the French had neither spirit to undertake it, nor fortitude to support it; and
now that there is one, he seeks an escape by condemning it.

Not sufficiently content with abusing the national assembly, a great part of his work is taken up with abusing Dr.
Price (one of the best hearted men that exists) and the two
societies in England, known by the name of the Revolution
and the Constitutional societies.

Dr. Price had preached a sermon on the 4th of Novem-
ber, 1789, being the anniversary of what is called in England the revolution, which took place in 1688. Mr. Burke,
speaking of this sermon, says, "the political divine proceeds dogmatically to assert, that, by the principles of the
revolution, the people of England have acquired three fundamental rights:

1st, To choose our own governors.

2d, To cashier them for misconduct.

3d. To frame a government for ourselves."

Dr. Price does not say that the right to do these things
exists in this or in that person, or in this or in that description of persons, but that it exists in the *whole*—that it is a
right resident in the nation. Mr. Burke, on the contrary,
denies that such a right exists in the nation, either in whole
or in part, or that it exists any where; and what is still
more strange and marvellous, he says, that "the people
of England utterly disclaim such right, and that they will
resist the practical assertion of it with their lives and fortunes." That men will take up arms, and spend their lives
and fortunes *not* to maintain their rights, but to maintain
that they have *not* rights, is an entire new species of discovery, and suited to the paradoxical genius of Mr. Burke.

The method which Mr. Burke takes to prove that the
people of England have no such rights, and that such rights
do not exist in the nation, either in whole or in part, or any
where at all, is of the same marvellous and monstrous kind
with what he has already said; for his arguments are, that
the persons, or the generation of persons in whom they did
exist, are dead, and with them the right is dead also. To
prove this, he quotes a declaration made by parliament
about an hundred years ago, to William and Mary, in these
words: "The lords spiritual and temporal, and commons,
do, in the name of the people aforesaid—(meaning the
people of England then living) most humbly and faithfully

submit themselves, their *heirs* and *posterity*, FOR EVER."—
He also quotes a clause of another act of parliament made
in the same reign, the terms of which, he says, " bind us—
(meaning the people of that day)—our *heirs* and our *posterity,* to *them,* their *heirs* and *posterity,* to the end of time."

Mr. Burke considers his point sufficiently established by
producing those clauses, which he enforces by saying that
they exclude the right of the nation *for ever:* and not yet
content with making such declarations, repeated over and
over again, he further says, " that if the people of England
possessed such a right before the revolution" (which he
acknowledges to have been the case, not only in England,
but throughout Europe, at an early period) " yet that the
English nation did, at the time of the revolution, most solemnly renounce and abdicate it, for themselves, and *for all
their posterity for ever.*"

As Mr. Burke occasionally applies the poison drawn
from his horrid principles (if it is not a profanation to call
them by the name of principles) not only to the English nation, but to the French revolution and the national assembly, and charges that august, illuminated and illuminating
body of men with the epithet of *usurpers,* I shall, *sans cere-
monie,* place another system of principles in opposition to
his.

The English parliament of 1688, did a certain thing,
which for themselves and their constituents, they had a right
to do, and which appeared right should be done; but, in
addition to this right, which they possessed by delegation,
they set up another right by assumption, that of binding and
controlling posterity to the end of time. The case, therefore, divides itself into two parts; the right which they
possessed by delegation, and the right which they set up
by assumption. The first is admitted; but with respect to
the second, I reply :—

There never did, nor never can exist a parliament, or
any description of men, or any generation of men, in any
country, possessed of the right or the power of binding or
controlling posterity to the " end of time," or of commanding for ever how the world shall be governed, or who shall
govern it; and therefore all such clauses, acts, or declarations, by which the makers of them attempt to do what
they have neither the right nor the power to do, nor the
power to execute, are in themselves null and void. Every
age and generation must be as free to act for itself, *in all*

cases, as the ages and generations which preceded it. The vanity and presumption of governing beyond the grave, is the most ridiculous and insolent of all tyrannies. Man has no property in man; neither has any generation a property in the generations which are to follow. The parliament or the people of 1688, or of any other period, had no more right to dispose of the people of the present day, or to bind or to control them *in any shape whatever*, than the parliament or the people of the present day have to dispose of, bind or control those who are to live an hundred or a thousand years hence. Every generation is and must be competent to all the purposes which its occasions require. It is the living and not the dead, that are to be accommodated. When man ceases to be, his power and his wants cease with him; and having no longer any participation in the concerns of this world, he has no longer any authority in directing who shall be its governors, or how its government shall be organized, or how administered.

I am not contending for, nor against, any form of government, nor for nor against any party, here or elsewhere. That which a whole nation chooses to do, it has a right to do. Mr. Burke denies it. Where then does the right exist? I am contending for the right of the *living*, and against their being willed away, and controlled and contracted for, by the manuscript-assumed authority of the dead; and Mr. Burke is contending for the authority of the dead over the rights and freedom of the living. There was a time when kings disposed of their crowns by will upon their death-beds, and consigned the people, like beasts of the field, to whatever successor they appointed. This is now so exploded as scarcely to be remembered, and so monstrous as hardly to be believed: but the parliamentary clauses upon which Mr. Burke builds his political church, are of the same nature.

The laws of every country must be analogous to some common principle. In England, no parent or master, nor all the authority of parliament, omnipotent as it has called itself, can bind or control the personal freedom even of an individual beyond the age of twenty-one years: on what ground of right then could the parliament of 1688, or any other parliament bind all posterity for ever?

Those who have quitted the world, and those who are not arrived yet in it, are as remote from each other as the utmost stretch of mortal imagination can conceive: what

possible obligation then can exist between them, what rule
or principle can be laid down, that two nonentities, the one
out of existence, and the other not in, and who never can
meet in this world, that the one should control the other
to the end of time?

In England, it is said that money cannot be taken out
of the pockets of the people without their consent: but
who authorized, and who could authorize the parliament
of 1688 to control and take away the freedom of posterity, and limit and confine their rights of acting in certain
cases for ever, who were not in existence to give or withhold their consent?

A greater absurdity cannot present itself to the understanding of man, than what Mr. Burke offers to his readers. He tells them, and he tells the world to come, that
a certain body of men who existed an hundred years ago,
made a law, and that there does not now exist in the nation, nor never will, nor never can, a power to alter it.—
Under how many subtleties, or absurdities, has the divine
right to govern been imposed on the credulity of mankind:
Mr. Burke has discovered a new one, and he has shortened
his journey to Rome, by appealing to the power of this in-
fallible parliament of former days; and he produces what
it has done, as of divine authority: for that power must be
certainly more than human, which no human power to the
end of time can alter.

But Mr. Burke has done some service, not to his cause,
but to his country, by bringing those clauses into public
view. They serve to demonstrate how necessary it is at
all times to watch against the attempted encroachment of
power, and to prevent its running to excess. It is somewhat extraordinary, that the offence for which James II.
was expelled, that of setting up power by *assumption*,
should be re-acted under another shape and form, by the
parliament that expelled him. It shows, that the rights of
man were but imperfectly understood at the revolution;
for certain it is that the right which that parliament set up
by *assumption* (for by delegation it had not, and could not
have it, because none could give it) over the persons and
freedom of posterity for ever, was of the same tyrannical,
unfounded kind which James attempted to set up over the
parliament and the nation, and for which he was expelled.
The only difference is, (for in principle they differ not) that
the one was an usurper over the living, and the other over

the unborn; and as the one has no better authority to stand
upon than the other, both of them must be equally null and
void, and of no effect.

From what or whence, does Mr. Burke prove the right
of any human power to bind posterity for ever? He has
produced his clauses; but he must produce also his proofs
that such a right existed, and show how it existed. If it
ever existed, it must now exist; for whatever appertains
to the nature of man, cannot be annihilated by man. It
is the nature of man to die, and he will continue to die
as long as he continues to be born. But Mr. Burke has set
up a sort of political Adam, in whom all posterity are
bound for ever; he must therefore prove that his Adam
possessed such a power or such a right.

The weaker any cord is, the less it will bear to be
stretched, and the worse is the policy to stretch it, unless it
is intended to break it. Had a person contemplated the
overthrow of Mr. Burke's positions, he would have proceeded as Mr. Burke has done. He would have magnified
the authorities, on purpose to have called the *right* of them
into question; and the instant the question of right was
started, the authorities must have been given up.

It requires but a very small glance of thought to perceive, that although laws made in one generation often continue in force through succeeding generations, yet they
continue to derive their force from the consent of the living.
A law not repealed continues in force, not because it *cannot* be repealed, but because it *is not* repealed; and the non-
repealing passes for consent.

But Mr. Burke's clauses have not even this qualification
in their favor. They become null, by attempting to become immortal. The nature of them precludes consent.
They destroy the right which they *might* have, by ground-
ing it on a right which they *cannot* have. Immortal power
is not a human right, and therefore cannot be a right of
parliament. The parliament of 1688 might as well have
passed an act to have authorized itself to live for ever, as
to make their authority live for ever. All, therefore, that
can be said of them is, that they are a formality of words,
of as much import, as if those who used them had address-
ed a congratulation to themselves, and, in the oriental style
of antiquity, had said, O! parliament, live for ever!

The circumstances of the world are continually changing, and the opinions of men change also; and as govern-

ment is for the living, and not for the dead, it is the living
only that has any right in it. That which may be thought
right and found convenient in one age, may be thought
wrong and found inconvenient in another. In such cases,
who is to decide, the living, or the dead?

As almost one hundred pages of Mr. Burke's book are
employed upon these clauses, it will consequently follow,
that if the clauses themselves, so far as they set up an *assumed, usurped* dominion over posterity for ever, are un-
authoritative, and in their nature, null and void, that all
his voluminous inferences and declamation drawn therefrom, or founded thereon, are null and void also: and on
this ground I rest the matter.

We now come more particularly to the affairs of France.
Mr. Burke's book has the appearance of being written as
instruction to the French nation; but if I may permit myself
the use of an extravagant metaphor, suited to the extravagance of the case, it is darkness attempting to illuminate
light.

While I am writing this, there is accidentally before me
some proposals for a declaration of rights by the marquis
de la Fayette (I ask his pardon for using his former address, and do it only for distinction's sake) to the national
assembly on the 11th of July 1789, three days before the
taking of the Bastile; and I cannot but be struck how opposite the sources are from which that gentleman and Mr.
Burke draw their principles. Instead of referring to mus-
ty records and mouldy parchments, to prove that the rights
of the living are lost, " renounced and abdicated for ever"
by those who are now no more, as Mr. Burke has done,
M. de la Fayette applies to the living world, and emphatically says, " Call to mind the sentiments which nature has
engraved in the heart of every citizen, and which take a
new force when they are solemnly recognized by all:—
for a nation to love liberty, it is sufficient that she knows
it; and to be free, it is sufficient that she wills it." How
dry, barren and obscure, is the source from which Mr.
Burke labors; and how ineffectual, though embellished
with flowers, is all his declamation and his argument, compared with these clear, concise and soul-animating sentiments: few and short as they are, they lead on to a vast
field of generous and manly thinking, and do not finish,
like Mr. Burke's periods, with music in the ear, and nothing
in the heart.

As I have introduced the mention of M. de la Fayette, I will take the liberty of adding an anecdote respecting his farewell address to the congress of America in 1783, and which occurred fresh to my mind when I saw Mr. Burke's thundering attack on the French revolution.—M. de la Fayette went to America at an early period of the war, and continued a volunteer in her service to the end. His conduct through the whole of that enterprise is one of the most extraordinary that is to be found in the history of a young man, scarcely then twenty years of age. Situated in a country that was like the lap of sensual pleasure, and with the means of enjoying it, how few are there to be found who would exchange such a scene for the woods and wilderness of America, and pass the flowery years of youth in unprofitable danger and hardship! But such is the fact. When the war ended, and he was on the point of taking his final departure, he presented himself to congress, and contemplating, in his affectionate farewell, the revolution he had seen, expressed himself in these words : *" May this great monument raised to Liberty, serve as a lesson to the oppressor, and an example to the oppressed !"* When this address came to the hands of Dr. Franklin, who was then in France, he applied to count Vergennes to have it inserted in the French gazette, but never could obtain his consent. The fact was, that count Vergennes was an aristocratical despot, at home, and dreaded the example of the American revolution in France, as certain other persons now dread the example of the French revolution in England ; and Mr. Burke's tribute of fear (for in this light his book must be considered) runs parallel with count Vergennes' refusal. But to return more particularly to his work.

"We have seen (says Mr. Burke) the French rebel against a mild and lawful monarch, with more fury, outrage and insult, than any people has been known to rise against the most illegal usurper, or the most sanguinary tyrant."— This is one among a thousand other instances, in which Mr. Burke shows that he is ignorant of the springs and principles of the French revolution.

It was not against Louis XVI. but against the despotic principle of the government, that the nation revolted. These principles had not their origin in him, but in the original establishment, many centuries back ; and they were become too deeply rooted to be removed, and the Augean stable of parasites and plunderers too abominably filthy to be cleansed, by any thing short of a complete and universal revolution.

When it becomes necessary to do a thing, the whole heart should join in the measure, or it should not be attempted. That crisis was then arrived, and there remained no choice but to act with determined vigor, or not to act at all. The king was known to be the friend of the nation, and this circumstance was favorable to the enterprise. Perhaps no man bred up in the style of an absolute king, ever possessed a heart so little disposed to the exercise of that species of power as the present king of France. But the principles of the government itself still remained the same. The monarch and monarchy were distinct and separate things; and it was against the established despotism of the latter, and not against the person or principles of the former, that the revolt commenced, and the revolution has been carried on.

Mr. Burke does not attend to this distinction between men and principles, and therefore he does not see that a revolt may take place against the despotism of the latter, while there lies no charge of despotism against the former.

The natural moderation of Louis XVI. contributed nothing to alter the hereditary despotism of the monarchy. All the tyrannies of former reigns, acted under that hereditary despotism, were still liable to be revived in the hands of a successor. It was not the respite of a reign that would satisfy France, enlightened as she was then become. A casual discontinuance of the *practice* of despotism, is not a discontinuance of its *principles ;* the former depends on the virtue of the individual who is in immediate possession of the power ; the latter, on the virtue and fortitude of the nation. In the case of Charles I. and James II. of England, the revolt was against the personal despotism of the men; whereas in France, it was against the hereditary despotism of the established government. But men who can consign over the the rights of posterity for ever on the authority of a mouldy parchment, like Mr. Burke, are not qualified to judge of this revolution. It takes in a field too vast for their views to explore, and proceeds with a mightiness of reason they cannot keep pace with.

But there are many points of view in which this revolution may be considered. When despotism has established itself for ages in a country, as in France, it is not in the person of the king only that it resides. It has the

appearance of being so in show, and in nominal authority;
but it is not so in practice, and in fact. It has its standard every where. Every office and department has its
despotism, founded upon custom and usage. Every place
has its Bastile, and every Bastile its despot. The original
hereditary despotism resident in the person of the king,
divides and sub-divides itself into a thousand shapes and
forms, till at last the whole of it is acted by deputation.—
This was the case in France; and against this species of
despotism, proceeding on through an endless labyrinth of
office till the source of it is scarcely perceptible, there is
no mode of redress. It strengthens itself by assuming the
appearance of duty, and tyrannizes under the pretence of
obeying.

When a man reflects on the condition which France was
in from the nature of her government, he will see other
causes for revolt than those which immediately connect
themselves with the person or character of Louis XVI.—
There were, if I may so express it, a thousand despotisms
to be reformed in France, which had grown up under the
hereditary despotism of the monarchy, and become so
rooted as to be in a great measure independent of it. Between the monarchy, the parliament, and the church, there
was a *rivalship* of despotism: besides the feudal despotism
operating locally, and the ministerial despotism operating
every where. But Mr. Burke, by considering the king as
the only possible object of a revolt, speaks as if France
was a village, in which every thing that passed must be
known to its commanding officer, and no oppression could
be acted but what he could immediately control. Mr.
Burke might have been in the Bastile his whole life, as
well under Louis XVI. as Louis XIV. and neither the one
nor the other known that such a man as Mr. Burke existed. The despotic principles of the government were the
same in both reigns, though the dispositions of the men
were as remote as tyranny and benevolence.

What Mr. Burke considers as a reproach to the French
revolution, that of bringing it forward under a reign more
mild than the preceding ones, is one of its highest honors.
The revolutions that have taken place in other European
countries, have been excited by personal hatred. The
rage was against the man, and he became the victim.—
But, in the instance of France, we see a revolution generated in the rational contemplation of the rights of man, and

distinguishing from the beginning between persons and
principles.

But Mr. Burke appears to have no idea of principles,
when he is contemplating governments. "Ten years ago,"
says he, "I could have felicitated France on her having a
government, without inquiring what the nature of that government was, or how it was administered." Is this the language of a rational man? Is it the language of a heart
feeling as it ought to feel for the rights and happiness of
the human race? On this ground, Mr. Burke must compliment every government in the world, while the victims
who suffer under them, whether sold into slavery or tortured out of existence, are wholly forgotten. It is power,
and not principles that Mr. Burke venerates; and under
this abominable depravity, he is disqualified to judge between them. Thus much for his opinion as to the occasion
of the French revolution. I now proceed to other consid-
erations.

I know a place in America called Point-no-Point; because as you proceed along the shore, gay and flowery as
Mr. Burke's language, it continually recedes and presents
itself at a distance a-head; and when you have got as far
as you can go, there is no point at all. Just thus is it with
Mr. Burke's three hundred and fifty-six pages. It is therefore difficult to reply to him. But as the points that he
wishes to establish may be inferred from what he abuses,
it is in his paradoxes that we must look for his arguments.

As to the tragic paintings by which Mr. Burke has out-
raged his own imagination, and seeks to work upon that of
his readers, they are very well calculated for theatrical
representation, where facts are manufactured for the sake
of show, and accommodated to produce, through the weakness of sympathy, a weeping effect. But Mr. Burke should
recollect that he is writing history, and not *plays*; and that
his readers will expect truth, and not the spouting rant of
high-toned exclamation.

When we see a man dramatically lamenting in a publication intended to be believed, that "*The age of chivalry is
gone;*" that "*the glory of Europe is extinguished forever!*"
that "*the unbought grace of life* (if any one knows what it
is,) *the cheap defence of nations, the nurse of manly sentiment
and heroic enterprise is gone!*" And all this because the
Quixote age of chivalric nonsense is gone, what opinion
can we form of his judgment, or what regard can we pay

to his facts? In the rhapsody of his imagination, he has discovered a world of windmills, and his sorrows are, that there are no Quixotes to attack them. But if the age of aristocracy, like that of chivalry, should fall, and they had originally some connexion, Mr. Burke, the trumpeter of the order, may continue his parody to the end, and finish with exclaiming—" *Othello's occupation's gone!*"

Notwithstanding Mr. Burke's horrid paintings, when the French revolution is compared with that of other countries, the astonishment will be, that it is marked with so few sacrifices; but this astonishment will cease when we reflect that it was *principles*, and not *persons*, that were the meditated objects of destruction. The mind of the nation was acted upon by a higher stimulus than what the consideration of persons could inspire, and sought a higher conquest than could be produced by the downfal of an enemy.— Among the few who fell, there do not appear to be any that were intentionally singled out. They all of them had their fate in the circumstances of the moment, and were not pursued with that long, cold-blooded, unabated revenge which pursued the unfortunate Scotch in the affair of 1745.

Through the whole of Mr. Burke's book I do not observe that the Bastile is mentioned more than once, and that with a kind of implication as if he was sorry it is pulled down, and wished it was built up again. "We have rebuilt Newgate (says he) and tenanted the mansion; and we have prisons almost as strong as the Bastile for those who dare to libel the queen of France."* As to what a madman, like the person called lord George Gordon, might say, and to whom Newgate is rather a bedlam than a prison, it is unworthy a rational consideration. It was a madman that libelled—and that is sufficient apology and it afforded an opportunity for confining him, which was the thing that was wished for: but certain it is that Mr. Burke, who does not call himself a madman, whatever other people may do, has libelled, in the most unprovoked manner,

---

* Since writing the above, two other places occur in Mr. Burke's pamphlet, in which the name of Bastile is mentioned but in the same manner.— In the one, he introduces it in a sort of obscure question, and asks—' Will any ministers who now serve such a king with but a decent appearance of respect, cordially obey the orders of those whom but the other day, in his name, they had committed to the Bastile?' In the other the taking it is mentioned as implying criminality in the French guards who assisted in demolishing it. "They have not" says he "forgot the taking the king's castles at Paris." This is Mr. Burke, who pretends to write on constitutional freedom.

and in the grossest style of the most vulgar abuse, the whole representative authority of France; and yet Mr. Burke takes his seat in the British house of commons!— From his violence and his grief, his silence on some points and his excess on others, it is difficult not to believe that Mr. Burke is sorry, extremely sorry, that arbitrary power, the power of the pope and the Bastile, are pulled down.

Not one glance of compassion, not one commiserating reflection, that I can find throughout his book, has he bestowed on those that lingered out the most wretched of lives, a life without hope, in the most miserable of prisons. It is painful to behold a man employing his talents to corrupt himself. Nature has been kinder to Mr. Burke than he has to her. He is not affected by the reality of distress touching upon his heart, but by the showy resemblance of it striking his imagination. He pities the plumage, but forgets the dying bird. Accustomed to kiss the aristocratical hand that hath purloined him from himself, he degenerates into a composition of art, and the genuine soul of nature forsakes him. His hero or his heroine must be a tragedy-victim, expiring in show, and not the real prisoner of misery, sliding into death in the silence of a dungeon.

As Mr. Burke has passed over the whole transaction of the Bastile (and his silence is nothing in his favor) and has entertained his readers with reflections on supposed facts, distorted into real falsehoods, I will give, since he has not, some account of the circumstances which preceded that transaction. They will serve to show, that less mischief could scarce have accompanied such an event, when considered with the treacherous and hostile aggravations of the enemies of the revolution.

The mind can hardly picture to itself a more tremendous scene than what the city of Paris exhibited at the time of taking the Bastile, and for two days before and after, nor conceive the possibility of its quieting so soon. At a distance, this transaction has appeared only as an act of heroism, standing on itself: and the close political connexion it had with the revolution is lost in the brilliancy of the achievement. But we are to consider it as the strength of the parties, brought man to man, and contending for the issue. The Bastile was to be either the prize or the prison of the assailants. The downfal of it included the idea of

the downfal of despotism; and this compounded image
was become as figuratively united as Bunyan's Doubting
Castle and giant Despair.

The national assembly, before and at the time of taking
the Bastile, was sitting at Versailles, twelve miles distant
from Paris. About a week before the rising of the Parisians and their taking the Bastile, it was discovered that a
plot was forming, at the head of which was the count
d'Artois, the king's youngest brother, for demolishing the
national assembly, seizing its members, and thereby crush-
ing, by a *coup de main*, all hopes and prospects of forming
a free government. For the sake of humanity, as well as
of freedom, it is well this plan did not succeed. Examples
are not wanting to show how dreadfully vindictive and
cruel are all old governments, when they are successful
against what they call a revolt.

This plan must have been some time in contemplation;
because in order to carry it into execution, it was necessary to collect a large military force round Paris, and to cut
off the communication between that city and the national
assembly at Versailles. The troops destined for this service were chiefly the foreign troops in the pay of France,
and who, for this particular purpose, were drawn from the
distant provinces where they were then stationed. When
they were collected, to the amount of between twenty-five
and thirty thousand, it was judged time to put the plan in
execution. The ministry who were then in office, and who
were friendly to the revolution, were instantly dismissed,
and a new ministry formed of those who had concerted
the project:—among whom was count de Broglio, and to
his share was given the command of those troops. The
character of this man, as described to me in a letter which
I communicated to Mr. Burke before he began to write his
book, and from an authority which Mr. Burke well knows
was good, was that of " an high-flying aristocrat, cool, and
capable of every mischief."

While these matters were agitating, the national assembly stood in the most perilous and critical situation that a
body of men can be supposed to act in. They were the
devoted victims, and they knew it. They had the hearts
and wishes of their country on their side, but military authority they had none. The guards of Broglio surrounded the hall where the assembly sat, ready, at the word of
command, to seize their persons, as had been done the

year before to the parliament in Paris. Had the national assembly deserted their trust, or had they exhibited signs of weakness or fear, their enemies had been encouraged, and the country depressed. When the situation they stood in, the cause they were engaged in, and the crisis then ready to burst which should determine their personal and political fate, and that of their country, and probably of Europe, are taken into one view, none but a heart callous with prejudice, or corrupted by dependance, can avoid interesting itself in their success.

The archbishop of Vienne was at this time president of the national assembly; a person too old to undergo the scene that a few days, or a few hours, might bring forth. A man of more activity, and bolder fortitude, was necessary; and the national assembly chose (under the form of vice-president, for the presidency still rested in the archbishop) M. de la Fayette; and this is the only instance of a vice-president being chosen. It was at the moment this storm was pending, July 11, that a declaration of rights was brought forward by M. de la Fayette, and is the same which is alluded to in page 51. It was hastily drawn up, and makes only a part of a more extensive declaration of rights, agreed upon and adopted afterwards by the national assembly. The particular reason for bringing it forward at this moment (M. de la Fayette has since informed me) was, that if the national assembly should fall in the threatened destruction that then surrounded it, some traces of its principles might have the chance of surviving the wreck.

Every thing now was drawing to a crisis. The event was freedom or slavery. On one side an army of nearly thirty thousand men; on the other an unarmed body of citizens, for the citizens of Paris on whom the national assembly must then immediately depend, were as unarmed and as undisciplined as the citizens of London are now.— The French guards had given strong symptoms of their being attached to the national cause; but their numbers were small, not a tenth part of the force that Broglio commanded, and their officers were in the interest of Broglio.

Matters being now ripe for execution, the new ministry made their appearance in office. The reader will carry in his mind, that the Bastile was taken the 14th of July: the point of time I am now speaking to, is the 12th. As soon as the news of the change of the ministry reached

Paris in the afternoon, all the play-houses and places of entertainment, shops and houses, were shut up. The change of ministry was considered as the prelude of hostilities, and the opinion was rightly founded.

The foreign troops began to advance towards the city. The prince de Lambesc, who commanded a body of German cavalry, approached by the palace of Louis XV. which connects itself with some of the streets. In his march he insulted and struck an old man with his sword. The French are remarkable for their respect to old age, and the insolence with which it appeared to be done, uniting with the general fermentation they were in, produced a powerful effect, and a cry of *to arms! to arms!* spread itself in a moment over the whole city.

Arms they had none, nor scarcely any who knew the use of them; but desperate resolution, when every hope is at stake, supplies, for a while, the want of arms. Near where the prince de Lambesc was drawn up, were large piles of stones collected for building the new bridge, and with these the people attacked the cavalry. A party of the French guards, upon hearing the firing, rushed from their quarters and joined the people; and night coming on the cavalry retreated.

The streets of Paris, being narrow, are favorable for defence; and the loftiness of the houses, consisting of many stories, from which great annoyance might be given, secured them against nocturnal enterprises; and the night was spent in providing themselves with every sort of weapon they could make or procure : guns, swords, blacksmiths' hammers, carpenters' axes, iron crows, pikes, halberds, pitchforks, spits, clubs, &c.

The incredible numbers with which they assembled the next morning, and the still more incredible resolution they exhibited, embarrassed and astonished their enemies.— Little did the new ministry expect such a salute. Accustomed to slavery themselves, they had no idea that liberty was capable of such inspiration, or that a body of unarmed citizens would dare to face the military force of thirty thousand men. Every moment of this day was employed in collecting arms, concerting plans, and arranging themselves in the best order which such an instantaneous movement could afford. Broglio continued lying round the city, but made no further advances this day, and the

succeeding night passed with as much tranquillity as such
a scene could possibly produce.

But the defence only was not the object of the citizens.
They had a cause at stake, on which depended their freedom or their slavery. They every moment expected an
attack, or to hear of one made on the national assembly ;
and in such a situation, the most prompt measures are
sometimes the best. The object that now presented itself,
was the Bastile ; and the *eclat* of carrying such a fortress
in the face of such an army, could not fail to strike terror
into the new ministry, who had scarcely yet had time to
meet. By some intercepted correspondence this morning,
it was discovered, that the mayor of Paris, M. de Flesseles
who appeared to be in their interest, was betraying them;
and from this discovery, there remained no doubt that
Broglio would reinforce the Bastile the ensuing evening.
It was therefore necessary to attack it that day ; but before this could be done, it was first necessary to procure a
better supply of arms than they were then possessed of.

There was, adjoining to the city, a large magazine of
arms deposited at the hospital of the invalids, which the
citizens summoned to surrender ; and as the place was not
defensible, nor attempted much defence, they soon succeeded. Thus supplied, they marched to attack the Bastile ; a vast mixed multitude of all ages, and of all degrees,
and armed with all sorts of weapons. Imagination would
fail of describing to itself the appearance of such a procession, and of the anxiety for the events which a few hours
or a few minutes might produce. What plans the ministry
was forming, were as unknown to the people within the city
as what the citizens were doing was unknown to them ; and
what movements Broglio might make for the support or relief of the place, were to the citizens equally unknown.
All was mystery and hazard.

That the Bastile was attacked with an enthusiasm of
heroism, such only as the highest animation of liberty
could inspire, and carried in the space of a few hours, is
an event which the world is fully possessed of. I am not
undertaking a detail of the attack, but bringing into view,
the conspiracy against the nation which provoked it, and
which fell with the Bastile. The prison to which the new
ministry were dooming the national assembly, in addition
to its being the high altar and castle of despotism, became
the proper object to begin with. This enterprise broke up

the new ministry, who began now to fly from the ruin they
had prepared for others.   The troops of Broglio dispersed
and himself fled also.

Mr. Burke has spoken a great deal about plots, but he
has never once spoken of this plot against the national assembly, and the liberties of the nation ; and that he might
not, he has passed over all the circumstances that might
throw it in his way. The exiles who have fled from France,
whose cause he so much interests himself in, and from
whom he has had his lesson, fled in consequence of the
miscarriage of this plot. No plot was formed against them :
it was they who were plotting against others ; and those
who fell, met, not unjustly, the punishment they were preparing to execute. But will Mr. Burke say, that if this
plot, contrived with the subtlety of an ambuscade, had
succeeded, the successful party would have restrained their
wrath so soon ? Let the history of all old governments answer the question.

Whom has the national assembly brought to the scaf-
fold ? None. They were themselves the devoted victims
of this plot, and they have not retaliated ; why then are
they charged with revenge they have not acted ? In the
tremendous breaking forth of a whole people, in which all
degrees, tempers and characters are confounded, and deliv-
ering themselves by a miracle of exertion, from the destruction meditated against them, is it to be expected that
nothing will happen ? When men are sore with the sense
of oppressions, and menaced with the prospect of new ones,
is the calmness of philosophy, or the palsy of insensibility
to be looked for ? Mr. Burke exclaims against outrage ;
yet the greatest is that which he has committed. His
book is a volume of outrage, not apologized for by the impulse of a moment, but cherished through a space of ten
months ; yet Mr. Burke had no provocation, no life, no interest at stake.

More citizens fell in this struggle than of their opponents;
but four or five persons were seized by the populace, and
instantly put to death ; the governor of the Bastile, and the
mayor of Paris, who was detected in the act of betraying
them ; and afterwards Foulon, one of the new ministry, and
Berthier, his son-in-law, who had accepted the office of in-
tendant of Paris. Their heads were stuck upon pikes,
and carried about the city ; and it is upon this mode of
punishment that Mr. Burke builds a great part of his tragic

scenes. Let us therefore examine how men came by the idea of punishing in this manner.

They learn it from the governments they live under; and retaliate the punishments they have been accustomed to behold. The heads stuck upon pikes, which remained for years upon Temple-bar, differed nothing in the horror of the scene from those carried about on pikes at Paris : yet this was done by the English government. It may perhaps be said, that it signifies nothing to a man what is done to him after he is dead; but it signifies much to the living : it either tortures their feelings, or hardens their hearts ; and in either case, it instructs them how to punish when power falls into their hands.

Lay then the axe to the root and teach governments humanity. It is their sanguinary punishments which corrupt mankind. In England, the punishment in certain cases, is by *hanging, drawing* and *quartering ;* the heart of the sufferer is cut out, and held up to the view of the populace. In France under the former government, the punishments were not less barbarous. Who does not remember the execution of Damien, torn to pieces by horses ? The effect of these cruel spectacles exhibited to the populace, is to destroy tenderness, or excite revenge ; and by the base and false idea of governing men by terror instead of reason, they become precedents. It is over the lowest class of mankind that government by terror is intended to operate, and it is on them that it operates to the worst effect. They have sense enough to feel that they are the objects aimed at ; and they inflict in their turn the examples of terror they have been instructed to practise.

There are in all European countries, a large class of people of that description which in England are called the " *mob.*" Of this class were those who committed the burnings and devastations in London in 1780, and of this class were those who carried the heads upon pikes in Paris. Foulon and Berthier were taken up in the country, and sent to Paris, to undergo their examination at the hotel de Ville ; for the national assembly immediately on the new ministry coming into office, passed a decree, which they communicated to the king and cabinet, that they (the national assembly) would hold the ministry, of which Foulon was one, responsible for the measures they were advising and pursuing ; but the mob incensed at the appearance of Foulon and Berthier, tore them from their conductors before they were carried to the hotel de Ville, and executed them on the spot. Why then does Mr. Burke charge outrages of this kind on a whole people? As well may he charge the riots and outrages of 1780 on all the people of London, or those in Ireland on all his country.

But every thing we see or hear offensive to our feelings, and derogatory to the human character, should lead to other reflections than those of reproach. Even the beings who commit them have some claim to our consideration. How then is it that such vast classes of mankind as are distinguished by the appellation of the vulgar, or the ignorant mob, are so numerous in all old countries? The instant we ask ourselves this question, reflection finds an answer. They arise, as an unavoidable consequence, out of the ill construction of all the old governments in Europe, England included with the rest. It is by distortedly exalting some men, that others are distortedly debased, till the whole is out of nature. A vast mass of mankind are degradedly thrown into the back ground of the human picture, to bring forward, with greater glare, the puppet-show of state and aristocracy. In the commencement of a revolution, those men are rather the followers of the *camp* than of the *standard* of liberty, and have yet to be instructed how to reverence it.

I give to Mr. Burke all his theatrical exaggerations for facts, and I then ask him, if they do not establish the certainty of what I here lay down? Admitting them to be true, they show the necessity of the French revolution, as much as any one thing he could have asserted. These outrages were not the effect of the principles of the revolution, but of the degraded mind that existed before the revolution, and which the revolution is calculated to reform. Place them then to their proper cause, and take the reproach of them to your own side.

It is to the honor of the national assembly, and the city of Paris, that during such a tremendous scene of arms and confusion, beyond the control of all authority, that they have been able, by the influence of example and exhortation, to restrain so much. Never was more pains taken to instruct and enlighten mankind, and to make them see that their interest consisted in their virtue, and not in their revenge, than what have been displayed in the revolution of France.—I now proceed to make some remarks on Mr.

Burke's account of the expedition to Versailles, on the 5th and 6th of October.

I can consider Mr. Burke's book in scarcely any other light than a dramatic performance; and he must, I think, have considered it in the same light himself, by the poetical liberties he has taken of omitting some facts, distorting others, and making the machinery bend to produce a stage effect. Of this kind is his account of the expedition to Versailles. He begins this account by omitting the only facts which as causes are known to be true; every thing beyond these is conjecture even in Paris: and he then works up a tale accommodated to his own passions and prejudices.

It is to be observed throughout Mr. Burke's book, that he never speaks of plots *against* the revolution; and it is from those plots that all the mischiefs have arisen. It suits his purpose to exhibit consequences without their causes. It is one of the arts of the drama to do so. If the crimes of men were exhibited with their suffering, the stage effect would sometimes be lost, and the audience would be inclined to approve where it was intended they should commiserate.

After all the investigations that have been made into this intricate affair (the expedition to Versailles,) it still remains enveloped in all that kind of mystery which ever accompanies events produced more from a concurrence of awkward circumstances, than from fixed design. While the characters of men are forming, as is always the case in revolutions, there is a reciprocal suspicion, and a disposition to misinterpret each other; and even parties directly opposite in principle, will sometimes concur in pushing forward the same movement with very different views, and with the hopes of its producing very different consequences. A great deal of this may be discovered in this embarrassed affair, and yet the issue of the whole was what nobody had in view.

The only things certainly known are, that considerable uneasiness was at this time excited in Paris, by the delay of the king in not sanctioning and forwarding the decrees of the national assembly, particularly that of the *declaration of the rights of man*, and the decrees of the *fourth of August*, which contained the foundation principles on which the constitution was to be erected. The kindest, and perhaps the fairest, conjecture upon this matter is, that some of the ministers intended to make observations upon certain parts of them, before they were finally sanctioned and sent to the provinces ; but be this as it may, the enemies of the revolution derived hopes from the delay, and the friends of the revolution, uneasiness.

During this state of suspense, the *gardes du corps*, which was composed, as such regiments generally are, of persons much connected with the court, gave an entertainment at Versailles (Oct. 1,) to some foreign regiments then arrived ; and when the entertainment was at its height, on a signal given, the *gardes du corps* tore the national cockade from their hats, trampled it under foot, and replaced it with a counter cockade prepared for the purpose. An indignity of this kind amounted to defiance. It was like declaring war ; and if men will give challenges, they must expect consequences. But all this Mr. Burke has carefully kept out of sight. He begins his account by saying, " History will record, that on the morning of the 6th of October, 1789, the king and queen of France, after a day of confusion, alarm, dismay and slaughter, lay down under the pledged security of public faith, to indulge nature in a few hours of respite, and troubled melancholy repose." This is neither the sober style of history, nor the intention of it. It leaves every thing to be guessed at, and mistaken. One would at least think there had been a battle ; and a battle there probably would have been, had it not been for the moderating prudence of those whom Mr. Burke involves in his censures. By his keeping the *gardes du corps* out of sight Mr. Burke has afforded himself the dramatic licence of putting the king and queen in their places, as if the object of the expedition was against them.—But, to return to my account—

This conduct of the *gardes du corps*, as might well be expected, alarmed and enraged the Parisians : the colors of the cause, and the cause itself, were become too united to mistake the intention of the insult and the Parisians were determined to call the *gardes du corps* to an account. There was certainly nothing of the cowardice of assassination in marching in the face of day to demand satisfaction, if such a phrase may be used, of a body of armed men who had voluntarily given defiance. But the circumstance which serves to throw this affair into embarrassment is, that the enemies of the revolution appear to have encouraged it, as well as its friends. The one hoped to prevent a civil war, by checking it in time, and the other to make one. The hopes of those opposed to the revolution, rested in making the king of their party, and getting him from Versailles to Metz, where they expected to collect a force, and set up a standard. We have therefore two different objects presenting themselves at the same time, and to be accomplished by the same means; the one, to chastise the *gardes du corps* which was the object of the Parisians; the other, to render the confusion of such a scene an inducement to the king to set off for Metz.

On the 5th of October, a very numerous body of women, and men in the disguise of women, collected round the hotel de Ville or town hall at Paris, and set off for Versailles. Their professed object was the *gardes du corps*; but prudent men readily recollected that mischief is easier begun than ended; and this impressed itself with the more force, from the suspicions already stated, and the irregularity of such a cavalcade. As soon therefore as a sufficient force could be collected, M. de la Fayette, by orders from the civil authority of Paris, set off after them at the head of twenty thousand of the Paris militia. The revolution could derive no benefit from confusion, and its opposers might. By an amiable and spirited manner of address, he had hitherto been fortunate in calming disquietudes, and in this he was extraordinarily successful; to frustrate, therefore, the hopes of those who might seek to improve this scene into a sort of justifiable necessity for the king's quitting Versailles and withdrawing to Metz, and to prevent at the same time, the consequences that might ensue between the *gardes du corps* and this phalanx of men and women, he forwarded expresses to the king, that he was on his march to Versailles, by the orders of the civil authority of Paris, for the purpose of peace and protection, expressing at the same time the necessity of restraining the *gardes du corps* from firing on the people.*

He arrived at Versailles between ten and eleven o'clock at night. The *gardes du corps* were drawn up, and the people had arrived some time before, but every thing had remained suspended. Wisdom and policy now consisted in changing a scene of danger into a happy event. M. de la Fayette became the mediator between the enraged parties;

* I am warranted in asserting this, as I had it from M. de la Fayette, with whom I have lived in habits of friendship for fourteen years.

and the king, to remove the uneasiness which had arisen from the delay already stated, sent for the president of the national assembly, and signed the *declaration of the rights of man*, and such other parts of the constitution as were in readiness.

It was now about one in the morning. Every thing appeared to be composed, and a general congratulation took place. At the beat of drum a proclamation was made, that the citizens of Versailles would give the hospitality of their houses to their fellow-citizens of Paris. Those who could not be accommodated in this manner, remained in the streets, or took up their quarters in the churches; and at two o'clock the king and queen retired.

In this state matters passed until the break of day, when a fresh disturbance arose from the censurable conduct of some of both parties; for such characters there will be in all such scenes. One of the *gardes du corps* appeared at one of the windows of the palace, and the people who had remained during the night in the streets accosted him with reviling and provocative language. Instead of retiring, as in such a case prudence would have dictated, he presented his musket, fired, and killed one of the Paris militia. The peace being thus broken, the people rushed into the palace in quest of the offender. They attacked the quarters of the *gardes du corps* within the palace, and pursued them through the avenues of it, and to the apartments of the king. On this tumult, not the queen only, as Mr. Burke has represented it, but every person in the palace, was awakened and alarmed; and M. de la Fayette had a second time to interpose between the parties, the event of which was, that the *gardes du corps* put on the national cockade, and the matter ended, as by oblivion, after the loss of two or three lives.

During the latter part of the time in which this confusion was acting, the king and queen were in public at the balcony, and neither of them concealed for safety's sake, as Mr. Burke insinuates. Matters being thus appeased, and tranquillity restored, a general acclamation broke forth, of *le roi a Paris—le roi a Paris*—the king to Paris. It was the shout of peace, and immediately accepted on the part of the king. By this measure, all future projects of trepanning the king to Metz, and setting up the standard of opposition to the constitution, were prevented, and the suspicions extinguished. The king and his family reached

Paris in the evening, and were congratulated on their arrival by M. Bailley, the mayor of Paris, in the name of
the citizens. Mr. Burke, who throughout his book confounds things, persons, and principles, has, in his remarks
on M. Bailley's address, confounded time also. He censures M. Bailley for calling it, " *un bon jour,*" a good day.
Mr. Burke should have informed himself, that this scene
took up the space of two days, the day on which it began
with every appearance of danger and mischief, and the
day on which it terminated without the mischiefs that
threatened ; and that it is to this peaceful termination that
M. Bailley alludes, and to the arrival of the king at Paris.
Not less than three hundred thousand persons arranged
themselves in the procession from Versailles to Paris, and
not an act of molestation was committed during the whole
march.

Mr. Burke, on the authority of M. Lally Tollendal, a
deserter from the national assembly, says, that on entering
Paris, the people shouted, " *tous les eveques a la lanterne.*"
All bishops to be hanged at the lantern or lamp-posts. It
is surprising that nobody should hear this but Lally Tollendal, and that nobody should believe it but Mr. Burke.
It has not the least connexion with any part of the transaction, and is totally foreign to every circumstance of it.
The bishops have never been introduced before into any
scene of Mr. Burke's drama : why then are they, all at
once, and together, *tout a coup et tous ensemble,* introduced
now ? Mr. Burke brings forward his bishops and his lantern, like figures in a magic lantern, and raises his scenes
by contrast instead of connexion. But it serves to show,
with the rest of his book, what little credit ought to be
given, where even probability is set at defiance, for the
purpose of defaming ; and with this reflection, instead of a
soliloquy in praise of chivalry, as Mr. Burke has done, I
close the account of the expedition to Versailles.*

I have now to follow Mr. Burke through a pathless wilderness of rhapsodies, and a sort of descant upon governments, in which he asserts whatever he pleases, on the presumption of its being believed, without offering either evidence or reasons for so doing.

* An account of the expedition to Versailles may be seen in No. 13, of the
'Revolution de Paris,' containing the events from the 3d to the 10th of October, 1789.

Before any thing can be reasoned upon to a conclusion, certain facts, principles, or data, to reason from, must be established, admitted, or denied. Mr. Burke, with his usual outrage, abuses the *declaration of the rights of man*, published by the national assembly of France, as the basis on which the constitution of France is built. This he calls "paltry and blurred sheets of paper about the rights of man." Does Mr. Burke mean to deny that *man* has any rights? If he does, then he must mean that there are no such things as rights any where, and that he has none himself; for who is there in the world but man? But if Mr. Burke means to admit that man has rights, the question then will be, what are those rights, and how came man by them originally?

The error of those who reason by precedents drawn from antiquity, respecting the rights of man, is, that they do not go far enough into antiquity. They do not go the whole way. They stop in some of the intermediate stages of an hundred or a thousand years, and produce what was then done as a rule for the present day. This is no authority at all. If we travel still further into antiquity, we shall find a directly contrary opinion and practice prevailing; and if antiquity is to be authority, a thousand such authorities may be produced, successively contradicting each other: but if we proceed on, we shall at last come out right: we shall come to the time when man came from the hand of his maker. What was he then? Man. Man was his high and only title, and a higher cannot be given him. But of titles I shall speak hereafter.

We have now arrived at the origin of man, and at the origin of his rights. As to the manner in which the world has been governed from that day to this, it is no further any concern of ours than to make a proper use of the errors or the improvements which the history of it presents. Those who lived an hundred or a thousand years ago, were then moderns as we are now. They had *their* ancients and those ancients had others, and we also shall be ancients in our turn. If the mere name of antiquity is to govern in the affairs of life, the people who are to live an hundred or a thousand years hence, may as well take us for a precedent, as we make a precedent of those who lived an hundred or a thousand years ago. The fact is, that portions of antiquity, by proving every thing, establish nothing. It is authority against authority all the way, till we come to the divine origin of the rights of man, at the creation. Here our inquiries find a resting-place, and our reason finds a home. If a dispute about the rights of man had arisen at the distance of an hundred years from the creation, it is to this source of authority they must have referred, and it is to the same source of authority that we must now refer.

Though I mean not to touch upon any sectarian principle of religion, yet it may be worth observing, that the genealogy of Christ is traced to Adam. Why then not trace the rights of man to the creation of man? I will answer the question. Because there have been an upstart of governments, thrusting themselves between, and presumptuously working to *un-make* man.

If any generation of men ever possessed the right of dictating the mode by which the world should be governed for ever, it was the first generation that existed; and if that generation did not do it, no succeeding generation can show any authority for doing it, nor set any up. The illuminating and divine principles of the equal rights of man (for it has its origin from the maker of man,) relates, not only to the living individuals, but to generations of men succeeding each other. Every generation is equal in rights to the generations which preceded it, by the same rule that every individual is born equal in rights with his contemporary.

Every history of the creation, and every traditionary account, whether from the lettered or unlettered world, however they may vary in their opinion or belief of certain particulars, all agree in establishing one point, *the unity of man*; by which I mean that man is all of *one degree*, and consequently that all men are born equal, and with equal natural rights, in the same manner as if posterity had been continued by *creation* instead of *generation*, the latter being only the mode by which the former is carried forward; and consequently, every child born into the world must be considered as deriving its existence from God. The world is as new to him as it was to the first man that existed, and his natural right in it is of the same kind.

The Mosaic account of the creation, whether taken as divine authority, or merely historical, is fully up to this point, *the unity or equality of man*. The expressions admit of no controversy. "And God said, let us make man in our own image. In the image of God created he him;

male and female created he them." The distinction of
sexes is pointed out, but no other distinction is even im-
plied. If this be not divine authority, it is at least historical
authority, and shows that the equality of man, so far from
being a modern doctrine, is the oldest upon record.

It is also to be observed, that all the religions known in
the world are founded, so far as they relate to man, on the
unity of man, as being all of one degree. Whether in
heaven or in hell, or in whatever state man may be supposed to exist hereafter, the good and the bad are the only
distinctions. Nay, even the laws of governments are obliged to slide into this principle, by making degrees to consist
in crimes, and not in persons.

It is one of the greatest of all truths, and of the highest
advantage to cultivate. By considering man in this light,
and by instructing him to consider himself in this light, it
places him in a close connexion with all his duties, whether
to his creator, or to the creation, of which he is a part;
and it is only when he forgets his origin, or, to use a more
fashionable phrase, his *birth and family*, that he becomes
dissolute. It is not among the least of the evils of the
present existing governments in all parts of Europe, that
man, considered as man, is thrown back to a vast distance
from his maker, and the artificial chasm filled up by a succession of barriers, or a sort of turnpike gates, through
which he has to pass. I will quote Mr. Burke's catalogue
of barriers that he has set up between man and his maker.
Putting himself in the character of a herald, he says—"We
fear God—we look with *awe* to kings—with affection to
parliaments—with duty to magistrates—with reverence to
priests, and with respect to nobility." Mr. Burke has
forgot to put in "chivalry." He has also forgot to put in
Peter.

The duty of man is not a wilderness of turnpike gates,
through which he is to pass by tickets from one to the
other. It is plain and simple, and consists but of two
points. His duty to God, which every man must feel; and
with respect to his neighbor, to do as he would be done by.
If those to whom power is delegated do well, they will be
respected; if not they will be despised; and with regard
to those to whom no power is delegated, but who assume it,
the rational world can know nothing of them.

Hitherto we have spoken only (and that but in part) of
the natural rights of man. We have now to consider the

civil rights of man, and to show how the one originates out of the other. Man did not enter into society to become *worse* than he was before, nor to have less rights than he had before, but to have those rights better secured. His natural rights are the foundation of all his civil rights. But in order to pursue this distinction with more precision, it is necessary to mark the different qualities of natural and civil rights.

A few words will explain this. Natural rights are those which always appertain to man in right of his existence. Of this kind are all the intellectual rights, or rights of the mind, and also all those rights of acting as an individual for his own comfort and happiness, which are not injurious to the rights of others.—Civil rights are those which appertain to man in right of his being a member of society. Every civil right has for its foundation some natural right pre-existing in the individual, but to which his individual power is not, in all cases, sufficiently competent. Of this kind are all those which relate to security and protection.

From this short review, it will be easy to distinguish between that class of natural rights which man retains after entering into society, and those which he throws into common stock as a member of society.

The natural rights which he retains, are all those in which the power to execute is as perfect in the individual as the right itself. Among this class, as is before mentioned, are all the intellectual rights, or rights of the mind: consequently, religion is one of those rights. The natural rights which are not retained, are all those in which, though the right is perfect in the individual, the power to execute them is defective. They answer not his purpose. A man, by natural right, has a right to judge in his own cause; and so far as the right of the mind is concerned, he never surrenders it: but what availeth it him to judge, if he has not power to redress? He therefore deposites this right in the common stock of society, and takes the arm of society, of which he is a part, in preference and in addition to his own. Society *grants* him nothing. Every man is a proprietor in society, and draws on the capital as a matter of right.

From these premises, two or three certain conclusions will follow.

1st, That every civil right grows out of a natural right; or, in other words, is a natural right exchanged.

2d, That civil power properly considered as such, is made up of the aggregate of that class of the natural rights of man, which becomes defective in the individual in point of power, and answers not his purpose, but when collected to a focus, becomes competent to the purpose of every one.

3d. That the power produced by the aggregate of natural rights, imperfect in power in the individual, cannot be applied to invade the natural rights which are retained in the individual, and in which the power to execute is as perfect as the right itself.

We have now, in a few words, traced man from a natural individual to a member of society, and shown, or endeavored to show, the quality of the natural rights retained, and of those which are exchanged for civil rights. Let us now apply those principles to government.

In casting our eyes over the world, it is extremely easy to distinguish the governments which have arisen out of society, or out of the social compact, from those which have not: but to place this in a clearer light than what a single glance may afford, it will be proper to take a review of the several sources from which governments have arisen, and on which they have been founded.

They may be all comprehended under three heads—1st, superstition : 2d, power : 3d. the common interests of society, and the common rights of man.

The first was a government of priest-craft, the second of conquerors, and the third of reason.

When a set of artful men pretended, through the medium of oracles, to hold intercourse with the deity, as familiarly as they now march up the back stairs in European courts, the world was completely under the government of superstition. The oracles were consulted, and whatever they were made to say, became the law; and this sort of government lasted just as long as this sort of superstition lasted.

After these a race of conquerors arose, whose government, like that of William the conqueror, was founded in power, and the sword assumed the name of a sceptre. Governments thus established, last as long as the power to support them lasts; but that they might avail themselves of every engine in their favor, they united fraud to force, and set up an idol which they called *divine right*, and which in imitation of the pope, who affects to be spiritual and temporal; and in contradiction to the founder of the Christian religion, twisted itself afterwards into an idol of another shape, called *church and state*. The key of St. Peter, and the key of the treasury, became quartered on one another, and the wondering, cheated multitude, worshipped the invention.

When I contemplate the natural dignity of man; when I feel (for nature has not been kind enough to me to blunt my feelings) for the honor and happiness of its character, I become irritated at the attempt to govern mankind by force and fraud, as if they were all knaves and fools, and can scarcely avoid feeling disgust for those who are thus imposed upon.

We have now to review the governments which arise out of society, in contradistinction to those which arose out of superstition and conquest.

It has been thought a considerable advance towards establishing the principles of freedom, to say, that government is a compact between those who govern and those who are governed: but this cannot be true, because it is putting the effect before the cause; for as man must have existed before governments existed, there necessarily was a time when governments did not exist, and consequently there could originally exist no governors to form such a compact with. The fact therefore must be, that the *individuals themselves*, each in his own personal and sovereign right, *entered into a compact with each other* to produce a government: and this is the only mode in which governments have a right to be established; and the only principle on which they have a right to exist.

To possess ourselves of a clear idea of what government is or ought to be, we must trace it to its origin. In doing this, we shall easily discover that governments must have arisen, either *out* of the people, or *over* the people. Mr. Burke has made no distinction. He investigates nothing to its source, and therefore he confounds every thing: but he has signified his intention of undertaking at some future opportunity, a comparison between the constitutions of England and France. As he thus renders it a subject of controversy by throwing the gauntlet, I take him up on his own ground. It is in high challenges that high truths have the right of appearing; and I accept it with the more readiness, because it affords me, at the same time, an opportunity of pursuing the subject with respect to governments arising out of society.

But it will be first necessary to define what is meant by a *constitution.* It is not sufficient that we adopt the word; we must fix also a standard signification to it.

A constitution is not a thing in name only, but in fact. It has not an ideal, but a real existence; and wherever it cannot be produced in a visible form there is none. A constitution is a thing antecedent to a government, and a government is only the creature of a constitution. The constitution of a country is not the act of its government, but of the people constituting a government. It is the body of elements, to which you can refer, and quote article by article; and contains the principles on which the government shall be established, the form in which it shall be organized, the powers it shall have, the mode of elections, the duration of parliaments, or by what other name such bodies may be called; the powers which the executive part of the government shall have; and, in fine, every thing that relates to the complete organization of a civil government, and the principle on which it shall act, and by which it shall be bound. A constitution, therefore is to a government, what the laws made afterwards by that government are to a court of judicature. The court of judicature does not make laws, neither can it alter them; it only acts in conformity to the laws made; and the government is in like manner governed by the constitution.

Can then Mr. Burke produce the English constitution? If he cannot we may fairly conclude, that though it has been so much talked about, no such thing as a constitution exists, or ever did exist, and consequently the people have yet a constitution to form.

Mr. Burke will not, I presume, deny the position I have already advanced; namely, that governments arise either *out* of the people, or *over* the people. The English government is one of those which arose out of a conquest, and not out of society, and consequently it arose over the people; and though it has been much modified from the opportunity of circumstances, since the time of William the conqueror, the country has never yet regenerated itself, and it is therefore without a constitution.

I readily perceive the reason why Mr. Burke declined going into the comparison between the English and French constitutions, because he could not but perceive, when he sat down to the task, that no constitution was in existence on his side of the question. His book is certainly bulky enough to have contained all he could say on this subject, and it would have been the best manner in which people could have judged of their separate merits. Why then has he declined the only thing that was worth while to write upon? It was the strongest ground he could take, if the advantages were on his side; but the weakest if they were not; and his declining to take it, is either a sign that he could not possess it, or could not maintain it.

Mr. Burke has said, in a speech last winter in parliament, that when the national assembly of France first met in three orders, (the *tiers etats*, the clergy, and the *noblesse*) that France had then a good constitution. This shows, among numerous other instances, that Mr. Burke does not understand what a constitution is. The persons so met, were not a *constitution*, but a *convention* to make a constitution.

The present national assembly of France is, strictly speaking, the personal social compact. The members of it are the delegates of the nation in its *original* character; future assemblies will be the delegates of the nation in its *organized* character. The authority of the present assembly is different to what the authority of future assemblies will be. The authority of the present one is to form a constitution: the authority of future assemblies will be to legislate according to the principles and forms prescribed in that constitution; and if experience should hereafter show that alterations, amendments, or additions are necessary, the constitution will point out the mode by which such things shall be done, and not leave it to the discretionary power of the future government.

A government on the principles on which constitutional governments, arising out of society, are established, cannot have the right of altering itself. If it had, it would be arbitrary. It might make itself what it pleased; and wherever such a right is set up, it shows that there is no constitution. The act by which the English parliament empowered itself to sit for seven years, shows there is no constitution in England. It might, by the same self-authority, have sat any greater number of years or for life. The bill which the present Mr. Pitt brought into parliament some years ago, to reform parliament, was on the same erroneous principle. The right of reform is in the

nation in its original character, and the constitutional method would be by a general convention elected for the purpose.   There is moreover a paradox in the idea of vitiat-
ed bodies reforming themselves.

From these preliminaries I proceed to draw some comparisons.   I have already spoken of the declaration of
rights ; and as I mean to be as concise as possible, I shall
proceed to other parts of the French constitution.

The constitution of France says, that every man who
pays a tax of sixty sous per annum (2s. and 6d. English)
is an elector.   What article will Mr. Burke place against
this ?   Can any thing be more limited, and at the same
time more capricious, than what the qualifications of electors are in England ?   Limited—because not one man in
an hundred (I speak much within compass) is admitted to
vote : capricious—because the lowest character that can
be supposed to exist, and who has not so much as the visible means of an honest livelihood, is ·an elector in some
places ; while, in other places, the man who pays very
large taxes, and with a fair, known character, and the
farmer who rents to the amount of three or four hundred
pounds a year, and with a property on that farm to three
or four times that amount, is not admitted to be an elector.
Every thing is out of nature, as Mr. Burke says on another occasion, in this strange chaos, and all sorts of follies
are blended with all sorts of crimes.   William the conqueror and his descendants parcelled out the country in
this manner, and bribed one part of it by what they called charters, to hold the other parts of it the better subjected to their will.   This is the reason why so many charters
abound in Cornwall.   The people were averse to the government established at the conquest, and the towns were
garrisoned and bribed to enslave the country.   All the old
charters are the badges of this conquest, and it is from this
source that the capriciousness of election arises.

The French constitution says, that the number of representatives for any place shall be in a ratio to the number of taxable inhabitants or electors.   What article will
Mr. Burke place against this ?   The county of Yorkshire,
which contains near a million of souls, sends two county
members ; and so does the county of Rutland, which contains not an hundredth part of that number.   The town of
old Sarum, which contains not three houses, sends two
members ; and the town of Manchester, which contains

upwards of sixty thousand souls, is not admitted to send any. Is there any principle in these things? Is there any thing by which you can trace the marks of freedom, or discover those of wisdom? No wonder then Mr. Burke has declined the comparison, and endeavored to lead his readers from the point by a wild, unsystematical display of paradoxical rhapsodies.

The French constitution says, that the national assembly shall be elected every two years. What article will Mr. Burke place against this? Why, that the nation has no right at all in the case: that the government is perfectly arbitrary with respect to this point; and he can quote for his authority, the precedent of a former parliament.

The French constitution says, there shall be no game laws; that the farmer on whose lands wild game shall be found (for it is by the produce of those lands they are fed) shall have a right to what he can take. That there shall be no monopolies of any kind, that all trades shall be free, and every man free to follow any occupation by which he can procure an honest livelihood, and in any place, town or city throughout the nation. What will Mr. Burke say to this? In England, game is made the property of those at whose expense it is not fed; and with respect to monopolies, the country is cut up into monopolies. Every chartered town is an aristocratic monopoly in itself, and the qualification of electors proceeds out of those chartered monopolies, Is this freedom? Is this what Mr. Burke means by a constitution?

In these chartered monopolies a man coming from another part of the country, is hunted from them as if he were a foreign enemy. An Englishman is not free in his own country: every one of those places presents a barrier in his way, and tells him he is not a freeman—that he has no rights. Within these monopolies, are other monopolies. In a city, such for instance as Bath, which contains between twenty and thirty thousand inhabitants, the right of electing representatives to parliament is monopolized into about thirty-one persons. And within these monopolies are still others. A man even of the same town, whose parents were not in circumstances to give him an occupation is debarred, in many cases, from the natural right of acquiring one, be his genius or industry what it may.

Are these things examples to hold out to a country regenerating itself from slavery, like France? Certainly they

are not; and certain am I, that when the people of England come to reflect upon them, they will, like France, an-
nihilate those badges of ancient oppression, those traces of
a conquered nation. Had Mr. Burke possessed talents
similar to the author "On the Wealth of Nations," he
would have comprehended all the parts which enter into,
and, by assemblage, form a constitution. He would have
reasoned from minutiæ to magnitude. It is not from his
prejudices only, but from the disorderly cast of his genius,
that he is unfitted for the subject he writes upon. Even
his genius is without a constitution. It is a genius at random, and not a genius constituted. But he must say something—He has therefore mounted in the air like a balloon,
to draw the eyes of the multitude from the ground they
stand upon.

Much is to be learned from the French constitution.
Conquest and tyranny transplanted themselves with William the conqueror, from Normandy into England, and the
country is yet disfigured with the marks. May then the
example of all France contribute to regenerate the freedom
which a province of it destroyed!

The French constitution says, that to preserve the national representation from being corrupt, no member of
the national assembly shall be an officer of government,
a placeman or a pensioner. What will Mr. Burke place
against this? I will whisper his answer: *loaves* and *fishes.*
Ah! this government of loaves and fishes has more mischief in it than people have yet reflected on. The national
assembly has made the discovery, and it holds out the example to the world. Had governments agreed to quarrel
on purpose to fleece their countries by taxes, they could
not have succeeded better than they have done.

Every thing in the English government appears to me
the reverse of what it ought to be, and of what it is said to
be. The parliament, imperfectly and capriciously elected
as it is, is nevertheless *supposed* to hold the national purse
in *trust* for the nation: but in the manner in which an English parliament is constructed, it is like a man being both
mortgager and mortgagee: and in the case of misapplica-
tion of trust, it is the criminal sitting in judgment on himself. If those persons who vote the supplies are the same
persons who receive the supplies when voted, and are to
account for the expenditure of those supplies to those who
voted them, it is *themselves accountable to themselves,* and the

Comedy of Errors concludes with the pantomime of *Hush.*
Neither the ministerial party, nor the opposition will touch
upon this case. The national purse is the common hack
which each mounts upon. It is like what the country people call, " Ride and tie—You ride a little way and then I."
They order these things better in France.

The French constitution says, that the right of war and
peace is in the nation. Where else should it reside, but in
those who are to pay the expense?

In England, this right is said to reside in a *metaphor,*
shown at the tower for sixpence or a shilling a-piece; so
are the lions; and it would be a step nearer to reason to
say it resided in them, for any inanimate metaphor is no
more than a hat or a cap. We can all see the absurdity
of worshipping Aaron's molten calf, or Nebuchadnezzar's
golden image; but why do men continue to practise in
themselves, the absurdities they despise in others?

It may with reason be said, that in the manner the English nation is represented it matters not where this right
resides, whether in the crown or in the parliament. War
is the common harvest of all those who participate in the
division and expenditure of public money, in all countries.
It is the art of *conquering at home:* the object of it is an
increase of revenue; and as revenue cannot be increased
without taxes, a pretence must be made for expenditures.
In reviewing the history of the English government, its
wars, and taxes, an observer, not blinded by prejudice,
nor warped by interest would declare, that taxes were not
raised to carry on wars, but that wars were raised to carry
on taxes.

Mr. Burke, as a member of the house of commons, is a
part of the English government; and though he professes
himself an enemy to war, he abuses the French constitution, which seeks to explode it. He holds up the English
government as a model in all its parts, to France ; but he
should first know the remarks which the French make upon
it. They contend, in favor of their own, that the portion of
liberty enjoyed in England, is just enough to enslave a
country by, more productively than by despotism; and
that as the real object of a despotism is revenue, a government so formed obtains more than it could either by direct
despotism, or in a full state of freedom, and is, therefore,
on the ground of interest, opposed to both. They account
also for the readiness which always appears in such

governments for engaging in wars, by remarking on the different motives which produce them. In despotic governments, wars are the effects of pride; but in those governments in which they become the means of taxation, they acquire thereby a more permanent promptitude.

The French constitution, therefore, to provide against both those evils, has taken away from kings and ministers the power of declaring war, and placed the right where the expense must fall.

When the question on the right of war and peace was agitating in the national assembly, the people of England appeared to be much interested in the event, and highly to applaud the decision. As a principle, it applies as much to one country as to another. William the conqueror, *as a conqueror*, held this power of war and peace in himself, and his descendants have ever since claimed it as a right.

Although Mr. Burke has asserted the right of the parliament at the revolution to bind and control the nation and posterity *for ever*, he denies, at the same time, that the parliament or the nation had any right to alter, what he calls, the succession of the crown, in any thing but in part, or by a sort of modification. By his taking this ground, he throws the case back to the *Norman conquest;* and by thus running a line of succession, springing from William the conqueror to the present day, he makes it necessary to inquire who and what William the conqueror was, and where he came from: and into the origin, history and nature of what are called prerogatives. Every thing must have had a beginning, and the fog of time and antiquity should be penetrated to discover it. Let then Mr. Burke bring forward his William of Normandy, for it is to this origin that his argument goes. It also unfortunately happens, in running this line of succession, that another line, parallel thereto, presents itself, which is, that if the succession runs in the line of the conquest, the nation runs in the line of being conquered, and it ought to rescue itself from this reproach.

But it will perhaps be said, that though the power of declaring war descends into the heritage of the conquest, it is held in check by the right of the parliament to withhold the supplies. It will always happen, when a thing is originally wrong, that amendments do not make it right, and it often happens that they do as much mischief one way as good the other: and such is the case here, for if the one rashly declares war as a matter of right, and the other peremptorily withholds the supplies as a matter of right, the remedy becomes as bad or worse than the disease. The one forces the nation to a combat, and the other ties its hands : but the more probable issue is, that the contrast will end in a collusion between the parties, and be made a screen to both.

On this question of war, three things are to be considered : 1st, the right of declaring it : 2d, the expense of supporting it : 3d, the mode of conducting it after it is declared. The French constitution places the *right* where the *expense* must fall, and this union can be only in the nation. The mode of conducting it after it is declared, it consigns to the executive department. Were this the case in all countries, we should hear but little more of wars.

Before I proceed to consider other parts of the French constitution, and by way of relieving the fatigue of argument, I will introduce an anecdote which I had from Dr. Franklin.

While the doctor resided in France, as minister from America, during the war, he had numerous proposals made to him by projectors of every country and of every kind, who wished to go to the land that floweth with milk and honey, America; and among the rest, there was one who offered himself to be king. He introduced his proposal to the doctor by letter, which is now in the hands of M. Beaumarchais, of Paris—stating, first, that as the Americans had dismissed or sent away their king, they would want another. Secondly, that himself was a Norman. Thirdly, that he was of a more ancient family than the dukes of Normandy, and of a more honorable descent, his line having never been bastardized. Fourthly, that there was already a precedent in England, of kings coming out of Normandy : and on these grounds he rested his offer, *enjoining* that the doctor would forward it to America. But as the doctor did not do this, nor yet send him an answer, the projector wrote a second letter; in which he did not, it is true, threaten to go over and conquer America, but only, with great dignity, proposed, that if his offer was not accepted, that an acknowledgment of about 30,000*l.* might be made to him for his generosity ! Now, as all arguments respecting succession must necessarily connect that succession with some beginning, Mr. Burke's arguments on this subject go to show, that there is no English origin of kings, and that they are descendants of the Norman line in right of the conquest. It may therefore be of service to his doctrine to make the story known, and to inform him, that in case of that natural extinction to which all mortality is subject, kings may again be had from Normandy, on more reasonable terms than William the conqueror; and consequently, that the good people of England, at the revolution of 1688, might have done much better, had such a generous Norman as *this* known *their* wants, and they *his*. The chivalric character which Mr. Burke so much admires, is certainly much easier to make a bargain with than a hard-dealing Dutchman. But, to return to the matters of the constitution—

The French constitution says, *there shall be no titles :* and of consequence, all that class of equivocal generation, which in some countries is called "*aristocracy*," and in others "*nobility*," is done away, and the *peer* is exalted into the *man.*

Titles are but nicknames, and every nickname is a title. The thing is perfectly harmless in itself, but it marks a sort of foppery in the human character which degrades it. It renders man diminutive in things which are great, and the counterfeit of woman in things which are little. It talks about its fine *riband* like a girl, and shows its *garter* like a child. A certain writer, of some antiquity, says, " When I was a child, I thought as a child; but when I became a man, I put away childish things."

It is, properly, from the elevated mind of France, that the folly of titles has been abolished. It has outgrown the baby-clothes of *count* and *duke,* and breeched itself in manhood. France has not levelled, it has exalted. It has put down the dwarf to set up the man. The insignificance of a senseless word like *duke, count,* or *earl,* has ceased to please. Even those who possessed them have disowned the gibberish, and, as they outgrew the rickets, have despised the rattle. The genuine mind of man, thirsting for its native home, society, contemns the gewgaws that separate him from it. Titles are like circles drawn by the magician's wand, to contract the sphere of man's felicity. He lives immured within the Bastile of a word, and surveys at a distance the envied life of man.

Is it then any wonder that titles should fall in France? Is it not a greater wonder they should be kept up any where? What are they? What is their worth and "what is their amount?" When we think or speak of a *judge* or a *general*, we associate with it the ideas of office and character; we think of gravity in the one and bravery in the other: but when we use a word merely as a title, no ideas associate with it. Through all the vocabulary of Adam, there is not such an animal as a duke or a count; neither can we connect any certain idea to the words. Whether they mean strength or weakness, wisdom or folly, a child or a man, or a rider or a horse, is all equivocal. What respect then can be paid to that which describes nothing, and which means nothing? Imagination has given figure and character to centaurs, satyrs, and down to all the fairy tribe; but titles baffle even the powers of fancy, and are a chimerical nondescript.

But this is not all—If a whole country is disposed to hold them in contempt, all their value is gone, and none will own them. It is common opinion only that makes them any thing or nothing, or worse than nothing. There is no occasion to take titles away, for they take themselves away when society concurs to ridicule them. This species of imaginary consequence has visibly declined in every part of Europe, and it hastens to its exit as the world of reason continues to rise. There was a time when the lowest class, of what are called nobility, was more thought of than the highest is now, and when a man in armor riding through Christendom in search of adventures was more stared at than a modern duke. The world has seen this folly fall, and it has fallen by being laughed at, and the farce of titles will follow its fate. The patriots of France have discovered in good time, that rank and dignity in society must take a new ground. The old one has fallen through. It must now take the substantial ground of character, instead of the chimerical ground of titles; and they have brought their titles to the altar, and made of them a burnt-offering to reason.

If no mischief had annexed itself to the folly of titles, they would not have been worth a serious and formal destruction, such as the national assembly have decreed them; and this makes it necessary to inquire further into the nature and character of aristocracy.

That, then, which is called aristocracy in some countries, and nobility in others, arose out of the governments founded upon conquest. It was originally a military order for the purpose of supporting military government; (for such were all governments founded in conquests) and to keep up a succession of this order for the purpose for which it was established, all the younger branches of those families were disinherited, and the law of *primogenitureship* set up.

The nature and character of aristocracy shows itself to us in this law. It is a law against every law of nature, and nature herself calls for its destruction. Establish family justice and aristocracy falls. By the aristocratical law of primogenitureship, in a family of six children, five are exposed.—Aristocracy has never but *one* child. The rest are begotten to be devoured. They are thrown to the cannibal for prey, and the natural parent prepares the unnatural repast.

As every thing which is out of nature in man, affects more or less, the interest of society, so does this. All the children which the aristocracy disowns (which are all, except the eldest) are, in general, cast like orphans on a parish, to be provided for by the public, but at a greater charge. Unnecessary offices and places in governments and courts are created at the expense of the public to maintain them.

With what kind of parental reflections can the father or mother contemplate their younger offspring. By nature they are children, and by marriage they are heirs; but by aristocracy they are bastards and orphans. They are the flesh and blood of their parents in one line, and nothing akin to them in the other. To restore, therefore, parents to their children, and children to their parents—relations to each other, and man to society—and to exterminate the monster aristocracy, root and branch—the French constitution has destroyed the law of *primogenitureship*. Here then lies the monster, and Mr. Burke, if he pleases, may write its epitaph.

Hitherto we have considered aristocracy chiefly in one point of view. We have now to consider it in another. But whether we view it before or behind, or side ways, or any way else, domestically or publicly, it is still a monster.

In France, aristocracy had one feature less in its countenance than what it has in some other countries. It did not compose a body of hereditary legislators. It was not *"a corporation of aristocracy,"* for such I have heard M. de la Fayette describe an English house of peers. Let us then examine the grounds upon which the French constitution has resolved against having such an house in France.

Because, in the first place, as is already mentioned, aristocracy is kept up by family tyranny and injustice.

2d, Because there is an unnatural unfitness in an aristocracy to be legislators for a nation. Their ideas of *distributive justice* are corrupted at the very source. They begin life trampling on all their younger brothers and sisters, and relations of every kind, and are taught and educated so to do. With what ideas of justice or honor can that man enter an house of legislation, who absorbs in his own person the inheritance of a whole family of children, or metes out some pitiful portion with the insolence of a gift?

3d, Because the idea of hereditary legislators is as inconsistent as that of hereditary judges, or hereditary juries ; and as absurd as an hereditary mathematician, or an hereditary wise man ; and as ridiculous as an hereditary poet-laureat.

4th, Because a body of men, holding themselves accountable to nobody, ought not to be trusted by any body.

5th, Because it is continuing the uncivilized principle of governments founded in conquest, and the base idea of man having property in man, and governing him by personal right.

6th. Because aristocracy has a tendency to degenerate the human species. By the universal economy of nature it is known, and by the instance of the Jews it is proved, that the human species has a tendency to degenerate, in any small number of persons, when separated from the general stock of society, and intermarrying constantly with each other. It defeats even its pretended end, and becomes in time the opposite of what is noble in man. Mr. Burke talks of nobility ; let him show what it is. The greatest characters the world has known, have rose on the democratic floor. Aristocracy has not been able to keep a proportionate pace with democracy. The artificial *noble* shrinks into a dwarf before the *noble* of nature ; and in the few instances (for there are some in all countries) in whom nature, as by a miracle, has survived in aristocracy, *those men despise it.* But it is time to proceed to a new subject.

The French constitution has reformed the condition of the clergy. It has raised the income of the lower and middle classes, and taken from the higher. None are now less than twelve hundred livres (fifty pounds sterling) nor any higher than two or three thousand pounds. What will Mr. Burke place against this? Hear what he says.

He says, that "the people of England can see, without pain or grudging, an archbishop precede a duke; they can see a bishop of Durham, or a bishop of Winchester, in possession of 10,000*l.* a-year; and cannot see why it is in worse hands than estates to the like amount in the hands of this earl or that 'squire." And Mr. Burke offers this as an example to France.

As to the first part, whether the archbishop precedes the duke, or the duke the bishop, it is, I believe, to the people in general, somewhat like *Sternhold* and *Hopkins*, or *Hopkins* and *Sternhold ;* you may put which you please first: and as I confess that I do not understand the merits of this case I will not contend it with Mr. Burke.

But with respect to the latter, I have something to say. Mr. Burke has not put the case right. The comparison is out of order by being put between the bishop and the earl or the 'squire. It ought to be put between the bishop and the curate, and then it will stand thus : *the people of England can see, without grudging or pain, a bishop of Durham, or a bishop of Winchester, in possession of ten thousand pounds a-year, and a curate on thirty or forty pounds a-year, or less.* No, sir, they certainly do not see these things without great pain and grudging. It is a case that applies itself to every man's sense of justice, and is one among many that calls aloud for a constitution.

In France, the cry of *" the church! the church!"* was repeated as often as in Mr. Burke's book, and as loudly as when the dissenters' bill was before parliament ; but the generality of the French clergy were not to be deceived by this cry any longer. They knew, that whatever the pretence might be, it was themselves who were one of the principal objects of it. It was the cry of the high beneficed clergy, to prevent any regulation of income taking place between those of ten thousand pounds a-year and the parish priest. They, therefore, joined their case to those of every other oppressed class of men, and by this union obtained redress.

The French constitution has abolished tithes, that source of perpetual discontent between the tithe-holder and the parishioner. When land is held on tithe, it is in the condition of an estate held between two parties; one receiving one tenth, and the other nine-tenths of the produce: and, consequently, on principles of equity, if the estate can be improved, and made to produce by that improvement double or treble what it did before, or in any other ratio, the expense of such improvement ought to be borne in like proportion between the parties who are to share the produce. But this is not the case in tithes; the farmer bears the whole expense, and the tithe-holder takes a tenth of the improvement, in addition to the original tenth, and by this means gets the value of two tenths instead of one. This is another case that calls for a constitution.

The French constitution hath abolished or renounced *toleration,* and *intoleration* also, and hath established *universal right of conscience.*

Toleration is not the *opposite* of intoleration, but is the *counterfeit* of it. Both are despotisms. The one assumes to itself the right of withholding liberty of conscience, and the other of granting it. The one is the pope, armed with fire and faggot, and the other is the pope selling or granting indulgences. The former is church and state, and the latter is church and traffic.

But toleration may be viewed in a much stronger light. Man worships not himself, but his maker; and the liberty of conscience which he claims, is not for the service of himself, but of his God. In this case, therefore, we must necessarily have the associated idea of two beings; the *mortal* who renders the worship, and the *immortal being* who is worshipped. Toleration, therefore, places itself, not between man and man, nor between church and church, nor between one denomination of religion and another, but between God and man; between the being who worships, and the *being* who is worshipped; and by the same act of assumed authority by which it tolerates man to pay his worship, it presumptuously and blasphemously sets up itself to tolerate the almighty to receive it.

Were a bill brought into parliament, entitled, " An *act* to tolerate or grant liberty to the almighty to receive the worship of a Jew or a Turk," or " to prohibit the almighty from receiving it," all men would startle, and call it blasphemy. There would be an uproar. The presumption of toleration in religious matters would then present itself unmasked: but the presumption is not the less because the name of " man" only appears to those laws, for the associated idea of the *worshipper* and the *worshipped* cannot be

separated.   Who, then, art thou, vain dust and ashes! by
whatever name thou art called, whether a king, a bishop.
a church or a state, a parliament or any thing else, that ob-
trudest thine insignificance between the soul of man and his
maker?   Mind thine own concerns.   If he believes not as
thou believest, it is a proof that thou believest not as he
believeth, and there is no earthly power can determine between you.

With respect to what are called denominations of religion, if every one is left to judge of his own religion, there
is no such thing as a religion that is wrong; but if they
are to judge of each other's religion, there is no such thing
as a religion that is right; and therefore, all the world is
right, or all the world is wrong.   But with respect to religion itself, without regard to names, and as directing itself from the universal family of mankind to the divine object of all adoration, *it is man bringing to his maker the fruits
of his heart;* and though these fruits may differ from each
other, like the fruits of the earth, the grateful tribute of
every one is accepted.

A bishop of Durham, or a bishop of Winchester, or the
archbishop who heads the dukes, will not refuse a tithe-
sheaf of wheat, because it is not a cock of hay; nor a
cock of hay, because it is not a sheaf of wheat; nor a pig,
because it is neither the one nor the other: but these same
persons, under the figure of an established church, will not
permit their maker to receive the varied tithes of man's devotion.

One of the continual choruses of Mr. Burke's book is,
" church and state;" he does not mean some one particular church, or some one particular state, but any church
and state; and he uses the term as a general figure to hold
forth the political doctrine of always uniting the church
with the state in every country, and he censures the national assembly for not having done this in France.   Let
us bestow a few thoughts on this subject.

All religions are in their nature mild and benign, and
united with principles of morality.   They could not have
made proselytes at first, by professing any thing that was
vicious, cruel, persecuting, or immoral.   Like every thing
else, they had their beginning; and they proceeded by
persuasion, exhortation, and example.   How then is it
that they lose their native mildness, and become morose
and intolerant?

It proceeds from the connexion which Mr. Burke recommends. By engendering the church with the state, a sort of mule animal, capable only of destroying, and not of breeding up, is produced, called, *the church established by law.* It is a stranger, even from its birth, to any parent mother on which it is begotten, and whom in time it kicks out and destroys.

The inquisition in Spain does not proceed from the religion originally professed, but from this mule animal, engendered between the church and the state. The burnings in Smithfield proceeded from the same heterogenous production; and it was the regeneration of this strange animal in England afterwards, that renewed rancor and irreligion among the inhabitants, and that drove the people called Quakers and Dissenters to America. Persecution is not an original feature in *any* religion; but it is always the strongly-marked feature of all law-religions, or religions established by law. Take away the law-establishment, and every religion re-assumes its original benignity. In America, a catholic priest is a good citizen, a good character, and a good neighbor; an episcopalian minister is of the same description: and this proceeds, independent of men, from there being no law-establishment in America.

If also we view this matter in a temporal sense, we shall see the ill effects it has had on the prosperity of nations. The union of church and state has impoverished Spain.—The revoking the edict of Nantz drove the silk manufacture from that country into England; and church and state are now driving the cotton manufacture from England to America and France. Let then Mr. Burke continue to preach his anti-political doctrine of church and state. It will do some good. The national assembly will not follow his advice, but will benefit by his folly. It was by observing the ill effects of it in England, that America has been warned against it; and it is by experiencing them in France, that the national assembly have abolished it, and, like America, has established *universal right of conscience, and universal right of citizenship.**

* When in any country we see extraordinary circumstances taking place, they naturally lead any man who has a talent for observation and investigation, to inquire into the causes. The manufacturers of Manchester, Birmingham, and Sheffield, are the principal manufacturers in England. From whence did this arise? A little observation will explain the case. The principal, and the generality of the inhabitants of those places, are not of what is

I will here cease the comparison with respect to the principles of the French constitution, and conclude this part of the subject with a few observations on the organization of the formal parts of the French and English governments.

The executive power in each country is in the hands of a person styled, the king; but the French constitution distinguishes between the king and the sovereign: it considers the station of king as official, and places sovereignty in the nation.

The representatives of the nation, which compose the national assembly, and who are the legislative power, originate in and from the people by election, as an inherent right in the people. In England it is otherwise; and this arises from the original establishment of what is called its monarchy; for, as by the conquest all the rights of the people or the nation were absorbed into the hands of the conqueror, and who added the title of king to that of conqueror, those same matters which in France are now held as rights in the people, or in the nation, are held in England as grants from what is called the crown. The parliament in England, in both its branches, was erected by patents from the descendants of the conqueror. The house of commons did not originate as a matter of right in the people, to delegate or elect, but as a grant or boon.

called in England, the church established by law : and they, or their fathers (for it is within but a few years) withdrew from the persecution of the chartered towns, where test-laws more particularly operate, and established a sort of asylum for themselves in those places. It was the only asylum then offered, for the rest of Europe was worse. But the case is now changing.— France and America bid all comers welcome, and initiate them into all the rights of citizenship. Policy and interest, therefore, will, but perhaps too late, dictate in England, what reason and justice could not. Those manufacturers are withdrawing to other places. There is now erecting at Passey, three miles from Paris, a large cotton manufactory. and several are already erected in America Soon after the rejecting the bill for repealing the test-law, one of the richest manufacturers in England said in my hearing, " England, sir, is not a country for a Dissenter to live in—we must go to France." These are truths, and it is doing justice to both parties to tell them. It is chiefly the Dissenters that have carried English manufactures to the height they are now at, and the same men have it in their power to carry them away; and though those manufactures would afterwards continue in those places, the foreign market will be lost. There frequently appears in the London Gazette, extracts from certain acts to prevent machines, and as far as it can extend to persons, from going out of the country. It appears from these, that the ill effects of the test-laws and church-establishment begin to be much suspected; but the remedy of force can never supply the remedy of reason. In the progress of less than a century, all the unrepresented part of England, of all denominations which is at least an hundred times the most numerous, may begin to feel the necessity of a constitution, and then all those matters will come regularly before them.

By the French constitution, the nation is always named before the king. The third article of the declaration of rights says, " *The nation is essentially the source* (or fountain) *of all sovereignty.*" Mr. Burke argues, that, in England, a king is the fountain—that he is the fountain of all honor. But as this idea is evidently descended from the conquest, I shall make no other remark upon it than that it is the nature of conquest to turn every thing upside down; and as Mr. Burke will not be refused the privilege of speaking twice, and as there are but two parts in the figure, the *fountain* and the *spout*, he will be right the second time.

The French constitution puts the legislative before the executive ; the law before the king; *la loi, le roi.* This also is in the natural order of things ; because laws must have existence, before they can have execution.

A king in France does not, in addressing himself to the national assembly, say, " my assembly," similar to the phrase used in England of " *my* parliament ;" neither can he use it consistent with the constitution, nor could it be admitted. There may be propriety in the use of it in England, because, as is before mentioned, both houses of parliament originated out of what is called the crown, by patent or boon—and not out of the inherent rights of the people, as the national assembly does in France, and whose name designates its origin.

The president of the national assembly does not ask the king *to grant to the assembly the liberty of speech*, as is the case with the English house of commons. The constitutional dignity of the national assembly cannot debase itself. Speech is, in the first place, one of the natural rights of man, always retained ; and with respect to the national assembly, the use of it is their *duty*, and the nation is their *authority*. They were elected by the greatest body of men exercising the right of election the European world ever saw. They sprung not from the filth of rotten boroughs, nor are they vassal representatives of aristocratical ones. Feeling the proper dignity of their character, they support it. Their parliamentary language, whether for or against a question, is free, bold, and manly, and extends to all the parts and circumstances of the case. If any matter or subject respecting the executive department, or the person who presides in it (the king,) comes before them, it is debated on with the spirit of men, and the language of gentlemen ; and their answer, or their address, is returned in the same style. They stand not aloof with the gaping vacuity of vulgar ignorance, nor bend with the cringe of sycophantic insignificance. The graceful pride of truth knows no extremes, and preserves, in every latitude of life the right-angled character of man.

Let us now look to the other side of the question. In the addresses of the English parliaments to their kings, we see neither the intrepid spirit of the old parliaments of France, nor the serene dignity of the present national assembly; neither do we see in them any thing of the style of English manners, which borders somewhat on bluntness. Since then they are neither of foreign extraction, nor naturally of English production, their origin must be sought for elsewhere, and that origin is the Norman conquest. They are evidently of the vassalage class of manners, and emphatically mark the prostrate distance that exists in no other condition of men than between the conqueror and the conquered. That this vassalage idea and style of speaking was not got rid of, even at the revolution of 1688, is evident from the declaration of parliament to William and Mary, in these words : "we do most humbly and faithfully *submit* ourselves, our heirs and posterity for ever." Submission is wholly a vassalage term, repugnant to the dignity of freedom, and an echo of the language used at the conquest.

As the estimation of all things is by comparison, the revolution of 1688, however from circumstances it may have been exalted above its value, will find its level. It is already on the wane, eclipsed by the enlarging orb of reason, and the revolutions of America and France. In less than another century, it will go, as well as Mr. Burke's labors, "to the family vault of all the Capulets." Mankind will then scarcely believe that a country calling itself free, would send to Holland for a man, and clothe him with power, on purpose to put themselves in fear of him, and give him almost a million sterling a-year for leave to *submit* themselves and their posterity, like bondmen and bondwomen for ever.

But there is a truth that ought to be made known; I have had the opportunity of seeing it : which is, *that, notwithstanding appearances, there is not any description of men that despise monarchy so much as courtiers.* But they well know, that if it were seen by others, as it is seen by them, the juggle could not be kept up. They are in the condition of

men who get their living by a show, and to whom the folly
of that show is so familiar that they ridicule it; but were
the audience to be made as wise, in this respect, as themselves, there would be an end to the show and the profits
with it. The difference between a republican and a courtier with respect to monarchy is, that the one opposes monarchy believing it to be something, and the other laughs at
it knowing it to be nothing.

As I used sometimes to correspond with Mr. Burke, believing him then to be a man of sounder principles than his
book shows him to be, I wrote to him last winter from Paris,
and gave him an account how prosperously matters were
going on. Among other subjects in that letter, I referred
to the happy situation the national assembly were placed
in; that they had taken a ground on which their moral
duty and their political interest were united. They have
not to hold out a language which they do not believe, for
the fraudulent purpose of making others believe it. Their
station requires no artifice to support it, and can only be
maintained by enlightening mankind. It is not their interest to cherish ignorance, but to dispel it. They are not in
the case of a ministerial or an opposition party in England,
who, though they are opposed, are still united to keep up
the common mystery. The national assembly must throw
open a magazine of light. It must show man the proper
character of man; and the nearer it can bring him to that
standard, the stronger the national assembly becomes.

In contemplating the French constitution, we see in it a
rational order of things. The principles harmonize with
the forms, and both with their origin. It may perhaps be
said as an excuse for bad forms, that they are nothing
more than forms; but this is a mistake. Forms grow out
of principles, and operate to continue the principles they
grow from. It is impossible to practice a bad form on any
thing but a bad principle. It cannot be ingrafted on a
good one; and wherever the forms in any government are
bad, it is a certain indication that the principles are bad
also.

I will here finally close this subject. I began it by remarking that Mr. Burke had *voluntarily* declined going into
a comparison of the English and French constitutions. He
apologizes (p. 241) for not doing it, by saying that he had
not time. Mr. Burke's book was upwards of eight months
in hand, and it extended to a volume of three hundred

and fifty-six pages. As his omission does injury to his cause, his apology makes it worse; and men on the English side of the water will begin to consider, whether there is not some radical defect in what is called the English constitution, that made it necessary in Mr. Burke to suppress the comparison, to avoid bringing it into view.

As Mr. Burke has not written on constitutions, so neither has he written on the French revolution. He gives no account of its commencement or its progress. He only expresses his wonder. "It looks," says he, "to me as if I were in a great crisis, not of the affairs of France alone, but of all Europe, perhaps of more than Europe. All circumstances taken together, the French revolution is the most astonishing that has hitherto happened in the world."

As wise men are astonished at foolish things, and other people at wise ones, I know not on which ground to account for Mr. Burke's astonishment; but certain it is that he does not understand the French revolution. It has apparently burst forth like a creation from a chaos, but it is no more than the consequence of mental revolution previously existing in France. The mind of the nation had changed before hand, and the new order of things has naturally followed a new order of thoughts.—I will here, as concisely as I can, trace out the growth of the French revolution, and mark the circumstances that have contributed to produce it.

The despotism of Louis XIV. united with the gaiety of his court, and the gaudy ostentation of his character, had so humbled, and at the same time so fascinated the mind of France, that the people appear to have lost all sense of their own dignity, in contemplating that of their grand monarch: and the whole reign of Louis XV. remarkable only for weakness and effeminacy, made no other alteration than that of spreading a sort of lethargy over the nation, from which it showed no disposition to rise.

The only signs which appeared of the spirit of liberty during those periods, are to be found in the writings of the French philosophers. Montesquieu, president of the parliament of Bourdeaux, went as far as a writer under a despotic government could well proceed; and being obliged to divide himself between principle and prudence, his mind often appears under a veil, and we ought to give him credit for more than he has expressed.

Voltaire, who was both the flatterer and satirist of despotism, took another line. His forte lay in exposing and ridiculing the superstitions which priest-craft, united with state-craft, had interwoven with governments. It was not from the purity of his principles, or his love of mankind, (for satire and philanthropy are not naturally concordant) but from his strong capacity of seeing folly in its true shape, and his irresistible propensity to expose it that he made those attacks. They were however as formidable as if the motives had been virtuous; and he merits the thanks rather than the esteem of mankind.

On the contrary, we find in the writings of Rousseau and abbe Raynal, a loveliness of sentiment in favor of liberty, that excites respect, and elevates the human faculties; yet having raised this animation, they do not direct its operations, but leave the mind in love with an object, without describing the means of possessing it.

The writings of Quisne, Turgot, and the friends of those authors, are of a serious kind; but they labored under the same disadvantage with Montesquieu; their writings abound with moral maxims of government, but are rather directed to economise and reform the administration of the government, than the government itself.

But all those writings and many others had their weight; and by the different manner in which they treated the subject of government, Montesquieu by his judgment and knowledge of laws; Voltaire by his wit; Rousseau and Raynal by their animation, and Quisne and Turgot by their moral maxims and systems of economy, readers of every class met with something to their taste, and a spirit of political inquiry began to diffuse itself through the nation at the time the dispute between England and the then colonies of America broke out.

In the war which France afterwards engaged in, it is very well known that the nation appeared to be beforehand with the French ministry. Each of them had its views: but those views were directed to different objects; the one sought liberty and the other retaliation on England. The French officers and soldiers who after this went to America, were eventually placed in the school of freedom, and learned the practice as well as the principles of it by heart.

As it was impossible to separate the military events which took place in America from the principles of the American revolution, the publication of those events in

France necessarily connected themselves with the princíples that produced them. Many of the facts were in themselves principles; such as the declaration of American independence, and the treaty of alliance between France and America, which recognized the natural rights of man, and justified resistance to oppression.

The then minister of France, count Vergennes, was not the friend of America: and it is both justice and gratitude to say, that it was the queen of France who gave the cause of America a fashion at the French court. Count Vergennes was the personal and social friend of Dr. Franklin; and the doctor had obtained by his sensible gracefulness, a sort of influence over him; but with respect to principles, count Vergennes was a despot.

The situation of Dr. Franklin as minister from America to France should be taken into the chain of circumstances. A diplomatic character is the narrowest sphere of society that man can act in. It forbids intercourse by a reciprocity of suspicion; and a diplomatist is a sort of unconnected atom, continually repelling and repelled. But this was not the case with Dr. Franklin. he was not the diplomatist of a court, but of *man.* His character as a philosopher had been long established, and his circle of society in France was universal.

Count Vergennes resisted for a considerable time the publication of the American constitutions in France, translated into the French language; but even in this he was obliged to give way to public opinion, and a sort of propriety in admitting to appear what he had undertaken to defend. The American constitutions were to liberty what a grammar is to language: they define its parts of speech, and practically construct them into syntax.

The peculiar situation of the then marquis de la Fayette is another link in the great chain. He served in America as an American officer, under a commission of congress, and by the universality of his acquaintance, was in close friendship with the civil government of America, as well as with the military line. He spoke the language of the country, entered into the discussions on the principles of government, and was always a welcome friend at any election.

When the war closed, a vast reinforcement to the cause of liberty spread itself over France, by the return of the French officers and soldiers. A knowledge of the practice was then joined to the theory ; and all that was wanting to give it real existence, was opportunity. Man, cannot, properly speaking, make circumstances for his purpose, but he always has it in his power to improve them when they occur : and this was the case in France.

M. Neckar was displaced in May 1781; and by the ill-management of the finances afterwards, and particularly during the extravagant administration of M. Calonne, the revenue of France which was nearly twenty-four millions sterling per year, was become unequal to the expenditures not because the revenue had decreased, but because the expenses had increased, and this was the circumstance which the nation laid hold of to bring forward a revolution, The English minister, Mr. Pitt, has frequently alluded to the state of the French finances in his budgets, without understanding the subject. Had the French parliaments been as ready to register edicts for new taxes, as an English parliament is to grant them, there had been no derangement in the finances, nor yet any revolution ; but this will better explain itself as I proceed.

It will be necessary here to show how taxes were formerly raised in France. The king, or rather the court or ministry, acting under the use of that name, framed the edicts for taxes at their own discretion, and sent them to the parliaments to be registered ; for until they were registered by the parliaments, they were not operative. Disputes had long existed between the court and the parliament with respect to the extent of the parliament's authority on this head. The court insisted that the authority of parliament went no further than to remonstrate or show reasons against the tax, reserving to itself the right of determining whether the reasons are well or ill-founded ; and in consequence thereof, either to withdraw the edict as a matter of choice, or to *order* it to be enregistered as a matter of authority. The parliaments on their part insisted, that they had not only a right to remonstrate, but to reject ; and on this ground they were always supported by the nation.

But, to return to the order of my narrative—M. Calonne wanted money ; and as he knew the sturdy disposition of the parliaments with respect to new taxes, he ingeniously sought either to approach them by a more gentle means than that of direct authority, or to get over their heads by a manœuvre : and, for this purpose, he revived the project of assembling a body of men from the several provinces, under the style of an "assembly of the notables," or men of note, who met in 1787, and who were either to recommend taxes to the parliaments, or to act as a parliament themselves. An assembly under this name had been called in 1687.

As we are to view this as the first practical step towards the revolution, it will be proper to enter into some particulars respecting it. The assembly of the notables has in some places been mistaken for the states-general, but was wholly a different body ; the states-general being always by election. The persons who composed the assembly of the notables were all nominated by the king, and consisted of one hundred and forty-members. But as M. Calonne could not depend upon a majority of this assembly in his favor, he very ingeniously arranged them in such a manner as to make forty-four a majority of one hundred and forty : to effect this, he disposed of them into seven separate committees, of twenty members each. Every general question was to be decided, not by a majority of persons, but by a majority of committees ; and as eleven votes would make a majority in a committee, and four committees a majority of seven, M. Calonne had good reason to conclude, that as forty-four would determine any general question, he could not be out-voted. But all his plans deceived him, and in the event became his overthrow.

The then marquis de la Fayette was placed in the second committee, of which count d'Artois was president ; and as money matters was the object, it naturally brought into view every circumstance connected with it. M. de la Fayette made a verbal charge against Calonne, for selling crown land to the amount of two millions of livres, in a manner that appeared to be unknown to the king. The count d'Artois (as if to intimidate, for the Bastile was then in being) asked the marquis, if he would render the charge in writing ? He replied that he would. The count d'Artois did not demand it, but brought a message from the king to that purport. M. de la Fayette then delivered in his charge in writing, to be given to the king, undertaking to support it. No further proceedings were had upon this affair ; but M. Calonne was soon after dismissed by the king, and went to England.

As M. de la Fayette, from the experience he had had in America, was better acquainted with the science of civil government than the generality of the members who composed the assembly of the notables could then be, the brunt of the business fell considerably to his share. The plan of those who had a constitution in view, was to contend with the court on the ground of taxes, and some of them openly professed their object. Disputes frequently arose between count d' Artois and M. de la Fayette upon various subjects. With respect to the arrears already incurred, the latter proposed to remedy them, by accommodating the expenses to the revenue, instead of the revenue to the expenses; and as objects of reform, he proposed to abolish the Bastile, and all the state-prisons throughout the nation (the keeping of which was attended with great expense) and to suppress *lettres de cachet:* but those matters were not then much attended to; and with respect to *lettres de cachet, a majority of the nobles appeared to be in favor of them.*

On the subject of supplying the treasury by new taxes, the assembly declined taking the matter on themselves, concurring in the opinion that they had not authority. In a debate on this subject, M. de la Fayette said, that raising money by taxes could only be done by a national assembly, freely elected by the people and acting as their representatives. Do you mean, said the count d'Artois, the states-general? M. de la Fayette replied, that he did. Will you, said the count d'Artois, sign what you say, to be given to the king? The other replied, that he not only would do this, but that he would go further, and say, that the effectual mode would be, for the king to agree to the establishment of a constitution.

As one of the plans had thus failed, that of getting the assembly to act as a parliament, the other came into view, that of recommending. On this subject, the assembly agreed to recommend two new taxes to be enregistered by the parliament, the one a stamp-act, and the other a territorial tax, or sort of land-tax. The two have been estimated at about five millions sterling, per annum. We have now to turn our attention to the parliaments, on whom the business was again devolving.

The archbishop of Thoulouse (since archbishop of Sens, and now a cardinal) was appointed to the administration of the finances, soon after the dismission of Calonne. He was also made prime minister, an office that did not always exist in France. When this office did not exist, the chief of each of the principal departments transacted busi-

ness immediately with the king; but when a prime minister was appointed, they did business only with him.   The
archbishop arrived to more state-authority than any minister since the duke de Choiseuil, and the nation was
strongly disposed in his favor; but by a line of conduct
scarcely to be accounted for, he perverted every opportunity, turned out a despot, and sunk into disgrace, and a
cardinal.

The assembly of the notables having broke up, the new
minister sent the edicts for the two new taxes recommended by the assembly to the parliaments, to be enregistered.
They of course came first before the parliament of Paris,
who returned for answer, *That with such a revenue as the nation then supported, the name of taxes ought not to be mentioned,
but for the purpose of reducing them;* and threw both the
edicts out.*

On this refusal, the parliament was ordered to Versailles, where, in the usual form, the king held, what under
the old government was called a bed of justice: and the
two edicts were enregistered in presence of the parliament,
by an order of state, in the manner mentioned, p. 99.   On
this, the parliament immediately returned to Paris, renewed
their session in form, and ordered the enregistering to be
struck out, declaring that every thing done at Versailles
was illegal.   All the members of parliament were then
served with *lettres de cachet*, and exiled to Trois; but as
they continued as inflexible in exile as before, and as ven-
geance did not supply the place of taxes, they were after a
short time recalled to Paris.

The edicts were again tendered to them, and the count
d'Artois undertook to act as representative for the king.—
For this purpose, he came from Versailles to Paris, in a
train of procession; and the parliament was assembled to
receive him.   But show and parade had lost their influence
in France; and whatever ideas of importance he might
set off with, he had to return with those of mortification
and disappointment.   On alighting from his carriage to as-
cend the steps of the parliament house, the crowd (which
was numerously collected) threw out trite expressions,
saying, " this is monsieur d'Artois, who wants more of our
money to spend."   The marked disapprobation which he

* When the English minister, Mr. Pitt, mentions the French finances
again in the English parliament, it would be well that he noticed this as an
example.

saw, impressed him with apprehensions; and the word *aux arms*, (*to arms*) was given out by the officer of the guard who attended him. It was so loudly vociferated, that it echoed through the avenues of the house, and produced a temporary confusion: I was then standing in one of the apartments through which he had to pass, and could not avoid reflecting how wretched is the condition of a disrespected man.

He endeavored to impress the parliament by great words, and opened his authority by saying, " The king, our lord and master." The parliament received him very coolly, and with their usual determination not to register the taxes: and in this manner the interview ended.

After this a new subject took place: in the various debates and contests that arose between the court and the parliaments on the subject of taxes, the parliament of Paris at last declared, that although it had been customary for parliaments to enregister edicts for taxes as a matter of convenience, the right belonged only to the states-general; and that therefore, the parliaments could no longer with propriety continue to debate on what it had not authority to act. The king after this, came to Paris, and held a meeting with the parliament, in which he continued from ten in the morning till about six in the evening; and, in a manner that appeared to proceed from him, as if unconsulted upon with the cabinet or the ministry, gave his word to the parliament, that the states-general should be convened.

But after this another scene arose, on a ground different from all the former. The minister and the cabinet were averse to calling the states-general: they well knew, that if the states-general were assembled, that themselves must fall; and as the king had not mentioned *any time*, they hit on a project calculated to elude, without appearing to oppose.

For this purpose, the court set about making a sort of constitution itself: it was principally the work of M. Lamoignon, keeper of the seals, who afterwards shot himself. The arrangement consisted in establishing a body under the name of a *cour pleniere*, or full court, in which were invested all the power that the government might have occasion to make use of. The persons composing this court to be nominated by the king; the contended right of taxation was given up on the part of the king, and a new criminal code of laws, and law proceedings, was substituted in the room of the former. The thing, in many points, contained better principles than those upon which the government had hitherto been administered: but with respect to the *cour pleniere*, it was no other than a medium through which despotism was to pass, without appearing to act directly from itself.

The cabinet had high expectations from their new contrivance. The persons who were to compose the *cour pleniere*, were already nominated; and as it was necessary to carry a fair appearance, many of the best characters in the nation were appointed among the number. It was to commence on the 8th of May, 1788: but an opposition arose to it, on two grounds—the one as to principle, the other as to form.

On the ground of principle it was contended, that government had not a right to alter itself; and that if the practice was once admitted, it would grow into a principle, and be made a precedent for any future alterations the government might wish to establish: that the right of altering the government was a national right, and not a right of government. And on the ground of form, it was contended, that the *cour pleniere* was nothing more than a large cabinet.

The then dukes de la Rochefoucault, Luxembourg, de Noailles, and many others, refused to accept the nomination, and strenuously opposed the whole plan. When the edict for establishing this new court was sent to the parliaments to be enregistered, and put into execution, they resisted also. The parliament of Paris not only refused, but denied the authority; and the contest renewed itself between the parliament and the cabinet more strongly than ever. While the parliament was sitting in debate on this subject, the ministry ordered a regiment of soldiers to surround the house, and form a blockade. The members sent out for beds and provision, and lived as in a besieged citadel; and as this had no effect, the commanding officer was ordered to enter the parliament house and seize them, which he did, and some the principal members were shut up in different prisons. About the same time a deputation of persons arrived from the province of Britanny, to remonstrate against the establishment of the *cour pleniere*; and those the archbishop sent to the Bastile. But the spirit of the nation was not to be overcome; and it was so fully sensible of the strong ground it had taken, that of withholding taxes, that it contented itself with keeping up a sort of quiet resistance, which effectually overthrew all the plans at that time formed against it. The project of the *cour pleniere* was at last obliged to be given up, and the prime minister not long afterwards followed its fate ; and M. Neckar was recalled into office.

The attempt to establish the *cour pleniere* had an effect upon the nation, which was not anticipated. It was a sort of new form of government, that insensibly served to put the old one out of sight, and to unhinge it from the superstitious authority of antiquity. It was government dethroning government; and the old one, by attempting to make a new one, made a chasm.

The failure of this scheme renewed the subject of convening the states-general ; and this gave rise to a new series of politics. There was no settled form for convening the states-general : all that it positively meant, was a deputation from what was then called the clergy, the nobility, and the commons; but their numbers, or their proportions, had not been always the same. They had been convened only on extraordinary occasions, the last of which was in 1614; their numbers were then in equal proportions, and they voted by orders.

It could not well escape the sagacity of M. Neckar, that the mode of 1614 would answer neither the purpose of the then government, nor of the nation. As matters were at that time circumstanced, it would have been too contentious to argue upon any thing. The debates would have been endless upon privileges and exemptions, in which neither the wants of the government, nor the wishes of the nation for a constitution, would have been attended to. But as he did not choose to take the decision upon himself, he summoned again the assembly of the *notables*, and referred it to them. This body was in general interested in the decision, being chiefly of the aristocracy and the high-paid clergy; and they decided in favor of the mode of 1614. This decision was against the sense of the nation, and also against the wishes of the court ; for the aristocracy opposed itself to both, and contended for privileges independent of either. The subject was then taken up by the parliament, who recommended that the number of the commons should be equal to the other two ; and that they should all sit in one house, and vote in one body. The number finally determined on was twelve hundred : six hundred to be chosen by the commons (and this was less than their

proportion ought to have been when their worth and consequence is considered on a national scale) three hundred by
the clergy, and three hundred by the aristocracy ; but with
respect to the mode of assembling themselves, whether together or apart, or the manner in which they should vote,
those matters were referred.*

The election that followed, was not a contested election,
but an animated one. The candidates were not men, but
principles. Societies were formed in Paris, and committees
of correspondence and communication established throughout the nation, for the purpose of enlightening the people,
and explaining to them the principles of civil government;
and so orderly was the election conducted, that it did not
give rise even to the rumor of tumult.

The states-general were to meet at Versailles in April,
1789, but did not assemble till May. They located themselves in three separate chambers, or rather the clergy and
the aristocracy withdrew each into a separate chamber.
The majority of the aristocracy claimed what they called
the privilege of voting as a separate body, and of giving
their consent or their negative in that manner ; and many
of the bishops and the high-beneficed clergy claimed the
same privilege on the part of their order.

The *tiers etat* (as they were called) disowned all knowledge of artificial orders and privileges ; and they were not
only resolute on this point but somewhat disdainful. They

* Mr. Burke, (and I must take the liberty of telling him that he is unacquainted with French affairs,) speaking upon this subject, says, "The first
thing that struck me in calling the states-general, was a great departure from
the ancient course ;" and he soon after says, "From the moment I read the
list, I saw distinctly, and very nearly as it has happened, all that was to follow."
Mr. Burke certainly did not see all that was to follow. I have endeavored to
impress him, as well before as after the states general met, that there would
be a *revolution ;* but was not able to make him see it, neither would he believe it. How then he could distinctly see all the parts, when the whole was
out of sight, is beyond my comprehension. And with respect to the "departure from the ancient course," besides the natural weakness of the remark, it shows that he is unacquainted with circumstances. The departure
was necessary, from the experience had upon it, that the ancient course was
a bad one. The states-general of 1614 were called at the commencement of
the civil war in the minority of Louis XIII. : but by the clash of arranging
them by orders, they increased the confusion they were called to compose.
The author of *l'Intrigue du Cabinet* (Intrigue of the Cabinet,) who wrote before any revolution was thought of in France, speaking of the states-general
of 1614, says, "They held the public in suspense five months: and by the
questions agitated therein, and the heat with which they were put, it appears that the great (*les grands*) thought more to satisfy their particular
passions, than to procure the good of the nation ; and the whole time passed
away in altercations, ceremonies and parade." l'Intrigue du Cabinet, vol. i.
p. 329.

began to consider aristocracy as a kind of fungus growing
out of the corruption of society, that could not be admitted
even as a branch of it; and from the disposition the aristocracy had shown, by upholding *lettres de cachet*, and in
sundry other instances, it was manifest that no constitution
could be formed by admitting men in any other character
than as national men.

After various altercations on this head, the *tiers etat*, or
commons, (as they were then called) declared themselves
(on a motion made for that purpose by the abbe Sieyes,)
" THE REPRESENTATIVES OF THE NATION ; *and that the two orders
could be considered but as deputies of corporations, and could
only have a deliberative voice but when they assembled in a national character, with the national representatives.*" This proceeding extinguished the style of *etas generaux* or states-general,
and erected it into the style it now bears, that of *l'assemble
nationale* or national assembly.

This motion was not made in a precipitate manner : it was
the result of cool deliberation, and concerted between the
national representatives and the patriotic members of the
two chambers, who saw into the folly, mischief, and injustice of artificial privileged distinctions. It was become
evident, that no constitution, worthy of being called by that
name, could be established on any thing less than a national ground. The aristocracy had hitherto opposed the
despotism of the court, and affected the language of patriotism ; but it opposed it as its rival; (as the English barons
opposed king John) and it now opposed the nation from the
same motives.

On carrying this motion the national representatives, as
had been concerted, sent an invitation to the two chambers,
to unite with them in a national character, and proceed to
business. A majority of the clergy, chiefly of the parish
priests, withdrew from the clerical chamber, and joined the
nation; and forty-five from the other chamber joined in
like manner. There is a sort of secret history belonging
to this last circumstance, which is necessary to its explanation : it was not judged prudent that all the patriotic members of the chamber, styling itself the nobles, should quit it
at once ; and in consequence of this arrangement, they
drew off by degrees, always leaving some, as well to reason the case, as to watch the suspected. In a little time,
the numbers increased from forty-five to eighty, and soon
after to a greater number ; which with a majority of the

clergy, and the whole of the national representatives, put the malcontents in a very diminutive condition.

The king, who, very different to the general class called by that name, is a man of a good heart, showed himself disposed to recommend a union of the three chambers, on the ground the national assembly had taken; but the malcontents exerted themselves to prevent it, and began now to have another project in view. Their numbers consisted of a majority of the aristocratical chamber, and a minority of the clerical chamber, chiefly of bishops and high-beneficed clergy; and these men were determined to put every thing at issue, as well by strength as by stratagem. They had no objection to a constitution; but it must be such an one as themselves should dictate, and suited to their own views and particular situations. On the other hand, the nation disowned knowing any thing of them but as citizens, and was determined to shut out all such upstart pretensions. The more aristocracy appeared, the more it was despised; there was a visible imbecility and want of intellects in the majority, a sort of *je ne scais quoi*, that while it affected to be more than citizen, was less than man. It lost ground more from contempt than from hatred; and was rather jeered at as an ass, than dreaded as a lion. This is the general character of aristocracy, or what are called nobles or nobility, or rather no-ability, in all countries.

The plan of the malcontents consisted now of two things; either to deliberate and vote by chambers (or orders,) more especially on all questions respecting a constitution (by which the aristocratical chamber would have had a negative on any article of the constitution) or, in case they could not accomplish this object, to overthrow the national assembly entirely.

To effect one or the other of these objects, they began now to cultivate a friendship with the despotism they had hitherto attempted to rival, and the count d'Artois became their chief. The king (who has since declared himself deceived into their measures) held, according to the old form, *a bed of justice*, in which he accorded to the deliberation and vote *par tete* (by head) upon several objects; but reserved the deliberation and vote upon all questions respecting a constitution to the three chambers separately. This declaration of the king was made against the advice of M. Neckar, who now began to perceive that he was growing out of fashion at court, and that another minister was in contemplation.

As the form of sitting in separate chambers was yet apparently kept up, though essentially destroyed, the national representatives, immediately after this declaration of the king, resorted to their chambers, to consult on a protest against it; and the minority of the chamber (calling itself the nobles) who had joined the national cause, retired to a private house, to consult in like manner. The malcontents had by this time concerted their measures with the court, which count d'Artois undertook to conduct: and as they saw, from the discontent which the declaration excited, and the opposition making against it, that they could not obtain a control over the intended constitution by a separate vote, they prepared themselves for their final object—that of conspiring against the national assembly, and overthrowing it.

The next morning, the door of the chamber of the national assembly was shut against them, and guarded by troops; and the members were refused admittance. On this, they withdrew to a tennis-ground in the neighborhood of Versailles, as the most convenient place they could find, and, after renewing their session, took an oath never to separate from each other, under any circumstances whatever, death excepted, until they had established a constitution. As the experiment of shutting up the house had no other effect than that of producing a closer connexion in the members, it was opened again the next day, and the public business re-commenced in the usual place.

We now are to have in view the forming the new ministry, which was to accomplish the overthrow of the national assembly. But as force would be necessary, orders were issued to assemble thirty thousand troops, the command of which was given to Broglio, one of the new-intended ministry, who was recalled from the country for this purpose. But as some management was necessary to keep this plan concealed till the moment it should be ready for execution, it is to this policy that a declaration made by the count d'Artois must be attributed, and which is here proper to be introduced.

It could not but occur, that while the malcontents continued to resort to their chambers separate from the national assembly, that more jealousy would be excited than if they were mixed with it, and that the plot might be suspected. But as they had taken their ground, and now wanted a pretence for quitting it, it was necessary that one should be devised. This was effectually accomplished by a declaration made by count d'Artois, that "*if they took not a part in the national assembly, the life of the king would be endangered,*" on which they quitted their chambers, and mixed with the assembly in one body.

At the time this declaration was made, it was generally treated as a piece of absurdity in the count d'Artois, and calculated merely to relieve the outstanding members of the two chambers from the diminutive situation they were put in; and if nothing more had followed, this conclusion would have been good. But as things best explain themselves by events, this apparent union was only a cover to the machinations that were secretly going on; and the declaration accommodated itself to answer that purpose. In a little time the national assembly found itself surrounded by troops, and thousands daily arriving. On this a very strong declaration was made by the national assembly to the king, remonstrating on the impropriety of the measure, and demanding the reason. The king, who was not in the secret of this business, as himself afterwards declared, gave substantially for answer, that he had no other object in view than to preserve public tranquillity, which appeared to be much disturbed.

But in a few days from this time the plot unravelled itself. M. Neckar and the ministry were displaced, and a new one formed, of the enemies of the revolution; and Broglio, with between twenty-five and thirty thousand foreign troops, was arrived to support them. The mask was now thrown off, and matters were come to a crisis. The event was, that in the space of three days, the new ministry and all their abettors, found it prudent to fly the nation; the Bastile was taken, and Broglio and his foreign troops dispersed; as is already related in a former part of this work.

There are some curious circumstances in the history of this short-lived ministry, and this brief attempt at a counter-revolution. The palace of Versailles, where the court was sitting, was not more than four hundred yards distant from the hall where the national assembly was sitting. The two places were at this moment like the separate head-quarters of two combatant enemies; yet the court was as perfectly ignorant of the information which had arrived from Paris to the national assembly, as if it had resided at an hundred miles distance. The then marquis de la Fayette, who (as has been already mentioned) was chosen to preside in the national assembly on this particular occasion, named, by order of the assembly, three successive deputations to the king, on the day, and up to the evening on which the Bastile was taken, to inform and confer with him on the state of affairs: but the ministry, who knew not so much as that it was attacked, precluded all communication, and were solacing themselves how dexterously they had succeeded: but in a few hours the accounts arrived so thick and fast, that they had to start from their desks and run: some set off in one disguise, and some in another, and none in their own character. Their anxiety now was to outride the news, lest they should be stopped, which, though it flew fast, flew not so fast as themselves.

It is worth remarking, that the national assembly neither pursued those fugitive conspirators, nor took any notice of them, nor sought to retaliate in any shape whatever. Occupied with establishing a constitution, founded on the rights of man and the authority of the people, the only authority on which government has a right to exist in any country, the national assembly felt none of those mean passions which mark the character of impertinent governments, founding themselves on their own authority, or on the absurdity of hereditary succession. It is the faculty of the human mind to become what it contemplates, and to act in unison with its object.

The conspiracy being thus dispersed, one of the first works of the national assembly, instead of vindictive proclamations, as has been the case with other governments, published a declaration of the rights of man, as the basis on which the new constitution was to be built, and which is here subjoined.

Declaration of the rights of man and of citizens: by the national assembly of France.

" The representatives of the people of France, formed into a national assembly, considering that ignorance, neglect, or contempt of human rights, are the sole causes of public misfortunes, and corruptions of government, have resolved to set forth, in a solemn declaration, these natural, imprescriptible, and unalienable rights: that this declara-

tion being constantly present to the minds of the body social, they may be ever kept attentive to their rights and
their duties: that the acts of the legislative and executive
powers of government, being capable of being every moment compared with the end of political institutions, may
be more respected: and also, that the future claims of the
citizens, being directed by simple and .incontestible principles, may always tend to the maintenance of the constitution and the general happiness.

"For these reasons the national assembly doth recog-
nize and declare, in the presence of the supreme being,
and with a hope of his blessing and favor, the following *sacred* rights of men and of citizens:

"I. Men are born and always continue free and equal
in respect of their rights.   Civil distinctions, therefore, can
only be founded on public utility.

"II. The end of all political associations is the preser-
vation of the natural and imprescriptible rights of man;
and these rights are liberty, property, security, and resistance of oppression.

"III. The nation is essentially the source of all sovereignty: nor can any *individual* or *any body of men,* be entitled to any authority which is not expressly derived
from it.

"IV. Political liberty consists in the power of doing
whatever does not injure another.   The exercise of the
natural rights of every man has no other limits than those
which are necessary to secure to every *other* man the free
exercise of the same rights; and these limits are determinable only by the law.

"V. The law ought to prohibit only actions hurtful to
society.   What is not prohibited by the law, should not
be hindered; nor should any one be compelled to that
which the law does not require.

"VI. The law is an expression of the will of the community.   All citizens have a right to concur, either per-
sonally, or by their representatives, in its formation.   It
should be the same to all, whether it protects or punishes;
and all being equal in its sight, are equally eligible to all
honors, places, and employments, according to their different abilities, without any other distinction than that created by their virtues and talents.

"VII. No man should be accused, arrested, or held in
confinement, except in cases determined by the law, and

according to the forms which it has prescribed. All who promote, solicit, execute, or cause to be executed, arbitrary orders, ought to be punished; and every citizen called upon or apprehended by virtue of the law, ought immediately to obey, and not render himself culpable by resistance.

" VIII. The law ought to impose no other penalties than such as are absolutely and evidently necessary: and no one ought to be punished, but in virtue of a law promulgated before the offence, and legally applied.

" IX. Every man being presumed innocent till he has been convicted, whenever his detention becomes indispensable, all rigor to him, more than is necessary to secure his person, ought to be provided against by the law.

" X. No man ought to be molested on account of his opinions, not even on account of his religious opinions, provided his avowal of them does not disturb the public order established by law.

" XI. The unrestrained communication of thoughts and opinions being one of the most precious rights of man, every citizen may speak, write, and publish freely, provided he is responsible for the abuse of this liberty in cases determined by the law.

" XII. A public force being necessary to give security to the rights of men and of citizens, that force is instituted for the benefit of the community, and not for the particular benefit of the persons with whom it is intrusted.

" XIII. A common contribution being necessary for the support of the public force, and for defraying the other expenses of government, it ought to be divided equally among the members of the community, according to their abilities.

" XIV. Every citizen has a right, either by himself or his representative, to a free voice in determining the necessity of public contributions, the appropriation of them, and their amount, mode of assessment, and duration.

" XV. Every community has a right to demand of all its agents, an account of their conduct.

" XVI. Every community in which a separation of powers and a security of rights is not provided for, wants a constitution.

" XVII. The right to property being inviolable and sacred, no one ought to be deprived of it, except in cases of

evident public necessity legally ascertained, and on condition of a previous just indemnity."

Observations on the declaration of rights.

The three first articles comprehend in general terms the
whole of a declaration of rights : all the succeeding articles either originate out of them, or follow as elucidations.
The 4th, 5th, and 6th, define more particularly what is
only generally expressed in the 1st, 2d, and 3d.

The 7th, 8th, 9th, 10th, and 11th articles are declaratory of *principles* upon which laws shall be construed con-
formable to *rights* already declared.   But it is questioned
by some very good people in France, as well as in other
countries, whether the 10th article sufficiently guarantees
the right it is intended to accord with : besides which, it
takes off from the divine dignity of religion, and weakens
its operative force upon the mind to make it a subject of
human laws.   It then presents itself to man, like light intercepted by a cloudy medium, in which the source of it is
obscured from his sight, and he sees nothing to reverence
in the dusky rays.*

The remaining articles, beginning with the twelfth, are
substantially contained in the principles of the preceding
articles ; but, in the particular situation which France then
was, having to undo what was wrong, as well as to set up
what was right, it was proper to be more particular than
what in another condition of things would be necessary.

While the declaration of rights was before the national
assembly, some of its members remarked, that if a declaration of rights was published, it should be accompanied

---

* There is a single idea, which, if it strikes rightly upon the mind, either
in a legal or a religious sense, will prevent any man, or any body of men, or
any government, from going wrong on the subject of religion : which is, that
before any human institutions of government were known in the world, there
existed, if I may so express it, a compact between God and man, from the
beginning of time ; and that as the relation and condition which man in his
individual person stands in towards his maker cannot be changed, by any human laws or human authority, that religious devotion, which is a part of this
compact, cannot so much as be made a subject of human laws ; and that all
laws must conform themselves to this prior existing compact, and not assume
to make the compact conform to the laws, which, besides being human, are
subsequent thereto.   The first act of man, when he looked around and saw
himself a creature which he did not make, and a world furnished for his re-
ception, must have been devotion ; and devotion must ever continue sacred
to every individual man, as it appears right to him ; and governments do mischief by interfering.

by a declaration of duties. The observation discovered a mind that reflected, and it only erred by not reflecting far enough. A declaration of rights is, by reciprocity, a declaration of duties also. Whatever is my right as a man, is also the right of another; and it becomes my duty to guarantee, as well as to possess.

The three first articles are the basis of liberty as well individual as national; nor can any country be called free, whose government does not take its beginning from the principles they contain, and continue to preserve them pure; and the whole of the declaration of rights is of more value to the world, and will do more good, than all the laws and statutes that have yet been promulgated.

In the declaratory exordium which prefaces the declaration of rights, we see the solemn and majestic spectacle of a nation opening its commission, under the auspices of its creator, to establish a government; a scene so new, and so transcendantly unequalled by any thing in the European world, that the name of a revolution is inexpressive of its character, and it rises into a regeneration of man. What are the present governments of Europe, but a scene of iniquity and oppression? What is that of England? Does not its own inhabitants say, it is a market where every man has his price, and where corruption is common traffic, at the expense of a deluded people? No wonder, then, that the French revolution is traduced. Had it confined itself merely to the destruction of flagrant despotism, perhaps Mr. Burke and some others had been silent. Their cry now is, "It has gone too far:" that is, gone to far for them. It stares corruption in the face, and the venal tribe are all alarmed. Their fear discovers itself in their outrage, and they are but publishing the groans of a wounded vice. But from such opposition, the French revolution, instead of suffering, receives homage. The more it is struck, the more sparks it will emit; and the fear is, it will not be struck enough. It has nothing to dread from attacks. Truth has given it an establishment; and time will record it with a name as lasting as its own.

Having now traced the progress of the French revolution through most of its principal stages, from its commencement to the taking of the Bastile, and its establishment by the declaration of rights, I will close the subject with the energetic apostrophe of M. de la Fayette—*May* *this great monument raised to liberty, serve as a lesson to the oppressor, and an example to the oppressed !**

MISCELLANEOUS CHAPTER.

To prevent interrupting the argument in the preceding part of this work, or the narrative that follows it, I reserved some observations to be thrown together into a miscellaneous chapter; by which variety might not be censured for confusion. Mr. Burke's book is *all* miscellany. His intention was to make an attack on the French revolution: but instead of proceeding with an orderly arrangement, he has stormed it with a mob of ideas, tumbling over and destroying one another.

But this confusion and contradiction in Mr. Burke's book, is easily accounted for. When a man in any cause attempts to steer his course by any thing else than some popular truth or principle, he is sure to be lost. It is beyond the compass of his capacity, to keep all the parts of an argument together, and make them unite in one issue, by any other means than having this guide always in view. Neither memory nor invention will supply the want of it. The former fails him, and the latter betrays him.

Notwithstanding the nonsense, for it deserves no better name, that Mr. Burke has asserted about hereditary rights, and hereditary succession, and that a nation has not a right to form a government for itself, it happened to fall in his way to give some account of what government is. " Government," says he, " is a contrivance of human wisdom."

Admitting that government is a contrivance of human wisdom, it must necessarily follow, that hereditary succession, and hereditary rights (as they are called) can make no part of it, because it is impossible to make wisdom hereditary; and on the other hand, *that* cannot be a wise contrivance, which in its operation may commit the government of a nation to the wisdom of an ideot. The

---

* See p. 52. of this work.—N. B. Since the taking the Bastile, the occurrences have been published : but the matters recorded in this narrative are prior to that period, and some of them, as may easily be seen, can be but very little known.

ground which Mr. Burke now takes is fatal to every part, of his cause. The argument changes from hereditary rights to hereditary wisdom; and the question is, who is the wisest man? He must now show that every one in the line of hereditary succession was · a Solomon, or his title is not good to be a king. What a stroke has Mr. Burke now made! to use a sailor's phrase he has *swabbed the deck*, and scarcely left a name legible in the list of kings; and he has mowed down and thinned the house of peers, with a scythe as formidable as death and time.

But, Mr. Burke appears to have been aware of this retort, and he has taken care to guard against it, by making government to be not only a *contrivance* of human wisdom, but a *monopoly* of wisdom. He puts the nation as fools on one side, and places his government of wisdom, all wise men of Gotham, on the other side; and he then proclaims, and says, that " *men have a* RIGHT *that their* WANTS *should be provided for by this wisdom.*" Having thus made proclamation, he next proceeds to explain to them what their *wants* are, and also what their *rights* are. In this he has succeeded dexterously, for he makes their wants to be a *want* of wisdom; but as this is but cold comfort, he then informs them, that they have a *right* (not to any of the wisdom) but to be governed by it: and in order to impress them with a solemn reverence for this monopoly-government of wisdom, and of its vast capacity for all purposes, possible or impossible, right or wrong, he proceeds with astrological, mysterious importance, to tell them its powers in these words—"The rights of men in government are their advantages; and these are often in balances between differences of good; and in compromises sometimes between *good* and *evil*, and sometimes between *evil* and *evil*. Political reason is a *computing principle;* adding, subtracting, multiplying, and dividing, morally and not metaphysically or mathematically, true moral demonstrations."

As the wondering audience whom Mr. Burke supposes himself talking to, may not understand all this jargon, I will undertake to be its interpreter. The meaning then, good people, of all this is, *that government is governed by no principle whatever: that it can make evil good, or good evil, just as it pleases. In short, that government is arbitrary power.*

But there are some things which Mr. Burke has forgotten: 1st, he has not shown where the wisdom originally came from: and, 2d, he has not shown by what authority it first began to act. In the manner he introduced the matters, it is either government stealing wisdom, or wisdom stealing government. It is without an origin, and its powers without authority. In short, it is usurpation.

Whether it be from a sense of shame, or from a consciousness of some radical defect in government necessary to be kept out of sight, or from both, or from some other cause, I undertake not to determine ; but so it is, that a monarchical reasoner never traces government to its source, or from its source. It is one of the *shibboleths* by which he may be known. A thousand years hence, those who shall live in America or in France will look back with contemplative pride on the origin of their governments, and say, *this was the work of our glorious ancestors!* But what can a monarchical talker say ? What has he to exult in ? Alas! he has nothing. A certain something forbids him to look back to a beginning, lest some robber or some Robin Hood should rise from the long obscurity of time, and say, *I am the origin.* Hard as Mr. Burke labored under the regency bill and hereditary succession two years ago, and much as he dived for precedents, he still had not boldness enough to bring up William of Normandy, and say, *there is the head of the list, there is the fountain of honor,* the son of a prostitute, and the plunderer of the English nation.

The opinions of men, with respect to government, are changing fast in all countries. The revolutions of America and France have thrown a beam of light over the world, which reaches into man. The enormous expense of governments have provoked people to think by making them feel : and when once the veil begins to rend, it admits not of repair. Ignorance is of a peculiar nature : once dispelled, it is impossible to re-establish it. It is not originally a thing of itself, but is only the absence of knowledge ; and though man may be *kept* ignorant, he cannot be *made* ignorant. The mind, in discovering truths, acts in the same manner as it acts through the eye in discovering an object ; when once any object has been seen, it is impossible to put the mind back to the same condition it was in before it saw it. Those who talk of a counter-revolution in France, show how little they understand of man. There does not exist in the compass of language, an arrangement of words to express so much as the means of effecting a counter-revolution. The means must be an obliteration of knowledge ;

and it has never yet been discovered how to make a man *unknow* his knowledge, or *unthink* his thoughts.

Mr. Burke is laboring in vain to stop the progress of knowledge ; and it comes with the worse grace from him, as there is a certain transaction known in the city, which renders him suspected of being a pensioner in a fictitious name. This may account for some strange doctrine he has advanced in his book, which, though he points it at the Revolution society, is effectually directed against the whole nation.

" The king of England," says he, " holds *his* crown (for it does not belong to the nation, according to Mr. Burke) in *contempt* of the choice of the Revolution society, who have not a single vote for a king among them either *individually* or *collectively ;* and his majesty's heirs, each in their time and order, will come to the crown *with the same contempt* of their choice, with which his majesty has succeeded to that which he now wears."

As to who is king in England or elsewhere, or whether there is any at all, or whether the people choose a Cherokee chief, or a Hessian hussar for a king, is not a matter that I trouble myself about, be that to themselves ; but with respect to the doctrine, so far as it relates to the rights of men and nations, it is as abominable as any thing ever uttered in the most enslaved country under heaven. Whether it sounds worse to my ear, by not being accustomed to hear such despotism, than it does to the ear of another person, I am not so well a judge of : but of its abominable principle, I am at no loss to judge.

It is not the Revolution society that Mr. Burke means ; it is the nation, as well in its *original,* as in its *representative* character ; and he has taken care to make himself understood, by saying that they have not a vote either *collectively* or *individually.* The Revolution society is composed of citizens of all denominations, and of members of both houses of parliament, and consequently, if there is not a right to vote in any of the characters, there can be no right to any, either in the nation or in its parliament. This ought to be a caution to every country, how it imports foreign families to be kings. It is somewhat curious to observe that although the people of England have been in the habit of talking about kings, it is always a foreign house of kings ; hating foreigners yet governed by them. It is now the house of Brunswick, one of the petty tribes of Germany.

It has hitherto been the practice of the English parliaments, to regulate what was called the succession, (taking it for granted, that the nation then continued to accord to the form of annexing a monarchical branch to its government; for without this, the parliament could not have had authority to have sent either to Holland or to Hanover, or to impose a king upon the nation against its will.) And this must be the utmost limit to which parliament can go upon the case; but the right of the nation goes to the *whole* case, because it has the right of changing its *whole* form of government. The right of a parliament is only a right in trust, a right by delegation, and that but from a very small part of the nation; and one of its houses has not even this. But the right of the nation is an original right, as universal as taxation. The nation is the paymaster of every thing, and every thing must conform to its general will.

I remember taking notice of a speech in what is called the English house of peers, by the then earl of Shelburne, and I think it was at the time he was minister, which is applicable to this case. I do not directly charge my memory with every particular; but the words and the purport as nearly as I remember, were these: *that the form of government was a matter wholly at the will of a nation at all times: that if it chose a monarchical form, it had a right to have it so, and if it afterwards chose to be a republic, it had a right to be a republic, and to say to a king, we have no longer any occasion for you.*

When Mr. Burke says that " his majesty's heirs and successors, each in their time and order, will come to the crown with the same contempt of their choice with which his majesty has succeeded to that he wears," it is saying too much even to the humblest individual in the country; part of whose daily labor goes towards making up the million sterling a-year, which the country give a person it styles a king. Government with insolence, is despotism; but when contempt is added, it becomes worse; and to pay for contempt is the excess of slavery. This species of government comes from Germany; and reminds me of what one of the Brunswick soldiers told me, who was taken prisoner by the Americans in the late war; " Ah !" said he, "America is a fine free country, it is worth people's fighting for; I know the difference by knowing my own; in my country, if the prince say, eat straw, we eat straw."—God help that country, thought I, be it England or elsewhere, whose liberties are to be protected by German principles of government and princes of Brunswick.

As Mr. Burke sometimes speaks of England, sometimes of France, and sometimes of the world, and of government in general, it is difficult to answer his book without apparently meeting him on the same ground. Although principles of government are general subjects, it is next to impossible in many cases to separate them from the idea of place and circumstance; and the more so when circumstances are put for arguments, which is frequently the case with Mr. Burke.

In the former part of his book, addressing himself to the people of France, he says, " no experience has taught us, (meaning the English) that in any other course or method than that of an *hereditary crown*, can our liberties be regularly perpetuated and preserved sacred as our *hereditary right*." I ask Mr. Burke who is to take them away ? M. de la Fayette, in speaking of France, says, " *For a nation to be free, it is sufficient that she wills it.*" But Mr. Burke represents England as wanting capacity to take care of itself ; and that its liberties must be taken care of by a king, holding it in " contempt." If England is sunk to this, it is preparing itself to eat straw, as in Hanover or in Brunswick. But besides the folly of the declaration, it happens that the facts are all against Mr. Burke. It was by the government *being hereditary*, that the liberties of the people were endangered. Charles I. and James II. are instances of this truth ; yet neither of them went so far as to hold the nation in contempt.

As it is sometimes of advantage to the people of one country, to hear what those of other countries have to say respecting it, it is possible that the people of France may learn something from Mr. Burke's book, and that the people of England may also learn something from the answers it will occasion. When nations fall out about freedom, a wide field of debate is opened. The argument commences with the rights of war, without its evils ; and as knowledge is the object contended for, the party that sustains the defeat obtains the prize.

Mr. Burke talks about what he calls an hereditary crown, as if it were some production of nature ; or as if like time, it had power to operate not only independently.

but in spite of man; or as if it were a thing or a subject universally consented to. Alas! it has none of those properties, but is the reverse of them all. It is a thing of imagination, the propriety of which is more than doubted, and the legality of which in a few years will be denied.

But, to arrange this matter in a clearer view than what general expressions can convey, it will be necessary to state the distinct heads under which (what is called) an hereditary crown, or, more properly speaking, an hereditary succession to the government of a nation, can be considered, which are,

1st, The right of a particular family to establish itself.

2d. The right of a nation to establish a particular family.

With respect to the *first* of these heads, that of a family establishing itself with hereditary powers on its own authority, and independent of the consent of a nation, all men will concur in calling it despotism; and it would be trespassing on their understanding to attempt to prove it.

But the *second* head, that of a nation establishing a particular family with *hereditary powers*, does not present itself as despotism on the first reflection; but if men will permit a second reflection to take place, and carry that reflection forward but one remove out of their own persons to that of their offspring, they will then see that hereditary succession becomes in its consequences the same despotism to others, which they reprobated for themselves. It operates to preclude the consent of the succeeding generation, and the preclusion of consent is despotism. When the person who at any time shall be in possession of a government, or those who stand in succession to him, shall say to a nation, I hold this power in " contempt " of you, it signifies not on what authority he pretends to say it. It is no relief, but an aggravation to a person in slavery, to reflect that he was sold by his parent; and as that which heightens the criminality of an act cannot be produced to prove the legality of it, hereditary succession cannot be established as a legal thing.

In order to arrive at a more perfect decision on this head it will be proper to consider the generation which undertakes to establish a family with *hereditary powers*, separately from the generations which are to follow; and also to consider the character in which the *first* generation acts with respect to succeeding generations.

The generation which first selects a person, and puts him at the head of its government, either with the title of king, or any other distinction, acts its *own choice*, be it wise or foolish, as a free agent for itself. The person so set up is not hereditary, but selected and appointed; and the generation who sets him up, does not live under an hereditary government, but under a government of its own choice and establishment. Were the generation who sets him up, and the person so set up, to live for ever, it never could become hereditary succession : hereditary succession can only follow on death of the first parties.

As therefore hereditary succession is out of the question with respect to the *first* generation, we have now to consider the character in which *that* generation acts with respect to the commencing generation, and to all succeeding ones.

It assumes a character, to which it has neither right nor title. It changes itself from a *legislator* to a *testator*, and affects to make its will, which is to have operation after the demise of the makers, to bequeath the government ; and it not only attempts to bequeath, but to establish on the succeeding generation, a new and different form of government under which itself lived. Itself, as is before observed, lived not under an hereditary government, but under a government of its own choice and establishment; and it now attempts, by virtue of a will and testament (and which it has not authority to make) to take from the commencing generation, and all future ones, the rights and free agency by which itself acted.

But, exclusive of the right which any generation has to act collectively as a testator, the objects to which it applies itself in this case, are not within the compass of any law, or of any will or testament.

The rights of men in society, are neither devisable, nor transferrable, nor annihilable but are descendable only ; and it is not in the power of any generation to intercept finally, and cut off the descent. If the present generation, or any other, are disposed to be slaves, it does not lessen the right of the succeeding generation to be free : wrongs cannot have a legal descent. When Mr. Burke attempts to maintain, that the *English nation did, at the revolution of* 1688, *most solemnly renounce and abdicate their rights for themselves, and for all their posterity for ever,* he speaks a language that merits not reply, and which can only excite contempt for his prostitute principles, or pity for his ignorance.

In whatever light hereditary succession, as growing out of the will and testament of some former generation, presents itself, it is an absurdity. A cannot make a will to take from B his property, and give it to C; yet this is the manner in which (what is called) hereditary succession by law, operates. A certain former generation made a will to take away the rights of the commencing generation and all future ones, and convey those rights to a third person, who afterwards comes forward, and tells them, in Mr. Burke's language, that they have *no rights*, that their rights are already bequeathed to him, and that he will govern in *contempt* of them. From such principles, and such ignorance, good Lord deliver the world!

But, after all, what is this metaphor, called a crown, or rather, what is monarchy? Is it a thing, or is it a name, or is it a fraud? Is it a "contrivance of human wisdom," or human craft, to obtain money from a nation under specious pretences? Is it a thing necessary to a nation? If it is, in what does that necessity consist, what service does it perform, what is its business, and what are its merits? Doth the virtue consist in the metaphor, or in the man? Doth the goldsmith that makes the crown, make the virtue also? Doth it operate like Fortunatus's wishing cap, or Harlequin's wooden sword? Doth it make a man a conjuror? In fine, what is it? It appears to be a something going much out of fashion, falling into ridicule, and rejected in some countries both as unnecessary and expensive. In America it is considered as an absurdity, and in France it has so far declined, that the goodness of the man, and the respect for his personal character, are the only things that preserve the appearance of its existence.

If government be what Mr. Burke describes it, "a contrivance of human wisdom," I might ask him, if wisdom was at such a low ebb in England, that it was become necessary to import it from Holland and from Hanover? But I will do the country the justice to say, that that was not the case; and even if it was, it mistook the cargo. The wisdom of every country, when properly exerted, is sufficient for all its purposes: and there could exist no more real occasion in England to have sent for a Dutch stadtholder, or a German elector, than there was in America to have done a similar thing. If a country does not understand its own affairs, how is a foreigner to understand them, who knows neither its laws, its manners, nor its language? If there existed a man so transcendantly wise above all others, that his wisdom was necessary to instruct a nation, some reason might be offered for monarchy; but when we cast our eyes about a country, and observe how every part understands its own affairs; and when we look around the world, and see that of all men in it, the race of kings are the most insignificant in capacity, our reason cannot fail to ask us—What are those men kept for?

If there is any thing in monarchy which we people of America do not understand, I wish Mr. Burke would be so kind as to inform us. I see in America, a government extending over a country ten times as large as England, and conducted with regularity for a fortieth part of the expense which government costs in England. If I ask a man in America, if he wants a king, he retorts, and asks me if I take him for an ideot. How is it that this difference happens; are we more or less wise than others? I see in America, the generality of people living in a style of plenty unknown in monarchical countries; and I see that the principle of its government, which is that of the *equal rights of man*, is making a rapid progress in the world.

If monarchy is a useless thing, why is it kept up any where? And if a necessary thing, how can it be dispensed with? That *civil government* is necessary, all civilized nations will agree in; but civil government is republican government. All that part of the government of England which begins with the office of constable, and proceeds through the department of magistrate, quarter-session, and general assize, including the trial by jury, is republican government. Nothing of monarchy appears in any part of it, except the name which William the conqueror imposed upon the English, that of obliging them to call him "their sovereign lord the king."

It is easy to conceive, that a band of interested men, such as placemen, pensioners, lords of the bed-chamber, lords of the kitchen, lords of the necessary-house, and the Lord knows what besides, can find as many reasons for monarchy as their salaries, paid at the expense of the country, amount to; but if I ask the farmer, the manufacturer, the merchant, the tradesman, and down through all the occupations of life to the common laborer, what service monarchy is to him, he can give me no answer. If I ask him what monarchy is, he believes it is something like a sinecure.

Notwithstanding the taxes of England amount to almost seventeen millions a-year, said to be for the expenses of government, it is still evident that the sense of the nation is left to govern itself, and does govern itself by magistrates and juries, almost at its own charge, on republican principles, exclusive of the expense of taxes. The salaries of the judges are almost the only charge that is paid out of the revenue. Considering that all the internal government is executed by the people, the taxes of England ought to be the lightest of any nation in Europe; instead of which, they are the contrary. As this cannot be accounted for on the score of civil government, the subject necessarily extends itself to the monarchical part.

When the people of England sent for George I. (and it would puzzle a wiser man than Mr. Burke to discover for what he could be wanted, or what service he could render) they ought at least to have conditioned for the abandonment of Hanover. Besides the endless German intrigues that must follow from a German elector's being king of England, there is a natural impossibility of uniting in the same person the principles of freedom and the principles of despotism, or, as it is called in England, arbitrary power. A German elector is, in his electorate, a despot: how then could it be expected that he should be attached to principles of liberty in one country, while his interest in another was to be supported by despotism? The union cannot exist: and it might easily have been foreseen, that German electors would make German kings, or in Mr. Burke's words, would assume government with "contempt." The English have been in the habit of considering a king of England only in the character in which he appears to them: whereas the same person, while the connexion lasts, has a home-seat in another country, the interest of which is at variance with their own, and the principles of the government in opposition to each other. To such a person England will appear as a town-residence, and the electorate as the estate. The English may wish, as I believe they do, success to the principles of liberty in France, or in Germany; but a German elector trembles for the fate of despotism in his electorate; and the duchy of Mecklenburg, where the present queen's family governs, is under the same wretched state of arbitrary power, and the people in slavish vassalage.

There never was a time when it became the English to watch continental intrigues more circumspectly than at the present moment, and to distinguish the politics of the electorate from the politics of the nation. The revolution of France has entirely changed the ground with respect to England and France, as nations: but the German despots, with Prussia at their head, are combining against liberty; and the fondness of Mr. Pitt for office, and the interest which all his family connexions have obtained, do not give sufficient security against this intrigue.

As every thing which passes in the world becomes matter for history, I will now quit this subject, and take a concise review of the state of parties and politics in England, as Mr. Burke has done in France.

Whether the present reign commenced with contempt, I leave to Mr. Burke: certain however it is, that it had strongly that appearance. The animosity of the English nation, it is very well remembered, ran high; and, had the true principles of liberty been as well understood then as they now promise to be, it is probable the nation would not have patiently submitted to so much. George I. and II. were sensible of a rival in the remains of the Stuarts: and as they could not but consider themselves as standing on their good behaviour, they had prudence to keep their German principles of government to themselves; but as the Stuart family wore away, the prudence became less necessary.

The contest between rights, and what were called prerogatives, continued to heat the nation till some time after the conclusion of the American revolution, when all at once it fell a calm; execration exchanged itself for applause, and court popularity sprung up like a mushroom in the night.

To account for this sudden transition, it is proper to observe, that there are two distinct species of popularity; the one excited by merit, the other by resentment. As the nation had formed itself into two parties, and each was extolling the merits of its parliamentary champions for and against the prerogative, nothing could operate to give a more general shock than an immediate coalition of the champions themselves. The partisans of each being thus suddenly left in the lurch, and mutually heated with disgust at the measure, felt no other relief than uniting in a common execration against both. A higher stimulus of resentment being thus excited, than what the contest on prerogatives had occasioned, the nation quitted all former objects of rights and wrongs, and sought only that of gratification.— The indignation at the coalition, so effectually superseded the indignation against the court, as to extinguish it; and without any change of principles on the part of the court, the same people who had reprobated its despotism, united with it, to revenge themselves on the coalition parliament. The case was not, which they liked best—but, which they hated most; and the least hated passed for love. The dissolution of the coalition parliament, as it afforded the means of gratifying the resentment of the nation, could not fail to be popular; and from hence arose the popularity of the court.

Transitions of this kind exhibit to us a nation under the government of temper, instead of a fixed and steady principle: and having once committed itself, however rashly, it feels itself urged along to justify by continuance its first proceeding. Measures which at other times it would censure, it now approves, and acts persuasion upon itself to suffocate its judgment.

On the return of a new parliament, the new minister, Mr. Pitt, found himself in a secure majority: and the nation gave him credit, not out of regard to himself, but because it had resolved to do it out of resentment to another. He introduced himself to public notice by a proposed reform of parliament, which in its operation would have amounted to a public justification of corruption. The nation was to be at the expense of buying up the rotten boroughs, whereas it ought to punish the persons who deal in the traffic.

Passing over the two bubbles, of the Dutch business, and the million a-year to sink the national debt, the matter which is most prominent, is the affair of the regency. Never in the course of my observation, was delusion more successfully acted, nor a nation more completely deceived. But, to make this appear, it will be necessary to go over the circumstances.

Mr. Fox had stated in the house of commons, that the prince of Wales, as heir in succession, had a right in himself to assume the government. This was opposed by Mr. Pitt; and, so far as the opposition was confined to the doctrine, it was just. But the principles which Mr. Pitt maintained on the contrary side, were as bad, or worse in their extent, than those of Mr. Fox ; because they went to establish an aristocracy over the nation, and over the small representation it has in the house of commons.

Whether the English form of government be good or bad, is not in this case the question ; but, taking it as it stands, without regard to its merits or demerits, Mr. Pitt was further from the point than Mr. Fox.

It is supposed to consist of three parts ; while, therefore, the nation is disposed to continue this form, the parts have a *national standing*, independent of each other, and are not the creatures of each other. Had Mr. Fox passed through parliament, and said, that the person alluded to claimed on the ground of the nation, Mr. Pitt must then have contended for (what he called) the right of the parliament, against the right of the nation.

By the appearance which the contest made, Mr. Fox took the hereditary ground ; and Mr. Pitt the parliamentary ground, but the fact is, they both took hereditary ground, and Mr. Pitt took the worst of the two.

What is called the parliament, is made up of two houses ; one of which is more hereditary, and more beyond the control of the nation, than what the crown (as it is called) is supposed to be. It is an hereditary aristocracy, assuming and asserting indefeasible, irrevocable rights and authority, wholly independent of the nation. Where then was the merited popularity of exalting this hereditary power over another hereditary power less independent of the nation than what itself assumed to be, and of absorbing the rights of the nation into a house over which it has neither election nor control ?

The general impulse of the nation was right ; but it acted without reflection. It approved the opposition made to the right set up by Mr. Fox, without perceiving that Mr. Pitt was supporting another indefeasible right more remote from the nation, in opposition to it.

With respect to the house of commons, it is elected but by a small part of the nation ; but were the election as universal as taxation, which it ought to be, it would still be only the organ of the nation, and cannot possess inherent rights. When the national assembly of France resolves a matter, the resolve is made in right of the nation ; but Mr. Pitt, on all national questions, so far as they refer to the house of commons, absorbs the rights of the nation into the organ, and makes the organ into a nation, and the nation itself into a cypher.

In a few words, the question on the regency was a question on a million a-year, which is appropriated to the executive department: and Mr. Pitt could not possess himself of any management of this sum, without setting up the supremacy of parliament; and when this was accomplished, it was indifferent who should be regent, as he must be regent at his own cost. Among the curiosities which this contentious debate afforded, was that of making the great seal into a king; the affixing of which to an act, was to be royal authority. If, therefore, royal authority is a great seal, it consequently is in itself nothing; and a good constitution would be of infinitely more value to the nation, than what the three nominal powers, as they now stand are worth.

The continual use of the word *constitution* in the English parliament, shows there is none; and that the whole is merely a form of government without a constitution, and constituting itself with what powers it pleases. If there was a constitution, it certainly would be referred to; and the debate on any constitutional point, would terminate by producing the constitution. One member says, this is constitutional? another says, that is constitutional—To-day it is one thing; and to-morrow, it is something else—while the maintaining the debate proves there is none. Constitution is now the cant word of parliament, turning itself to the ear of the nation. Formerly it was the *universal supremacy and the omnipotence of parliament.* But, since the progress of liberty in France, those phrases have a despotic harshness in their note; and the English parliament has caught the fashion from the national assembly, but without the substance, of speaking of *a constitution.*

As the present generation of people in England did not make the government, they are not accountable for any of its defects; but that sooner or later it must come into their hands to undergo a constitutional reformation, is as certain as that the same thing has happened in France. If France, with a revenue of nearly twenty-four millions sterling, with an extent of rich and fertile country above four times larger than England, with a population of twenty-four millions of inhabitants to support taxation, with upwards of ninety millions sterling of gold and silver circulating in the nation, and with a debt less than the present debt of England—still found it necessary, from whatever cause, to come to a settlement of its affairs, it solves the problem of funding for both countries.

It is out of the question to say how long, what is called the English constitution, has lasted, and to argue from thence how long it is to last; the question is, how long can the funding system last? It is a thing but of modern invention, and has not yet continued beyond the life of a man; yet in that short space it has so far accumulated, that, together with the current expenses, it requires an amount of taxes at least equal to the whole landed rental of the nation in acres, to defray the annual expenditures. That a government could not always have gone on by the same system which has been followed for the last seventy years, must be evident to every man; and for the same reason it cannot always go on.

The funding system is not money; neither is it, properly speaking, credit. It in effect, creates upon paper the sum which it appears to borrow, and lays on a tax to keep the imaginary capital alive by the payment of interest, and sends the annuity to market, to be sold for paper already in circulation. If any credit is given, it is to the disposition of the people to pay the tax, and not to the government which lays it on. When this disposition expires, what is supposed to be the credit of government expires with it. The instance of France under the former government shows that it is impossible to compel the payment of taxes by force, when a whole nation is determined to take its stand upon that ground.

Mr. Burke, in his review of the finances of France, states the quantity of gold and silver in France, at about eighty-eight millions sterling. In doing this he has, I presume, divided by the difference of exchange, instead of the standard of twenty-four livres to a pound sterling; for M. Neckar's statement, from which Mr. Burke's is taken, is *two thousand two hundred millions of livres*, which is upwards of ninety-one millions and an half sterling.

M. Neckar in France, and Mr. George Chalmers of the office of trade and plantation in England, of which lord Hawkesbury is president, published nearly about the same time (1786) an account of the quantity of money in each nation, from the returns of the mint of each nation. Mr. Chalmers from the returns of the English mint at the Tower of London, states the quantity of money in England, including Scotland and Ireland, to be twenty millions sterling.[*]

M. Neckar[†] says, that the amount of money in France, recoined from the old coin which was called in, was two thousand five hundred millions of livres (upwards of one hundred and four millions sterling,) and, after deducting for waste, and what may be in the West-Indies, and other possible circumstances, states the circulating quantity at home, to be ninety-one millions and an half sterling; but, taking it as Mr. Burke has put it, it is sixty-eight millions more than the national quantity in England.

That the quantity of money in France cannot be under this sum, may at once be seen from the state of the French revenue, without referring to the records of the French mint for proofs. The revenue of France prior to the revolution, was nearly twenty-four millions sterling; and as paper had then no existence in France, the whole revenue was collected upon gold and silver; and it would have been impossible to have collected such a quantity of revenue upon a less national quantity than M. Neckar has stated. Before the establishment of paper in England, the revenue was about a fourth part of the national amount of gold and silver, as may be known by referring to the revenue prior to king William, and the quantity of money stated to be in the nation at that time, which was nearly as much as it is now.

It can be of no real service to a nation, to impose upon itself, or to permit itself to be imposed upon; but the prejudices of some, and the imposition of others, have always represented France as a nation possessing but little money, whereas the quantity is not only more than four times what the quantity is in England, but is considerably greater on a proportion of numbers. To account for this deficiency on the part of England, some reference should be had to the English system of funding. It operates to multiply paper, and to substitute it in the room of money, in various shapes; and the more paper is multiplied, the more opportunities are afforded to export the specie; and it admits of a possibility (by extending it to small notes) of increasing paper, till there is no money left.

---

[*] See Estimate of the Comparative Strength of Great Britain, by Geo. Chalmers.

[†] See Administration of the Finances of France, vol. iii. by M. Neckar.

I know this is not a pleasant subject to English readers; but the matters I am going to mention, are so important in themselves, as to require the attention of men interested in money transactions of a public nature. There is a circumstance stated by M. Neckar, in his treatise on the administration of the finances, which has never been attended to in England, but which forms the only basis whereon to estimate the quantity of money (gold and silver) which ought to be in every nation in Europe, to preserve a relative proportion with other nations.

Lisbon and Cadiz are the two ports into which (money) gold and silver from South America are imported, and which afterwards divides and spreads itself over Europe by means of commerce, and increases the quantity of money in all parts of Europe. If, therefore, the amount of the annual importation into Europe can be known, and the relative proportion of the foreign commerce of the several nations by which it is distributed can be ascertained, they give a rule, sufficiently true, to ascertain the quantity of money which ought to be found in any nation at any given time.

M. Neckar shows from the registers of Lisbon and Cadiz, that the importation of gold and silver into Europe, is five millions sterling annually. He has not taken it on a single year, but on an average of fifteen succeeding years, from 1763, to 1777, both inclusive; in which time, the amount was one thousand eight hundred million livres, which is seventy-five millions sterling.*

From the commencement of the Hanover succession in 1714, to the time Mr. Chalmers published, is seventy-two years; and the quantity imported into Europe, in that time, would be three hundred and sixty millions sterling.

If the foreign commerce of Great Britain be stated at a sixth part of what the whole foreign commerce of Europe amounts to (which is probably an inferior estimation to what the gentlemen at the exchange would allow) the proportion which Britain should draw by commerce, of this sum, to keep herself on a proportion with the rest of Europe, would be also a sixth part, which is sixty millions sterling; and if the same allowance for waste and accident be made for England, which M. Neckar makes for France, the quantity remaining after these deductions, would be

---

* Administration of the Finances of France, vol. iii.

fifty-two millions, and this sum ought to have been in the nation (at the time Mr. Chalmers published) in addition to the sum which was in the nation at the commencement of the Hanover succession, and to have made in the whole at least sixty-six millions sterling; instead of which there were but twenty millions, which is forty-six millions below its proportionate quantity.

As the quantity of gold and silver, imported into Lisbon and Cadiz is more easily ascertained than that of any commodity imported into England; and as the quantity of money coined at the Tower of London, is still more positively known, the leading facts do not admit of a controversy. Either, therefore, the commerce of England is unproductive of profit, or the gold and silver which it brings in, leak continually away by unseen means, at the average rate of about three quarters of a million a-year, which in the course of seventy-two years, accounts for the deficiency; and its absence is supplied by paper.*

---

* Whether the English commerce does not bring in money, or whether the government sends it out after it is brought in, is a matter which the parties concerned can best explain : but that the deficiency exists, is not in the power of either to disprove. While Dr. Price, Mr. Eden, (now Auckland) Mr. Chalmers, and others, were debating whether the quantity of money was greater or less than at the revolution, the circumstance was not adverted to, that since the revolution, there cannot have been less than four hundred millions sterling imported into Europe : and therefore the quantity in England ought at least to have been four times greater than it was at the revolution, to be on a proportion with Europe. What England is now doing by paper, is what she should have been able to do by solid money, if gold and silver had come into the nation in the proportion it ought, or had not been sent out; and she is endeavoring to restore by paper, the balance she has lost by money. It is certain, that the gold and silver which arrive annually in the register-ships to Spain and Portugal, do not remain in those countries. Taking the value half in gold and half in silver, it is about four hundred tons annually : and from the number of ships and galleons employed in the trade of bringing those metals from South-America to Portugal and Spain, the quantity sufficiently proves itself, without referring to the registers.

In the situation England now is, it is impossible she can increase in money. High taxes not only lessen the property of the individuals but they lessen also the money capital of the nation, by inducing smuggling, which can only be carried on by gold and silver. By the politics which the British government have carried on with the inland powers of Germany and the continent, it has made an enemy of all the maritime powers, and is therefore obliged to keep up a large navy : but though the navy is built in England, the naval stores must be purchased from abroad, and that from countries where the greatest part must be paid for in gold and silver. Some fallacious rumors have been set afloat in England to induce a belief of money, and, among others, that of the French refugees bringing great quantities. The idea is ridiculous. The general part of the money in France is silver ; and it would take upwards of twenty of the largest broad wheel wagons, with ten horses each, to remove one million sterling of silver. Is it then to be supposed, that a few people fleeing on horseback or in post-chaises, in a secret manner, and having the French custom-house to pass, and the sea to cross, could bring even a sufficiency for their own expenses ?

The revolution of France is attended with many novel circumstances, not only in the political sphere, but in the circle of money transactions. Among others, it shows that a government may be in a state of insolvency, and a nation rich. So far as the fact is confined to the late government of France, it was insolvent; because the nation would no longer support its extravagance, and therefore it could no longer support itself—but with respect to the nation all the means existed. A government may be said to be insolvent every time it applies to a nation to discharge its arrears. The insolvency of the late government of France, and the present government of England, differed in no other respect than as the disposition of the people differ. The people of France refused their aid to the old government, and the people of England submit to taxation without inquiry. What is called the crown in England has been insolvent several times; the last of which, publicly known, was in May 1777, when it applied to the nation to discharge upwards of 600,000*l*. private debts, which otherwise it could not pay.

It was the error of Mr. Pitt, Mr. Burke, and all those who were unacquainted with the affairs of France, to confound the French nation with the French government. The French nation in effect, endeavored to render the late government insolvent, for the purpose of taking government into its own hands; and it reserved its means for the support of the new government. In a country of such vast extent and population as France, the natural means cannot be wanting; and the political means appear the instant the nation is disposed to permit them. When Mr. Burke, in a speech last winter in the British parliament, *cast his eyes over the map of Europe, and saw a chasm that once was France*, he talked like a dreamer of dreams. The same natural France existed as before, and all the natural means existed with it. The only chasm was that which the extinction of despotism had left, and which was to be filled

---

When millions of money are spoken of, it should be recollected, that such sums can only accumulate in a country by slow degrees, and a long procession of time. The most frugal system that England could now adopt, would not recover in a century the balance she has lost in money since the commencement of the Hanover succession. She is seventy millions behind France, and she must be in some considerable proportion behind every country in Europe, because the returns of the English mint do not show an increase of money, while the registers of Lisbon and Cadiz show an European increase of between three and four hundred millions sterling.

up with a constitution more formidable in resources than the power which had expired.

Although the French nation rendered the late government insolvent, it did not permit the insolvency to act towards the creditors; and the creditors considering the nation as the real paymaster, and the government only as the agent, rested themselves on the nation, in preference to the government. This appears greatly to disturb Mr. Burke, as the precedent is fatal to the policy by which governments have supposed themselves secure. They have contracted debts, with a view of attaching what is called the monied interest of a nation to their support; but the example in France shows, that the permanent security of the creditor is in the nation, and not in the government; and that in all possible revolutions that may happen in governments, the means are always with the nation, and the nation always in existence. Mr. Burke argues, that the creditors ought to have abided the fate of the government which they trusted; but the national assembly considered them as the creditors of the nation, and not of the government— of the master, and not of the steward.

Notwithstanding the late government could not discharge the current expenses, the present government has paid off a great part of the capital. This has been accomplished by two means; the one by lessening the expenses of government, and the other by the sale of the monastic and ecclesiastical landed estates. The devotees and penitent debauchees, extortioners and misers of former days, to ensure themselves a better world than that they were about to leave, had bequeathed immense property in trust to the priesthood for *pious uses;* and the priesthood kept it for themselves. The national assembly has ordered it to be sold for the good of the whole nation, and the priesthood to be decently provided for.

In consequence of the revolution, the annual interest of the debt of France will be reduced at least six millions sterling, by paying off upwards of one hundred millions of the capital; which, with lessening the former expenses of government at least three millions, will place France in a situation worthy the imitation of Europe.

Upon a whole review of the subject, how vast is the contrast! While Mr. Burke has been talking of a general bankruptcy in France, the national assembly have been paying off the capital of the national debt; and while taxes have increased near a million a-year in England, they have lowered several millions a-year in France. Not a word has either Mr. Burke or Mr. Pitt said about French affairs, or the state of the French finances, in the present session of parliament. The subject begins to be too well understood, and imposition serves no longer.

There is a general enigma running through the whole of Mr. Burke's book. He writes in a rage against the national assembly; but what is he enraged about? If his assertions were as true as they are groundless, and if France by her revolution had annihilated her power, and become what he calls a *chasm*, it might excite the grief of a Frenchman (considering himself as a national man) and provoke his rage against the national assembly; but why should it excite the rage of Mr. Burke? Alas! it is not the nation of France that Mr. Burke means, but the *court;* and every court in Europe, dreading the same fate, is in mourning. He writes neither in the character of a Frenchman nor an Englishman, but in the fawning character of that creature, known in all countries, as a friend to none, a *courtier.* Whether it be the court of Versailles, or the court of St. James or of Carlton-house, or the court in expectation, signifies not; for the caterpillar principles of all courts and courtiers are alike. They form a common policy throughout Europe, detached and separate from the interest of the nations, and while they appear to quarrel, they agree to plunder. Nothing can be more terrible to a court or a courtier, than the revolution of France. That which is a blessing to nations, is bitterness to them; and as their existence depends on the duplicity of a country, they tremble at the approach of principles, and dread the precedent that threatens their overthrow.

CONCLUSION.

Reason and ignorance, the opposites of each other, influence the great bulk of mankind. If either of these can be rendered sufficiently extensive in a country, the machinery of government goes easily on. Reason shows itself, and ignorance submits to whatever is dictated to it.

The two modes of government which prevail in the world, are, 1st, government by election and representation : 2d, government by hereditary succession. The former is generally known by the name of republic; the latter by that of monarchy and aristocracy.

Those two distinct and opposite forms, erect themselves on the two distinct and opposite bases of reason and ignorance. As the exercise of government requires talents and abilities, and as talents and abilities cannot have hereditary descent, it is evident that hereditary succession requires a belief from man, to which his reason cannot subscribe, and which can only be established upon his ignorance; and the more ignorant any country is, the better it is fitted for this species of government.

On the contrary, government in a well constituted republic, requires no belief from man beyond what his reason authorizes. He sees the *rationale* of the whole system, its origin and its operation; and as it is best supported when best understood, the human faculties act with boldness, and acquire, under this form of government, a gigantic manliness.

As, therefore, each of those forms acts on a different basis, the one moving freely by the aid of reason, the other by ignorance; we have next to consider, what it is that gives motion to that species of government which is called mixed government, or, as it is sometimes ludicrously styled, a government of *this, that, and t'other.*

The moving power in this species of government is, of necessity, corruption. However imperfect election and representation may be in mixed governments, they still give exertion to a greater portion of reason than is convenient to the hereditary part; and therefore it becomes necessary to buy the reason up. A mixed government is an imperfect every-thing, cementing and soldering the discordant parts together by corruption, to act as a whole. Mr. Burke appears highly disgusted, that France, since she had resolved on a revolution, did not adopt what he calls " a British constitution;" and the regret which he expresses on this occasion, implies a suspicion, that the British constitution needed something to keep its defects in countenance.

In mixed governments there is no responsibility; the parts cover each other till responsibility is lost; and the corruption which moves the machine, contrives at the same time its own escape. When it is laid down as a maxim, that *a king can do no wrong*, it places him in a state of similar security with that of ideots and persons insane, and responsibility is out of the question with respect to himself. It then descends upon the minister, who shelters himself under a majority in parliament, which, by places, pensions, and corruption, he can always command; and that majority justifies itself by the same authority with which it protects the minister. In this rotatory motion, responsibility is thrown off from the parts, and from the whole.

When there is a part in a government which can do no wrong, it implies that it does nothing; and is only the machine of another power, by whose advice and direction it acts. What is supposed to be the king, in mixed governments, is the cabinet; and as the cabinet is always a part of the parliament, and the members justifying in one character what they act in another, a mixed government becomes a continual enigma; entailing upon a country, by the quantity of corruption necessary to solder the parts, the expense of supporting all the forms of government at once, and finally resolving itself into a government by committee; in which the advisers, the actors, the approvers, the justifiers, the persons responsible, and the persons not responsible, are the same persons.

By this pantomimical contrivance, and change of scene and character, the parts help each other out in matters, which, neither of them singly, would presume to act. When money is to be obtained, the mass of variety apparently dissolves, and a profusion of parliamentary praises passes between the parts. Each admires, with astonishment, the wisdom, the liberality and disinterestedness of the other; and all of them breathe a pitying sigh at the burdens of the nation.

But in a well-conditioned republic, nothing of this soldering, praising, and pitying, can take place; the representation being equal throughout the country, and complete in itself, however it may be arranged into legislative and executive, they have all one and the same natural source. The parts are not foreigners to each other, like democracy, aristocracy and monarchy. As there are no discordant distinctions, there is nothing to corrupt by compromise, nor confound by contrivance. Public measures appeal of themselves to the understanding of the nation, and, resting on their own merits, disown any flattering application to vanity. The continual whine of lamenting the burden of taxes, however successfully it may be practised in mixed governments, is inconsistent with the sense and spirit of a republic. If taxes are necessary, they are of course advantageous; but if they require an apology, the apology itself implies an impeachment. Why then is man thus imposed upon, or why does he impose upon himself?

When men are spoken of as kings and subjects, or when government is mentioned under distinct or combined heads of monarchy, aristocracy, and democracy, what is it that *reasoning* man is to understand by the terms? If there really existed in the world two more distinct and separate *elements* of human power, we should then see the several origins to which those terms would descriptively apply: but as there is but one species of man, there can be but one element of human power, and that element is man himself. Monarchy, aristocracy and democracy are but creatures of imagination; and a thousand such may be contrived as well as three.

. . . .

From the revolutions of America and France, and the symptoms that have appeared in other countries, it is evident that the opinion of the world is changing with respect to systems of government, and that revolutions are not within the compass of political calculations. The progress of time and circumstances, which men assign to the accomplishment of great changes, is too mechanical to measure the force of the mind, and the rapidity of reflection, by which revolutions are generated: all the old governments have received a shock from those that already appear, and which were once more improbable, and are a greater subject of wonder, than a general revolution in Europe would be now.

When we survey the wretched condition of man under the monarchical and hereditary systems of government, dragged from his home by one power, or driven by another, and impoverished by taxes more than by enemies, it becomes evident that those systems are bad, and that a general revolution in the principle and construction of governments is necessary.

What is government more than the management of the affairs of a nation? It is not, and from its nature cannot be, the property of any particular man or family, but of the whole community, at whose expense it is supported; and though by force or contrivance it has been usurped into an inheritance, the usurpation cannot alter the right of things. Sovereignty, as a matter of right, appertains to the nation only, and not to any individual; and a nation has at all times an inherent, indefeasible right to abolish any form of government it finds inconvenient, and establish such as accords with its interest, disposition and happiness. The romantic and barbarous distinctions of men into kings and subjects, though it may suit the condition of courtiers cannot that of citizens; and is exploded by the principle upon which governments are now founded. Every citizen is a member of the sovereignty, and as such, can acknowledge no personal subjection; and his obedience can be only to the laws.

When men think of what government is, they must necessarily suppose it to possess a knowledge of all the objects and matters upon which its authority is to be exercised. In this view of government, the republican system, as established by America and France, operates to embrace the whole of a nation; and the knowledge necessary to the interest of all the parts, is to be found in the centre, which the parts by representation form: but the old governments are on a construction that excludes knowledge as well as happiness; government by monks, who know nothing of the world beyond the walls of a convent, is as consistent as government by kings.

What were formerly called revolutions, were little more than a change of persons, or an alteration of local circumstances. They rose and fell like things of course, and had nothing in their existence or their fate that could influence beyond the spot that produced them. But what we now see in the world, from the revolutions of America and France, are a renovation of the natural order of things, a system of principles as universal as truth and the existence of man, and combining moral with political happiness and national prosperity.

"I. Men are born and always continue free and equal in respect to their rights. Civil distinctions, therefore, can be founded only on public utility.

" II. The end of all political associations is the preser-
vation of the natural and imprescriptible rights of man,
and these rights are liberty, property, security and resistance of oppression.

" III. The nation is essentially the source of all sovereignty; nor can any individual, or any body of men, be
entitled to any authority which is not expressly derived
from it."

In these principles there is nothing to throw a nation
into confusion, by inflaming ambition. They are. calculated to call forth wisdom and abilities, and to exercise
them for the public good, and not for the emolument or
aggrandizement of particular descriptions of men or families. Monarchical sovereignty, the enemy of mankind and
the source of misery, is abolished; and sovereignty itself
is restored to its natural and original place, the nation.—
Were this the case throughout Europe, the cause of wars
would be taken away.

It is attributed to Henry IV. of France, a man of an enlarged and benevolent heart, that he proposed, about the
year 1620, a plan for abolishing war in Europe. The plan
consisted in constituting an European congress, or, as the
French authors style it, a pacific republic; by appointing
delegates from the several nations, who were to act, as a
court of arbitration, in any disputes that might arise between nation and nation.

Had such a plan been adopted at the time it was proposed, the taxes of England and France, as two of the
parties, would have been at least ten millions sterling annually, to each nation, less than they were at the commencement of the French revolution.

To conceive a cause why such a plan has not been
adopted (and that instead of a congress for the purpose of
preventing war, it has been called only to *terminate* a war,
after a fruitless expense of several years) it will be necessary to consider the interest of governments as a distinct
interest to that of nations.

Whatever is the cause of taxes to a nation, becomes also
the means of revenue to a government. Every war ter-
minates with an addition of taxes, and consequently with
an addition of revenue; and in any event of war, in the
manner they are now commenced and concluded, the power and interest of governments are increased. War, therefore, from its productiveness, as it easily furnishes the

pretence of necessity for taxes and appointments to places and offices, becomes the principal part of the system of old governments; and to establish any mode to abolish war, however advantageous it might be to nations, would be to take from such government the most lucrative of its branches. The frivolous matters upon which war is made, show the disposition and avidity of governments to uphold the system of war, and betray the motives upon which they act.

Why are not republics plunged into war, but because the nature of their government does not admit of an interest distinct from that of the nation? Even Holland, though an ill-constructed republic, and with a commerce extending over the world, existed nearly a century without war: and the instant the form of government was changed in France, the republican principles of peace, and domestic prosperity and economy, arose with the new government; and the same consequences would follow the same causes in other nations.

As war is the system of government on the old construction, the animosity which nations reciprocally entertain, is nothing more than what the policy of their governments excite, to keep up the spirit of the system. Each government accuses the other of perfidy, intrigue and ambition, as a means of heating the imagination of their respective nations, and incensing them to hostilities. Man is not the enemy of man, but through the medium of a false system of government. Instead therefore of exclaiming against the ambition of kings, the exclamation should be directed against the principle of such governments; and instead of seeking to reform the individual, the wisdom of a nation should apply itself to reform the system.

Whether the forms and maxims of governments which are still in practice, were adapted to the condition of the world at the period they were established, is not in this case the question. The older they are the less correspondence can they have with the present state of things. Time, and change of circumstances and opinions have the same progressive effect in rendering modes of government obsolete, as they have upon customs and manners. Agriculture, commerce, manufactures and the tranquil arts, by which the prosperity of nations is best promoted, require a different system of government, and a different species of knowledge to direct its operations, to what might have been the former condition of the world.

As it is not difficult to perceive, from the enlightened state of mankind, that hereditary governments are verging to their decline, and that revolutions on the broad basis of national sovereignty, and government by representation, are making their way in Europe, it would be an act of wisdom to anticipate their approach, and produce revolutions by reason and accommodation, rather than commit them to the issue of convulsions.

From what we now see, nothing of reform in the political world ought to be held improbable. It is an age of revolutions, in which every thing may be looked for. The intrigue of courts, by which the system of war is kept up, may provoke a confederation of nations to abolish it : and an European congress to patronize the progress of free government, and promote the civilization of nations with each other is an event nearer in probability, than once were the revolutions and alliance of France and America.

RIGHTS OF MAN.

PART II.

COMBINING PRINCIPLES AND PRACTICE.

TO M. DE LA FAYETTE.

AFTER an acquaintance of nearly fifteen years, in difficult situations in America, and various consultations in Europe, I feel a pleasure in presenting you this small treatise, in gratitude for your services to my beloved America, and as a testimony of my esteem for the virtues, public and private, which I know you to possess.

The only point upon which I could ever discover that we differed, was not as to principles of government, but as to time. For my own part, I think it equally as injurious to good principles to permit them to linger, as to push them on too fast. That which you suppose accomplishable in fourteen or fifteen years, I may believe practicable in a much shorter period. Mankind, as it appears to me, are always ripe enough to understand their true interest, provided it be presented clearly to their understanding, and that in a manner not to create suspicion by any thing like self-design, nor to offend by assuming too much. Where we would wish to reform we must not reproach.

When the American revolution was established, I felt a disposition to sit serenely down and enjoy the calm. It did not appear to me that any object could afterwards arise great enough to make me quit tranquillity, and feel as I had felt before. But when principle, and not place, is the energetic cause of action, a man, I find, is every where the same.

I am now once more in the public world; and as I have not a right to contemplate on so many years of remaining life as you have, I am resolved to labor as fast as I can; and as I am anxious for your aid and your company, I wish you to hasten your principles and overtake me.

If you make a campaign the ensuing spring, which it is most probable there will be no occasion for, I will come and join you. Should the campaign commence, I hope it will terminate in the extinction of German despotism, and in establishing the freedom of all Germany, When France shall be surrounded with revolutions, she will be in peace and safety, and her taxes, as well as those of Germany, will consequently become less.

Your sincere,

Affectionate friend,

THOMAS PAINE.

London, Feb. 9, 1792.

PREFACE.

WHEN I began the chapter entitled the *Conclusion*, in the former part of the Rights of Man, published last year, it was my intention to have extended it to a greater length; but in casting the whole matter in my mind which I wished to add, I found that I must either make the work too bulky, or contract my plan too much. I therefore brought it to a close as soon as the subject would admit, and reserved what I had further to say to another opportunity.

Several other reasons contributed to produce this determination. I wished to know the manner in which a work, written in a style of thinking and expression at variance with what had been customary in England, would be received before I proceeded further. A great field was opening to the view of mankind by means of the French revolution. Mr. Burke's outrageous opposition thereto brought the controversy into England. He attacked principles which he knew (from information) I would contest with him, because they are principles I believe to be good and which I have contributed to establish, and conceive myself bound to defend. Had he not urged the controversy, I had most probably been a silent man.

Another reason for deferring the remainder of the work was, that Mr. Burke promised in his first publication to renew the subject at another opportunity, and to make a comparison of what he called the English and French constitutions. I therefore held myself in reserve for him. He has published two works since, without doing this;

which he certainly would not have omitted, had the comparison been in his favor.

In his last work, his " Appeal from the New to the Old Whigs," he has quoted about ten pages from the Rights of Man, and having given himself the trouble of doing this, says, " he shall not attempt in the smallest degree to refute them," meaning the principles therein contained. I am enough acquainted with Mr. Burke, to know, that he would if he could. But instead of contesting them, he immediately after consoles himself with saying that " he has done his part."—He has not done his part. He has not performed his promise of a comparison of constitutions. He started a controversy, he gave the challenge, and has fled from it; and he is now a *case in point* with his own opinion that " *the age of chivalry is gone !*"

The title, as well as the substance of his last work, his Appeal, is his condemnation. Principles must rest on their own merits, and if they are good they certainly will. To put them under the shelter of other men's authority, as Mr. Burke has done, serves to bring them into suspicion. Mr. Burke is not very fond of dividing his honors, but in this case he is artfully dividing the disgrace.

But who are those to whom Mr. Burke has appealed? A set of childish thinkers and half-way politicians born in the last century ; men who went no further with any principle than as it suited their purpose as a party ; the nation sees nothing in such works, or such politics worthy its attention. A little matter will move a party, but it must be something great that moves a nation.

Though I see nothing in Mr. Burke's Appeal worth taking notice of, there is, however, one expression upon which I shall offer a few remarks.—After quoting largely from the Rights of Man, and declining to contest the principles contained in that work, he says, " This will most probably be done (*if such writings shall be thought to deserve any other refutation than that of criminal justice*) by others, who may think with Mr. Burke and with the same zeal."

In the first place, it has not been done by any body. Not less, I believe, than eight or ten pamphlets, intended as answers to the former part of the Rights of Man have been published by different persons, and not one of them, to my knowledge, has extended to a second edition, nor are even the titles of them so much as generally remembered. As I am averse to unnecessarily multiplying publications, I have answered none of them. And as I believe that a man may write himself out of reputation when nobody else can do it, I am careful to avoid that rock.

But as I decline unnecessary publications on the one hand, so would I avoid any thing that looked like sullen pride on the other. If Mr. Burke, or any person on his side the question, will produce an answer to the Rights of Man, that shall extend to an half, or even a fourth part of the number of copies to which the Rights of Man extended, I will reply to his work. But until this be done, I shall so far take the sense of the public for my guide (and the world knows I am not a flatterer) that what they do not think worth while to read, is not worth mine to answer. I suppose the number of copies to which the first part of the Rights of Man extended, taking England, Scotland, and Ireland, is not less than between forty and fifty thousand.

I now come to remark on the remaining part of the quotation I have made from Mr. Burke.

"If," says he, "such writings shall be thought to deserve any other refutation than that of *criminal* justice."

Pardoning the pun, it must be *criminal* justice indeed that should condemn a work as a substitute for not being able to refute it. The greatest condemnation that could be passed upon it would be a refutation. But in proceeding by the method Mr. Burke alludes to, the condemnation would in the final event, pass upon the criminality of the process and not upon the work, and in this case, I had rather be the author, than be either the judge or the jury that should condemn it.

But to come at once to the point. I have differed from some professional gentlemen on the subject of prosecutions, and I since find they are falling into my opinion, which I shall here state as fully, but as concisely as I can.

I will first put a case with respect to any law, and then compare it with a government, or with what in England is, or has been, called a constitution.

It would be an act of despotism, or what in England is called arbitrary power, to make a law to prohibit investigating the principles, good or bad, on which such a law, or any other is founded.

If a law be bad, it is one thing to oppose the practice of it, but it is quite a different thing to expose its errors, to reason on its defects, and to show cause why it should be repealed, or why another ought to be substituted in its place. I have always held it an opinion (making it also my practice) that it is better to obey a bad law, making use at the same time of every argument to show its errors, and procure its repeal, than forcibly to violate it; because the precedent of breaking a bad law might weaken the force, and lead to a discretionary violation, of those which are good.

The case is the same with respect to principles and forms of government, or to what are called constitutions, and the parts of which they are composed.

It is for the good of nations, and not for the emolument or aggrandizement of particular individuals, that government ought to be established, and that mankind are at the expense of supporting it. The defects of every government and constitution both as to principle and form, must, on a parity of reasoning, be as open to discussion as the defects of a law, and it is a duty which every man owes to society to point them out. When those defects and the means of remedying them, are generally seen by a nation that nation will reform its government or its constitution in the one case, as the government repealed or reformed the law in the other. The operation of government is restricted to the making and the administering of laws; but it is to a nation that the right of forming or reforming, generating or regenerating constitutions and governments belong ; and consequently those subjects, as subjects of investigation, are always before a country *as a matter of right,* and cannot, without invading the general rights of that country, be made subjects for prosecution. On this ground I will meet Mr. Burke whenever he pleases. It is better that the whole argument should come out, than to seek to stifle it. It was himself that opened the controversy, and he ought not to desert it.

I do not believe that monarchy and aristocracy will continue seven years longer in any of the enlightened countries of Europe. If better reasons can be shown for them than against them, they will stand ; if the contrary, they will not. Mankind are not now to be told they shall not think, or they shall not read : and publications that go no further than to investigate principles of government, to invite men to reason and to reflect, and to show the errors and excellencies of different systems, have a right to appear. If they do not excite attention, they are not worth the trouble of a prosecution ; and if they do the prosecution will amount to nothing, since it cannot amount to a prohibition of reading. This would be a sentence on the public, instead of the author, and would also be the most effectual mode of making or hastening revolutions.

On all cases that apply universally to a nation, with respect to systems of government, a jury of *twelve* men is not competent to decide. Where there are no witnesses to be examined, no facts to be proved, and where the whole matter is before the whole public, and the merits or demerits of it resting on their opinion ; and where there is nothing to be known in a court, but what every body knows out of it, every twelve men are equally as good a jury as the other and would most probably reverse each other's verdict; or from the variety of their opinions, not be able to form one.

It is one case whether a nation approve a work, or a plan; but it is quite another case whether it will commit to any such jury the power of determining whether that nation has a right to, or shall reform its government, or not. I mention these cases, that Mr. Burke may see I have not written on government without reflecting on what is law, as well as on what are rights.—The only effectual jury in such cases would be a convention of the whole nation fairly elected; for in all such cases the whole nation is the vicinage.

As to the prejudices which men have from education and habit, in favor of any particular form or system of government, those prejudices have yet to stand the test of reason and reflection. In fact such prejudices are nothing. No man is prejudiced in favor of a thing knowing it to be wrong. He is attached to it on the belief of its being right; and when he sees it is not so, the prejudice will be gone. We have but a defective idea of what prejudice is. It might be said that until men think for themselves the whole is prejudice and *not opinion;* for that only is opinion which is the result of reason and reflection. I offer this remark, that Mr. Burke may not confide too much in what has been the customary prejudices of the country.

But admitting governments to be changed all over Europe, it certainly may be done without convulsion or revenge. It is not worth making changes or revolutions, unless it be for some great national benefit, and when this shall appear to a nation, the danger will be, as in America and France, to those who oppose; and with this reflection I close my preface.

THOMAS PAINE.

London, Feb. 9, 1792.

RIGHTS OF MAN.

PART II.

INTRODUCTION.

WHAT Archimedes said of the mechanical powers, may be applied to reason and liberty: " *Had we,*" said he, "*a place to stand upon, we might raise the world.*"

The revolution in America presented in politics what was only theory in mechanic's. So deeply rooted were all the governments of the old world, and so effectually had the tyranny and the antiquity of habit established itself over the mind, that no beginning could be made in Asia, Africa, or Europe, to reform the political condition of man. Freedom had been hunted round the globe; reason was considered as rebellion; and the slavery of fear had made men afraid to think.

But such is the irresistible nature of truth, that all it asks, and all it wants, is the liberty of appearing. The sun needs no inscription to distinguish him from darkness, and no sooner did the American governments display themselves to the world, than despotism felt a shock, and man began to contemplate redress.

The independence of America, considered merely as a separation from England, would have been a matter but of little importance, had it not been accompanied by a revolution in the principles and practice of government. She made a stand, not for herself only, but for the world, and looked beyond the advantages which *she* could receive. Even the Hessian, though hired to fight against her, may

live to bless his defeat; and England, condemning the
viciousness of its government, rejoice in its miscarriage.

As America was the only spot in the political world
where the principles of universal reformation could begin,
so also was it the best in the natural world. An assemblage of circumstances conspired, not only to give birth,
but to add gigantic maturity to its principles. The scene
which that country presents to the eye of the spectator,
has something in it which generates and enlarges great
ideas. Nature appears to him in magnitude. The mighty
objects he beholds, act upon his mind by enlarging it, and
he partakes of the greatness he contemplates. Its first
settlers were emigrants from different European nations,
and of diversified professions of religion, retiring from the
governmental persecutions of the old world, and meeting in
the new, not as enemies, but as brothers. The wants which
necessarily accompany the cultivation of a wilderness,
produced among them a state of society, which countries
long, harassed by the quarrels and intrigues of governments, had neglected to cherish. In such a situation man
becomes what he ought to be. He sees his species, not
with the inhuman idea of a natural enemy, but as kindred;
and the example shows to the artificial world, that man
must go back to nature for information.

From the rapid progress which America makes in every
species of improvement, it is rational to conclude, that if
the governments of Asia, Africa and Europe, had begun
on a principle similar to that of America, or had they not
been very early corrupted therefrom, those countries must,
by this time, have been in a far superior condition to what
they are. Age after age has passed away, for no other
purpose than to behold their wretchedness. Could we
suppose a spectator who knew nothing of the world, and
who was put into it merely to make his observations, he
would take a great part of the old world to be new, just
struggling with the difficulties and hardships of an infant
settlement. He could not suppose that the hordes of miserable poor, with which old countries abound, could be any
other than those who had not yet been able to provide for
themselves. Little would he think they were the consequence of what in such countries is called government.

If, from the more wretched parts of the old world, we
look at those which are in an advanced state of improvement, we still find the greedy hand of government thrusting

itself into every corner and crevice of industry, and grasping the spoil of the multitude. Invention is continually exercised, to furnish new pretences for revenue and taxation. It watches prosperity as its prey, and permits none to escape without a tribute.

As revolutions have begun, (and as the probability is always greater against a thing beginning, than of proceeding after it has begun) it is natural to expect that other revolutions will follow. The amazing and still increasing expenses with which old governments are conducted, the numerous wars they engage in or provoke, the embarrassments they throw in the way of universal civilization and commerce, and the oppression and usurpation acted at home, have wearied out the patience, and exhausted the property of the world. In such a situation, and with such examples already existing, revolutions are to be looked for. They are become subjects of universal conversation, and may be considered as the *order of the day*.

If systems of government can be introduced less expensive, and more productive of general happiness, than those which have existed, all attempts to oppose their progress will in the end prove fruitless. Reason, like time, will make its own way, and prejudice will fall in the combat with interest. If universal peace, harmony, civilization and commerce are ever to be the happy lot of man, it cannot be accomplished but by a revolution in the present system of governments. All the monarchical governments are military. War is their trade, plunder and revenue their objects. While such governments continue, peace has not the absolute security of a day. What is the history of all monarchical governments but a disgustful picture of human wretchedness, and the accidental respite of a few years repose? Wearied with war, and tired with human butchery, they sat down to rest and called it peace. This certainly is not the condition that heaven intended for man; and if *this be monarchy*, well might monarchy be reckoned among the sins of the Jews.

The revolutions which formerly took place in the world, had nothing in them that interested the bulk of mankind. They extended only to a change of persons and measures but not of principles, and rose or fell among the common transactions of the moment. What we now behold, may not improperly be called a " *counter revolution.*" Conquest and tyranny, at some early period, dispossessed man of his rights, and he is now recovering them. And as the tide of human affairs has its ebb and flow in directions contrary to each other, so also is it in this. Government founded on a *moral theory, on a system of universal peace, on the indefeasible, hereditary rights of man,* is now revolving from west to east by a stronger impulse than the government of the sword revolved from east to west. It interests not particular individuals but nations in its progress, and promises a new era to the human race.

The danger to which the success of revolutions is most exposed, is that of attempting them before the principles on which they proceed, and the advantages to result from them, are sufficiently understood. Almost every thing appertaining to the circumstances of a nation has been absorbed and confounded under the general and mysterious word *government.* Though it avoids taking to its account the errors it commits, and the mischiefs it occasions, it fails not to arrogate to itself whatever has the appearance of prosperity. It robs industry of its honors, by pedantically making itself the cause of its effects; and purloins from the general character of man, the merits that appertain to him as a social being.

It may therefore be of use, in this day of revolutions, to discriminate between those things which are the effect of government, and those which are not. This will best be done by taking a review of society and civilization, and the consequences resulting thereform, as things distinct from what are called governments. By beginning with this investigation, we shall be able to assign effects to their proper causes, and analyze the mass of common errors.

CHAPTER I.

OF SOCIETY AND CIVILIZATION.

A GREAT part of that order which reigns among mankind is not the effect of government. It had its origin in the principles of society, and the natural constitution of man. It existed prior to government, and would exist if the formality of government was abolished. The mutual dependance and reciprocal interest which man has in man, and all the parts of a civilized community upon each other, create that great chain of connexion which holds it together. The landholder, the farmer, the manufacturer, the merchant, the tradesman, and every occupation prospers by the aid which each receives from the other, and from the whole. Common interest regulates their concerns, and forms their laws; and the laws which common usage ordains, have a greater influence than the laws of government. In fine, society performs for itself almost every thing which is ascribed to government.

To understand the nature and quantity of government proper for man, it is necessary to attend to his character. As nature created him for social life, she fitted him for the station she intended. In all cases she made his natural wants greater than his individual powers. No one man is capable, without the aid of society, of supplying his own wants; and those wants acting upon every individual, impel the whole of them into society, as naturally as gravitation acts to a centre.

But she has gone further. She has not only forced man into society by a diversity of wants, which the reciprocal aid of each other can supply, but she has implanted in him a system of social affections, which though not necessary to his existence, are essential to his happiness. There is no period in life when this love for society ceases to act. It begins and ends with our being.

If we examine, with attention, into the composition and constitution of man, the diversity of his wants, and the diversity of talents in different men for reciprocally accommodating the wants of each other, his propensity to society, and consequently to preserve the advantages resulting from it, we shall easily discover, that a great part of what is called government is mere imposition.

Government is no further necessary than to supply the few cases to which society and civilization are not conveniently competent; and instances are not wanting to show that every thing which government can usefully add thereto, has been performed by the common consent of society, without government.

For upwards of two years from the commencement of the American war, and a longer period, in several of the American states, there were no established forms of government. The old governments had been abolished, and the country was too much occupied in defence, to employ its attention in establishing new governments; yet during this interval, order and harmony were preserved as inviolate as in any country in Europe. There is a natural aptness in man, and more so in society, because it embraces a greater variety of abilities and resources, to accommodate itself to whatever situation it is in. The instant formal government is abolished, society begins to act. A general association takes place, and common interest produces common security.

So far is it from being true, as has been pretended, that the abolition of any formal government is the dissolution of society, it acts by a contrary impulse, and brings the latter the closer together. All that part of its organization which it had committed to its government, devolves again upon itself, and acts through its medium. When men, as well from natural instinct, as from reciprocal benefits, have habituated themselves to social and civilized life, there is always enough of its principles in practice to carry them through any changes they may find necessary or convenient to make in their government. In short, man is so naturally a creature of society, that it is almost impossible to put him out of it.

Formal government makes but a small part of civilized life; and when even the best that human wisdom can devise is established, it is a thing more in name and idea, than in fact. It is to the great and fundamental principles of society and civilization—to the common usage universally consented to, and mutually and reciprocally maintained—to the unceasing circulation of interest, which, passing through its innumerable channels, invigorates the whole mass of civilized man—it is to these things, infinitely more than to any thing which even the best instituted government can perform, that the safety and prosperity of the individual and of the whole depends.

The more perfect civilization is, the less occasion has it for government, because the more does it regulate its own affairs, and govern itself; but so contrary is the practice of old governments to the reason of the case, that the expenses of them increase in the proportion they ought to diminish. It is but few general laws that civilized life requires, and those of such common usefulness, that whether they are enforced by the forms of government or not, the effect will be nearly the same. If we consider what the principles are that first condense men into society, and what the motives that regulate their mutual intercourse afterwards, we shall find, by the time we arrive at what is called government, that nearly the whole of the business is performed by the natural operation of the parts upon each other.

Man, with respect to all those matters, is more a creature of consistency than he is aware of, or than governments would wish him to believe. All the great laws of society are laws of nature. Those of trade and commerce, whether with respect to the intercourse of individuals, or of nations, are laws of mutual and reciprocal interest. They are followed and obeyed, because it is the interest of the parties so to do, and not on account of any formal laws their governments may impose or interpose.

But how often is the natural propensity to society disturbed or destroyed by the operations of government! When the latter, instead of being ingrafted on the principles of the former, assumes to exist for itself, and acts by partialities of favor and oppression, it becomes the cause of the mischiefs it ought to prevent.

If we look back to the riots and tumults, which at various times have happened in England, we shall find, that they did not proceed from the want of a government, but that government was itself the generating cause; instead of consolidating society, it divided it; it deprived it of its natural cohesion, and engendered discontents and disorders, which otherwise would not have existed. In those associations which men promiscuously form for the purpose of trade, or of any concern, in which government is totally out of the question, and in which they act merely on the principles of society, we see how naturally the various parties unite; and this shows, by comparison, that governments, so far from being always the cause or means of order, are often the destruction of it. The riots of 1780 had no other source than the remains of those prejudices, which the government itself had encouraged. But with respect to England there are also other causes.

Excess and inequality of taxation, however disguised in the means, never fail to appear in their effect. As a great mass of the community are thrown thereby into poverty and discontent, they are constantly on the brink of commotion; and, deprived, as they unfortunately are, of the means of information, are easily heated to outrage. Whatever the apparent cause of any riots may be, the real one is always want of happiness. It shows that something is wrong in the system of government, that injures the felicity by which society is to be preserved.

But as fact is superior to reasoning, the instance of America presents itself to confirm these observations.— If there is a country in the world, where concord, according to common calculation, would be least expected, it is America. Made up, as it is, of people from different nations,* accustomed to different forms and habits of government, speaking different languages, and more different in their modes of worship, it would appear that the union of such a people was impracticable; but by the simple operation of constructing government on the principles of society and the rights of man, every difficulty retires, and all the parts are brought into cordial unison. There, the poor are not oppressed, the rich are not privileged. Industry is not mortified by the splendid extravagance of a court rioting at its expense. Their taxes are few, because their government is just; and as there is nothing to render them wretched, there is nothing to engender riots and tumults.

A metaphysical man, like Mr. Burke, would have tortured his invention to discover how such a people could be governed. He would have supposed that some must be managed by fraud, others by force, and all by some contrivance; that genius must be hired to impose upon ignorance, and show and parade to fascinate the vulgar. Lost in the abundance of his researches, he would have resolved and re-resolved, and finally overlooked the plain and easy road that lay directly before him.

One of the great advantages of the American revolution has been, that it led to a discovery of the principles, and laid open the imposition of governments. All the revolutions till then had been worked within the atmosphere of

* That part of America which is generally called New England, including New-Hampshire, Massachusetts, Rhode-Island, and Connecticut, is peopled chiefly by English descendants. In the state of New-York, about half are Dutch, the rest English, Scotch, and Irish. In New-Jersey, a mixture of English and Dutch, with some Scotch and Irish. In Pennsylvania, about one third are English, another Germans, and the remainder Scotch and Irish, with some Swedes. The states to the southward have a greater proportion of English than the middle states, but in all of them there is a mixture; and besides those enumerated, there are a considerable number of French, and some few of all the European nations, lying on the coast. The most numerous religious denomination are the Presbyterians; but no one sect is established above another, and all men are equally citizens.

a court, and never on the great floor of a nation. The parties were always of the class of courtiers; and whatever was their rage for reformation, they carefully preserved the fraud of the profession.

In all cases they took care to represent government as a thing made up of mysteries, which only themselves understood: and they hid from the understanding of the nation, the only thing that was beneficial to know, namely, *that government is nothing more than a national association acting on the principles of society.*

Having thus endeavored to show, that the social and civilized state of man is capable of performing within itself, almost every thing necessary to its protection and government, it will be proper, on the other hand, to take a review of the present old governments, and examine whether their principles and practice are correspondent thereto.

CHAPTER II.

OF THE ORIGIN OF THE PRESENT OLD GOVERNMENTS.

It is impossible that such governments as have hitherto existed in the world, could have commenced by any other means than a total violation of every principle, sacred and moral. The obscurity in which the origin of all the present old governments is buried, implies the iniquity and disgrace with which they began. The origin of the present governments of America and France will ever be remembered, because it is honorable to record it; but with respect to the rest, even flattery has consigned them to the tomb of time, without an inscription.

It could have been no difficult thing in the early and solitary ages of the world, while the chief employment of men was that of attending flocks and herds, for a banditti of ruffians to overrun a country, and lay it under contribution. Their power being thus established, the chief of the band contrived to lose the name of robber in that of monarch; and hence the origin of monarchy and kings.

The origin of the government of England, so far as relates to what is called its line of monarchy, being one of the latest, is perhaps the best recorded. The hatred which the Norman invasion and tyranny begat, must have been deeply rooted in the nation, to have outlived the contrivance to obliterate it. Though not a courtier will talk of the curfew-bell, not a village in England has forgotten it.

Those bands of robbers having parcelled out the world, and divided it into dominions, began, as is naturally the case, to quarrel with each other. What at first was obtained by violence, was considered by others as lawful to be taken, and a second plunderer succeeded the first. They alternately invaded the dominions which each had assigned to himself, and the brutality with which they treated each other explains the original character of monarchy.— It was ruffian torturing ruffian. The conqueror considered the conquered not as his prisoner, but his property.— He led him in triumph rattling in chains, and doomed him, at pleasure, to slavery or death. As time obliterated the history of their beginning, their successors assumed new appearances, to cut off the entail of their disgrace, but their principles and objects remained the same. What at first was plunder assumed the softer name of revenue ; and the power originally usurped, they affected to inherit.

From such beginning of governments, what could be expected, but a continual system of war and extortion ? It has established itself into a trade. The vice is not peculiar to one more than to another, but is the common principle of all. There does not exist within such governments a stamina whereon to ingraft reformation ; and the shortest and most effectual remedy is to begin anew.

What scenes of horror, what perfection of iniquity, present themselves in contemplating the character, and reviewing the history of such governments ! If we would delineate human nature with a baseness of heart, and hypocrisy of countenance, that reflection would shudder at and humanity disown, it is kings, courts, and cabinets, that must sit for the portrait. Man, as he is naturally, with all his faults about him, is not up to the character.

Can we possibly suppose that if government had originated in a right principle, and had not an interest in pursuing a wrong one, that the world could have been in the wretched and quarrelsome condition we have seen it ?— What inducement has the farmer, while following the plough, to lay aside his peaceful pursuits, and go to war with the farmer of another country? Or what inducement has the manufacturer? What is dominion to them, or to any class of men in a nation? Does it add an acre to any man's estate, or raise its value? Are not conquest and defeat each of the same price, and taxes the never-failing consequence? Though this reasoning may be good to a nation, it is not so to a government. War is the faro-table of governments, and nations the dupes of the game.

If there is any thing to wonder at in this miserable scene of governments, more than might be expected, it is the progress which the peaceful arts of agriculture, manufacture, and commerce have made, beneath such a long accumulating load of discouragement and oppression. It serves to show, that instinct in animals does not act with stronger impulse than the principles of society and civilization operate in man. Under all discouragements, he pursues his object, and yields to nothing but impossibilities.

———

CHAPTER III.

OF THE OLD AND NEW SYSTEMS OF GOVERNMENT.

NOTHING can appear more contradictory than the principles on which the old governments began, and the condition to which society, civilization, and commerce, are capable of carrying mankind. Government on the old system, is an assumption of power, for the aggrandizement of itself; on the new, a delegation of power, for the common benefit of society. The former supports itself by keeping up a system of war; the latter promotes a system of peace, as the true means of enriching a nation. The one encourages national prejudices; the other promotes universal society, as the means of universal commerce.— The one measures its prosperity by the quantity of revenue it extorts; the other proves its excellence, by the small quantity of taxes it requires.

Mr. Burke has talked of old and new whigs. If he can amuse himself with childish names and distinctions, I shall not interrupt his pleasure. It is not to him, but to the Abbe Sieyes, that I address this chapter. I am alre dy engaged to the latter gentleman, to discuss the subject of monarchical government; and as it naturally occurs in comparing the old and new systems, I make this the opportunity of presenting to him my observations. I shall occasionally take Mr. Burke in my way.

Though it might be proved that the system of government now called the *new*, is the most ancient in principle of all that have existed, being founded on the original inherent rights of man : yet its tyranny and the sword have suspended the exercise of those rights for many centuries past, it serves better the purpose of distinction to call it the *new*, than to claim the right of calling it the old.

The first general distinction between those two systems, is, that the one now called the old is *hereditary*, either in whole or in part; and the new is entirely *representative*. It rejects all hereditary government :

1st, As being an imposition on mankind.

2d, As inadequate to the purposes for which government is necessary.

With respect to the first of these heads—It cannot be proved by what right hereditary government could begin : neither does there exist within the compass of mortal power, a right to establish it. Man has no authority over posterity in matters of personal right; and therefore, no man, or body of men, had, or can have, a right to set up hereditary government. Were even ourselves to come again into existence, instead of being succeeded by posterity, we have not now the right of taking from ourselves the rights which would then be ours. On what ground, then, do we pretend to take them from others?

All hereditary government is in its nature tyranny. An heritable crown, or an heritable throne, or by what other fanciful name such things may be called, have no other significant explanation than that mankind are heritable property. To inherit a government, is to inherit the people, as if they were flocks and herds.

With respect to the second head, that of being inadequate to the purposes for which government is necessary, we have only to consider what government essentially is, and compare it with the circumstances to which hereditary succession is subject.

Government ought to be a thing always in full maturity. It ought to be so constructed as to be superior to all the accidents to which individual man is subject; and therefore, hereditary succesion, by being *subject to them all*, is the most irregular and imperfect of all the systems of government.

We have heard the *rights of man* called a *levelling* system; but the only system to which the word *levelling* is truly applicable, is the hereditary monarchical system. It is a system of *mental levelling*. It indiscriminately admits every species of character to the same authority. Vice and virtue, ignorance and wisdom, in short, every quality, good or bad, is put on the same level. Kings succeed each other, not as rationals, but as animals. Can we then be surprised at the abject state of the human mind in monarchical countries, when the government itself is formed on such an abject levelling system?—It has no fixed character. To-day it is one thing; and to-morrow it is something else. It changes with the temper of every succeeding individual, and is subject to all the varieties of each. It is government through the medium of passions and accidents. It appears under all the various characters of childhood, decrepitude, dotage, a thing at nurse, in leading strings, or on crutches. It reverses the wholesome order of nature. It occasionally puts children over men, and the conceits of non-age over wisdom and experience. In short, we cannot conceive a more ridiculous figure of government, than hereditary succession, in all its cases, presents.

Could it be made a decree in nature, or an edict registered in heaven, and man could know it, that virtue and wisdom should invariably appertain to hereditary succession, the objections to it would be removed; but when we see that nature acts as if she disowned and sported with the hereditary system; that the mental characters of successors, in all countries, are below the average of human understanding; that one is a tyrant, another an ideot, a third insane, and some all three together, it is impossible to attach confidence to it, when reason in man has power to act.

It is not to the abbe Sieyes that I need apply this reasoning; he has already saved me that trouble, by giving his own opinion upon the case. "If it be asked," says he, "what is my opinion with respect to hereditary right, I answer, without hesitation, that, in good theory, an hereditary transmission of any power or office, can never accord with the laws of true representation.   Hereditaryship, is, in this sense, as much an attaint upon principle, as an outrage upon society.   But let us," continues he, " refer to the history of all elective monarchies and principalities ; is there one in which the elective mode is not worse than the hereditary succession."

As to debating on which is the worst of the two, is admitting both to be bad ; and herein we are agreed.   The preference which the abbe has given, is a condemnation of the thing he prefers.   Such a mode of reasoning on such a subject is inadmissible, because it finally amounts to an accusation of providence, as if she had left to man no other choice with respect to government than between two evils, the best of which he admits to be, " *an attaint upon principle, and an outrage upon society.*"

Passing over, for the present, all the evils and mischiefs which monarchy has occasioned in the world, nothing can more effectually prove its uselessness in a state of *civil government*, than making it hereditary.   Would we make any office hereditary that required wisdom and abilities to fill it ? And where wisdom and abilities are not necessary, such an office, whatever it may be, is superfluous or insignificant.

Hereditary succession is a burlesque upon monarchy. It puts it in the most ridiculous light, by presenting it as an office which any child or ideot may fill.   It requires some talents, to be a common mechanic ; but, to be a king, requires only the animal figure of man—a sort of breathing automaton.   This sort of superstition may last a few years more, but it cannot long resist the awakened reason and interest of man.

As to Mr. Burke, he is a stickler for monarchy, not altogether as a pensioner, if he is one, which I believe, but as a political man.   He has taken up a contemptible opinion of mankind, who, in their turn, are taking up the same of him.   He considers them as a herd of beings that must be governed by fraud, effigy, and show ; and an idol would be as good a figure of monarchy with him, as a man.   I will, however, do him the justice to say, that, with respect to America, he has been very complimentary.   He always contended, at least in my hearing, that the people of America were more enlightened than those of England, or of any country in Europe; and that therefore the imposition of show was not necessary in their governments.

Though the comparison between hereditary and elective monarchy, which the abbe had made, is unnecessary to the case, because the representative system rejects both; yet were I to make the comparison, I should decide contrary to what he has done.

The civil wars which have originated from contested hereditary claims, are more numerous, and have been more dreadful, and of longer continuance, than those which have been occasioned by election. All the civil wars in France arose from the hereditary system; they were either produced by hereditary claims, or by the imperfection of the hereditary form, which admits of regencies, or monarchy at nurse. With respect to England, its history is full of the same misfortunes. The contests for succession between the houses of York and Lancaster, lasted a whole century; and others of a similar nature, have renewed themselves since that period. Those of 1715 and 1745, were of the same kind. The succession-war for the crown of Spain, embroiled almost half of Europe. The disturbances in Holland are generated from the hereditaryship of the stadtholder. A government calling itself free, with an hereditary office, is like a thorn in the flesh, that produces a fermentation which endeavors to discharge it.

But I might go further, and place also foreign wars, of whatever kind, to the same cause. It is by adding the evil of hereditary succession to that of monarchy, that a permanent family interest is created, whose constant objects are dominion and revenue. Poland, though an elective monarchy, has had fewer wars than those which are hereditary; and it is the only government that has made a voluntary essay, though but a small one, to reform the condition of the country.

Having thus glanced at a few of the defects of the old, or hereditary systems of government, let us compare it with the new, or representative system.

The representative system takes society and civilization for its basis; nature, reason, and experience for its guide.

Experience, in all ages, and in all countries has demonstrated, that it is impossible to control nature in her distribution of mental powers. She gives them as she pleases. Whatever is the rule by which she, apparently to us, scatters them among mankind, that rule remains a secret to man. It would be as ridiculous to attempt to fix the hereditaryship of human beauty, as of wisdom.

Whatever wisdom constituently is, it is like a seedless plant; it may be reared when it appears; but it cannot be voluntarily produced. There is always a sufficiency somewhere in the general mass of society for all purposes; but with respect to the parts of society, it is continually changing its place. It rises in one to-day, in another to-morrow and has most probably visited in rotation every family of the earth, and again withdrawn.

As this is the order of nature, the order of government must necessarily follow it, or government will, as we see it does, degenerate into ignorance. The hereditary system, therefore, is as repugnant to human wisdom, as to human rights; and is as absurd, as it is unjust.

As the republic of letters brings forward the best literary productions, by giving to genius a fair and universal chance; so the representative system of government is calculated to produce the wisest laws, by collecting wisdom where it can be found. I smile to myself when I contemplate the ridiculous insignificance into which literature and all the sciences would sink, were they made hereditary; and I carry the same idea into governments. An hereditary governor is as inconsistent as an hereditary author. I know not whether Homer or Euclid had sons; but I will venture an opinion, that if they had, and had left their works unfinished, those sons could not have completed them.

Do we need a stronger evidence of the absurdity of hereditary government, than is seen in descendants of those men, in any line of life, who once were famous? Is there scarcely an instance in which there is not a total reverse of the character? It appears as if the tide of mental faculties flowed as far as it could in certain channels, and then forsook its course, and arose in others. How irrational then is the hereditary system which establishes channels of power, in company with which wisdom refuses to flow! By continuing this absurdity, man is perpetually in contradiction with himself; he accepts, for a king, or a chief magistrate, or a legislator, a person whom he would not elect for a constable.

It appears to general observation, that revolutions create genius and talents; but those events do no more than bring them forward. There exists in man, a mass of sense lying in a dormant state, and which, unless something excites it to action, will descend with him, in that condition, to the grave. As it is to the advantage of society that the whole of its faculties should be employed, the construction of government ought to be such as to bring forward, by a quiet and regular operation, all that extent of capacity which never fails to appear in revolutions.

This cannot take place in the insipid state of hereditary government, not only because it prevents, but because it operates to benumb. When the mind of a nation is bowed down by any political superstition in its government, such as hereditary succession is, it loses a considerable portion of its powers on all other subjects and objects. Hereditary succession requires the same obedience to ignorance, as to wisdom; and when once the mind can bring itself to pay this indiscriminate reverence, it descends below the statute of mental manhood. It is fit to be great only in little things. It acts a treachery upon itself, and suffocates the sensations that urge to detection.

Though the ancient governments present to us a miserable picture of the condition of man, there is one which above all others exempts itself from the general description. I mean the democracy of the Athenians. We see more to admire and less to condemn, in that great, extraordinary people, than in any thing which history affords.

Mr. Burke is so little acquainted with constituent principles of government, that he confounds democracy and representation together. Representation was a thing unknown in the ancient democracies. In those the mass of the people met and enacted laws (grammatically speaking) in the first person. Simple democracy was no other than the common hall of the ancients. It signifies the *form*, as well as the public principle of the government. As these democracies increased in population, and the territory extended, the simple democratical form became unwieldly and impracticable; and as the system of representation was not known, the consequence was, they either degenerated convulsively into monarchies, or became absorbed into such as then existed. Had the system of representation been then understood, as it now is, there is no reason to believe that those forms of government, now called monarchical or aristocratical would ever have taken place. It was the want of some method to consolidate the parts of society, after it became too populous, and too extensive for the simple democratical form, and also the lax and solitary condition of shepherds and herdsmen in other parts of the world, that afforded opportunities to those unnatural modes of government to begin.

As it is necessary to clear away the rubbish of errors, into which the subject of government has been thrown, I shall proceed to remark on some others.

It has always been the political craft of courtiers and court governments, to abuse something which they called republicanism; but what republicanism was, or is, they never attempt to explain. Let us examine a little into this case.

The only forms of government are, the democratical, the aristocratical, the monarchical, and what is now called the representative.

What is called a *republic*, is not any *particular form* of government. It is wholly characteristical of the purport, matter, or object for which government ought to be instituted, and on which it is to be employed, *res-publica*, the public affairs, or the public good; or, literally translated, the *public thing*. It is a word of a good original, referring to what ought to be the character and business of government; and in this sense it is naturally opposed to the word *monarchy*, which has a base original signification. It means arbitrary power in an individual person; in the exercise of which, *himself*, and not the *res-publica*, is the object.

Every government that does not act on the principle of a republic, or, in other words, that does not make the *res-publica* its whole and sole object, is not a good government. Republican government is no other than government established and conducted for the interest of the public, as well individually as collectively. It is not necessarily connected with any particular form, but it most naturally associates with the representative form, as being best calculated to secure the end for which a nation is at the expense of supporting it.

Various forms of government have affected to style themselves republics. Poland calls itself a republic, but is in fact an hereditary aristocracy, with what is called an elective monarchy. Holland calls itself a republic, which is chiefly aristocratical, with an hereditary stadtholdership. But the government of America, which is wholly on the system of representation, is the only real republic in character and practice, that now exists. Its government has no other object than the public business of the nation, and therefore it is properly a republic; and the Americans have taken care that *this*, and no other, shall be the object of their government, by their rejecting every thing hereditary, and establishing government on the system of representation only.

Those who have said that a republic is not a *form* of government calculated for countries of great extent, mistook, in the first place, the *business* of a government, for a *form* of government; for the *res-publica* equally appertains to every extent of territory and population. And, in the second place, if they meant any thing with respect to *form*, it was the simple democratical form, such as was the mode of government in the ancient democracies, in which there was no representation. The case, therefore, is not, that a republic cannot be extensive, but that it cannot be extensive on the simple democratic form; and the question naturally presents itself, *What is the best form of government for conducting the* RES-PUBLICA *or* PUBLIC BUSINESS *of a nation, after it becomes too extensive and populous for the simple democratical form?*

It cannot be monarchy, because monarchy is subject to an objection of the same amount to which the democratical form was subject.

It is possible that an individual may lay down a system of principles, on which government shall be constitutionally established to any extent of territory. This is no more than an operation of the mind, acting by its own powers. But the practice upon those principles, as applying to the various and numerous circumstances of a nation, its agriculture, manufactures, trade, commerce, &c. require a knowledge, of a different kind, and which can be had only from the various parts of society. It is an assemblage of practical knowledge, which no one individual can possess; and therefore the monarchical form is as much limited, in useful practice, from the incompetency of knowledge, as was the democratical form, from the multiplicity of population. The one degenerates, by extension, into confusion; the other, into ignorance and incapacity, of which all the great monarchies are an evidence. The monarchical form, therefore, could not be a substitute for the democratical, because it has equal inconveniences.

Much less could it when made hereditary. This is the most effectual of all forms to preclude knowledge. Neither could the high democratical mind have voluntarily yielded itself to be governed by children and ideots, and all the motley insignificance of character, which attends such a mere animal system, the disgrace and the reproach of reason and of man.

As to the aristocratical form, it has the same vices and defects with the monarchical, except that the chance of abilities is better from the proportion of numbers, but there is still no security for the right use and application of them.*

Referring, then, to the original simple democracy, it affords the true data from which government on a large scale can begin. It is incapable of extension, not from its principle, but from the inconvenience of its form; and monarchy and aristocracy from their incapacity. Retaining, then, democracy as the ground, and rejecting the corrupt systems of monarchy and aristocracy, the representative system naturally presents itself; remedying at once the defects of the simple democracy as to form, and the incapacity of the other two with regard to knowledge.

Simple democracy was society governing itself without the use of secondary means. By ingrafting representation upon democracy, we arrive at a system of government capable of embracing and confederating all the various interests and every extent of territory and population; and that also with advantages as much superior to hereditary government, as the republic of letters is to hereditary literature.

It is on this system that the American government is founded. It is representation ingrafted upon democracy. It has settled the form by a scale parallel in all cases to the extent of the principle. What Athens was in miniature, America will be in magnitude. The one was the wonder of the ancient world—the other is becoming the admiration and model of the present. It is the easiest of all the forms of government to be understood, and the most eligible in practice; and excludes at once the ignorance and insecurity of the hereditary mode, and the inconvenience of the simple democracy.

It is impossible to conceive a system of government capable of acting over such an extent of territory, and such a circle of interests, as is produced by the operation of

* For a character of aristocracy, the reader is referred to Rights of Man, part i. p. 84. et seq.

representation. France, great and populous as it is, is but a spot in the capaciousness of the system. It adapts itself to all possible cases. It is preferable to simple democracy even in small territories. Athens, by representation, would have surpassed her own democracy.

That which is called government, or rather that which we ought to conceive government to be, is no more than some common centre, in which all the parts of society unite. This cannot be established by any method so conducive to the various interests of the community, as by the representative system. It concentrates the knowledge necessary to the interests of the parts, and of the whole. It places government in a state of constant maturity. It is, as has been already observed, never young, never old. It is subject neither to nonage nor dotage. It is never in the cradle nor on crutches. It admits not of a separation between knowledge and power, and is superior, as government ought always to be, to all the accidents of individual man, and is therefore superior to what is called monarchy.

A nation is not a body, the figure of which is to be represented by the human body; but is like a body contained within a circle, having a common centre, in which every radius meets; and that centre is formed by representation. To connect representation with what is called monarchy, is eccentric government. Representation is of itself the delegated monarchy of a nation, and cannot debase itself by dividing it with another.

Mr. Burke has two or three times in his parliamentary speeches, and in his publications, made use of a jingle of words that convey no ideas. Speaking of government, he says, " It is better to have monarchy for its basis, and republicanism for its corrective, than republicanism for its basis, and monarchy for its corrective." If he means that it is better to correct folly with wisdom, than wisdom with folly, I will no otherwise contend with him, than to say, it would be much better to reject the folly altogether.

But what is this thing which Mr. Burke calls monarchy? Will he explain it: all mankind can understand what representation is; and that it must necessarily include a variety of knowledge and talents. But what security is there for the same qualities on the part of monarchy? Or, when this monarchy is a child, where then is the wisdom? What does it know about government? Who then is the monarch?

or where is the monarchy? If it is to be performed by regency, it proves it to be a farce. A regency is a mock species of republic, and the whole of monarchy deserves no better appellation. It is a thing as various as imagination can paint. It has none of the stable character that government ought to possess. Every succession is a revolution, and every regency a counter-revolution. The whole of it is a scene of perpetual court cabal and intrigue, of which Mr. Burke is himself an instance.

Whether I have too little sense to see, or too much to be imposed upon : whether I have too much or too little pride, or of any thing else, I leave out of the question; but certain it is, that what is called monarchy, always appears to me a silly, contemptible thing. I compare it to something kept behind a curtain, about which there is a great deal of bustle and fuss, and a wonderful air of seeming solemnity ; but when, by any accident, the curtain happens to be open and the company see what it is, they burst into laughter.

In the representative system of government, nothing like this can happen. Like the nation itself, it possesses a perpetual stamina, as well of body as of mind, and presents itself on the open theatre of the world in a fair and manly manner. Whatever are its excellencies or its defects, they are visible to all. It exists not by fraud and mystery; it deals not in cant and sophistry ; but inspires a language, that, passing from heart to heart, is felt and understood.

We must shut our eyes against reason, we must basely degrade our understanding, not to see the folly of what is called monarchy. Nature is orderly in all her works ; but this is a mode of government that counteracts nature. It turns the progress of the human faculties upside down. It subjects age to be governed by children, and wisdom by folly.

On the contrary, the representative system is always parallel with the order and immutable laws of nature, and meets the reason of man in every part. For example :

In the American federal government, more power is delegated to the president of the United States, than to any other individual member of congress. He cannot, therefore, be elected to this office under the age of thirty-five years. By this time the judgment of man becomes matured, and he has lived long enough to be acquainted with men and things, and the country with him. But on the monarchical plan (exclusive of the numerous chances there are against every man born into the world, of drawing a prize in the lottery of human faculties,) the next in succession, whatever he may be, is put at the head of a nation, and of a government at the age of eighteen years. Does this appear like an act of wisdom? Is it consistent with the proper dignity and the manly character of a nation? Where is the propriety of calling such a lad the father of the people?—In all other cases, a person is a minor until the age of twenty-one years. Before this period, he is not trusted with the management of an acre of land, or with the heritable property of a flock of sheep, or an herd of swine; but wonderful to tell! he may at the age of eighteen years, be trusted with a nation.

That monarchy is all a bubble, a mere court artifice to procure money, is evident (at least to me,) in every character in which it can be viewed. It would be almost impossible, on the rational system of representative government, to make out a bill of expenses to such an enormous amount as this deception admits. Government is not of itself a very chargeable institution. The whole expense of the federal government of America, founded, as I have already said, on the system of representation, and extending over a country nearly ten times as large as England, is but six hundred thousand dollars, or one hundred and thirty thousand pounds sterling.

I presume that no man in his sober senses will compare the character of any of the kings of Europe, with that of general Washington. Yet, in France, and also in England, the expense of the civil list only, for the support of one man, is eight times greater than the whole expense of the federal government of America. To assign a reason for this, appears almost impossible. The generality of people in America, especially the poor, are more able to pay taxes, than the generality of people either in France or England.

But the case is, that the representative system diffuses such a body of knowledge throughout the nation, on the subject of government, as to explode ignorance and preclude imposition. The craft of courts cannot be acted on that ground. There is no place for mystery; no where for it to begin. Those who are not in the representation, know as much of the nature of business as those who are. An affectation of mysterious importance would there be scouted. Nations can have no secrets; and the secrets of courts, like those of individuals, are always their defects.

In the representative system, the reason for every thing must publicly appear. Every man is a proprietor in government, and considers it a necessary part of his business to understand. It concerns his interest because it affects his property. He examines the cost, and compares it with the advantages ; and above all, he does not adopt the slavish custom of following what in other governments are called *leaders.*

It can only be by blinding the understanding of man, and making him believe that government is some wonderful mysterious thing, that excessive revenues are obtained. Monarchy is well calculated to ensure this end. It is the popery of government; a thing kept up to amuse the ignorant, and quiet them into paying taxes.

The government of a free country, properly speaking, is not in the persons, but in the laws. The enacting of those requires no great expense ; and when they are administered, the whole of civil government is performed—the rest is all court contrivance.

CHAPTER IV.

ON CONSTITUTIONS.

That men mean distinct and separate things when they talk of constitutions and of governments, is evident; or, why are those terms distinctly and separately used? A constitution is not the act of a government, but of a people constituting a government; and government without a constitution, is power without a right.

All power exercised over a nation, must have some beginning. It must be either delegated, or assumed. There are no other sources. All delegated power is trust, and all assumed power is usurpation. Time does not alter the nature and quality of either.

In viewing this subject, the case and circumstances of America present themselves as in the beginning of a world; and our inquiry into the origin of government is shortened, by referring to the facts that have arisen in our day. We have no occasion to roam for information into the obscure field of antiquity, nor hazard ourselves upon conjecture. We are brought at once to the point of seeing government begin, as if we had lived in the beginning of time. The real volume, not of history, but of facts, is directly before us, unmutilated by contrivance, or the errors of tradition.

I will here concisely state the commencement of the American constitutions; by which the difference between constitutions and governments will sufficiently appear.

It may not be improper to remind the reader, that the United States of America consist of thirteen states, each of which established a government for itself, after the declaration of independence, of the fourth of July 1776. Each state acted independently of the rest, in forming its government ; but the same general principle pervades the whole. When the several state governments were formed, they proceeded to form the federal government, that acts over the whole in all matters which concern the interest of the whole, or which relate to the intercourse of the several states with each other, or with foreign nations. I will begin with giving an instance from one of the state governments (that of Pennsylvania) and then proceed to thef edral government.

The state of Pennsylvania, though nearly of the same extent of territory as England, was then divided into twelve counties. Each of those counties had elected a committee at the commencement of the dispute with the English government ; and as the city of Philadelphia, which also had its committee, was the most central for intelligence, it became the centre of communication to the several county committees. When it became necessary to proceed to the formation of a government, the committee of Philadelphia proposed a conference of all the county committees, to be held in that city, and which met the latter end of July, 1776.

Though these committees had been elected by the people, they were not elected expressly for the purpose, nor invested with the authority of forming a constitution : and as they could not, consistently with the American idea of rights, assume such a power, they could only confer upon

the matter, and put it into a train of operation. The con-
ferees, therefore did no more than state the case, and recommend to the several counties to elect six representatives for each county, to meet in convention at Philadelphia,
with powers to form a constitution, and propose it for public consideration.

This convention, of which Benjamin Franklin was president, having met and deliberated, and agreed upon a constitution, they next ordered it to be published, not as a thing
established, but for the consideration of the whole people,
their approbation or rejection, and then adjourned to a
stated time. When the time of adjournment was expired,
the convention re-assembled; and as the general opinion
of the people in approbation of it was then known, the constitution was signed, sealed, and proclaimed on the *authority of the people,* and the original instrument deposited as a
public record. The convention then appointed a day for
the general election of the representatives who were to compose the government, and the time it should commence;
and having done this, they dissolved, and returned to their
several homes and occupations.

In this constitution were laid down, first, a declaration of
rights. Then followed the form which the government
should have, and the powers it should possess—the authority of the courts of judicature, and of juries—the manner in which elections should be conducted, and the proportion of representatives to the number of electors—the time
which each succeeding assembly should continue, which
was one year—the mode of levying, and of accounting for
the expenditure, of public money—of appointing public
officers, &c.

No article of this constitution could be altered or infringed at the discretion of the government that was to ensue.—
It was to that government a law. But as it would have
been unwise to preclude the benefit of experience, and in
order also to prevent the accumulation of errors, if any
should be found, and to preserve an unison of government
with the circumstances of the state at all times, the constitution provided, that, at the expiration of every seven
years, a convention should be elected; for the express purpose of revising the constitution, and making alterations,
additions, or abolitions therein, if any such should be found
necessary.

Here we see a regular process—a government issuing out of a constitution, formed by the people in their original character; and that constitution, serving, not only as an authority, but as a law of control to the government. It was the political bible of the state. Scarcely a family was without it. Every member of the government had a copy; and nothing was more common, when any debate arose on the principle of a bill, or on the extent of any species of authority, than for the members to take the printed constitution out of their pocket, and read the chapter with which such matter in debate was connected.

Having thus given an instance from one of the states, I will show the proceedings by which the federal constitution of the United States arose and was formed.

Congress, at its two first meetings, in September 1774, and May 1775, was nothing more than a deputation from the legislatures of the several provinces, afterwards states; and had no other authority than what arose from common consent, and the necessity of its acting as a public body. In every thing which related to the internal affairs of America, congress went no further than to issue recommendations, to the several provincial assemblies, who at discretion adopted them or not. Nothing on the part of congress was compulsive; yet, in this situation, it was more faithfully and affectionately obeyed, than was any government in Europe. This instance, like that of the national assembly of France, sufficiently shows, that the strength of government does not consist in any thing *within* itself, but in the attachment of a nation, and the interest which the people feel in supporting it. When this is lost, government is but a child in power; and though, like the old government of France, it may harass individuals for a while, it but facilitates its own fall.

After the declaration of independence, it became consistent with the principle on which representative government is founded, that the authority of congress should be defined and established. Whether that authority should be more or less than congress then discretionately exercised, was not then the question. It was merely the rectitude of the measure.

For this purpose the act, called the act of confederation (which was a sort of imperfect federal constitution) was proposed, and, after long deliberation, was concluded in the year 1781. It was not the act of congress, because it is repugnant to the principles of representative government that a body should give power to itself. Congress first informed the several states, of the powers which it conceived were necessary to be invested in the union, to enable it to perform the duties and services required from it; and the states severally agreed with each other, and concentrated in congress those powers.

It may not be improper to observe, that in both those instances (the one of Pennsylvania, and the other of the United States) there is no such thing as the idea of a compact between the people on one side, and the government on the other. The compact was that of the people with each other, to produce and constitute a government. To suppose that any government can be a party in a compact with the whole people, is to suppose it to have existence before it can have a right to exist. The only instance in which a compact can take place between the people and those who exercise the government, is, that the people shall pay them, while they choose to employ them.

Government is not a trade which any man or body of men has a right to set up and exercise for his own emolument, but is altogether a trust, in right of those by whom that trust is delegated, and by whom it is always resumable. It has of itself no rights; they are altogether duties.

Having thus given two instances of the original formation of a constitution, I will show the manner in which both have been changed since their first establishment.

The powers vested in the governments of the several states, by the state constitutions, were found, upon experience, to be too great; and those vested in the federal government, by the act of confederation, too little. The defect was not in the principle, but in the distribution of power.

Numerous publications, in pamphlets and in the newspapers, appeared on the propriety and necessity of new-modelling the federal government. After some time of public discussion, carried on through the channel of the press, and in conversations, the state of Virginia, experiencing some inconvenience with respect to commerce, proposed holding a continental conference; in consequence of which a deputation from five or six of the state assemblies met at Annapolis in Maryland, in 1786. This meeting, not conceiving itself sufficiently authorized to go into the business of a reform, did no more than state their

general opinions of the propriety of the measure, and recommend that a convention of all the states should be held
the year following.

This convention met at Philadelphia, in May 1787, of
which general Washington was elected president. He was
not at that time connected with any of the state governments, or with congress. He delivered up his commission when the war ended, and since then had lived a private citizen.

The convention went deeply into all the subjects; and
having, after a variety of debate and investigation, agreed
among themselves upon the several parts of a federal constitution, the next question was, the manner of giving it authority and practice.

For this purpose, they did not, like a cabal of courtiers,
send for a Dutch stadtholder, or a German elector; but
they referred the whole matter to the sense and interest of
the country.

They first directed, that the proposed constitution should
be published. Second, that each state should elect a convention, expressly for the purpose of taking it into consideration, and of ratifying or rejecting it; and that as soon
as the approbation and ratification of any nine states
should be given, that those states should proceed to the
election of their proportion of members to the new federal
government; and that the operation of it should then begin, and the former federal government cease.

The several states proceeded accordingly to elect their
conventions; some of those conventions ratified the constitution by very large majorities, and two or three unanimously. In others there were much debate and division
of opinion. In the Massachusetts convention, which met
at Boston, the majority was not above nineteen or twenty,
in about three hundred members; but such is the nature
of representative government, that it quietly decides all
matters by majority. After the debate in the Massachusetts convention was closed, and the vote taken, the ob-
jecting members rose, and declared, " *That though they had
argued and voted against it, because certain parts appeared to
them in a different light to what they appeared to other members ;
yet, as the vote had been decided in favor of the constitution as
proposed, they should give it the same practical support as if they
had voted for it.*"

As soon as nine states had concurred, (and the rest followed in the order their conventions were elected) the old fabric of the federal government was taken down, and a new one erected, of which general Washington is president. In this place I cannot help remarking, that the character and services of this gentleman are sufficient to put all those men called kings to shame. While they are receiving from the sweat and labors of mankind, a prodigality of pay, to which neither their abilities nor their services can entitle them, he is rendering every service in his power, and refusing every pecuniary reward. He accepted no pay as commander-in-chief; he accepts none as president of the United States.

After the new federal constitution was established, the state of Pennsylvania, conceiving that some parts of its own constitution required to be altered, elected a convention for that purpose. The proposed alterations were published, and the people concurring therein, they were established.

In forming those constitutions, or in altering them, little or no inconvenience took place. The ordinary course of things was not interrupted, and the advantages have been much. It is always the interest of a far greater number of people in a nation to have things right, than to let them remain wrong; and when public matters are open to debate, and the public judgment free, it will not decide wrong, unless it decides too hastily.

In the two instances of changing the constitutions, the government then in being were not actors either way.— Government has no right to make itself a party in any debate respecting the principles or modes of forming, or of changing constitutions. It is not for the benefit of those who exercise the powers of government, that constitutions, and the governments issuing from them, are established. In all those matters, the right of judging and acting are in those who pay, and not in those who receive.

A constitution is the property of a nation, and not of those who exercise the government. All the constitutions of America are declared to be established on the authority of the people. In France, the word nation is used instead of the people; but in both cases, a constitution is a thing antecedent to the government, and always distinct therefrom.

In England, it is not difficult to perceive that every thing has a constitution, except the nation. Every society and association that is established, first agreed upon a number of original articles, digested into form, which are its constitution. It then appointed its officers, whose powers and authorities are described in that constitution, and the government of that society then commenced. Those officers, by whatever name they are called, have no authority to add to, alter, or abridge the original articles. It is only to the constituting power that this right belongs.

From the want of understanding the difference between a constitution and a government, Dr. Johnson, and all writers of his description, have always bewildered themselves. They could not but perceive, that there must necessarily be a *controlling* power existing somewhere, and they placed this power in the discretion of the persons exercising the government, instead of placing it in a constitution formed by the nation. When it is in a constitution, it has the nation for its support, and the natural and the political controlling powers are together. The laws which are enacted by governments, control men only as individuals, but the nation, through its constitution, controls the whole government, and has a natural ability so to do.— The final controlling power, therefore, and the original constituting power, are one and the same power.

Dr. Johnson could not have advanced such a position in any country where there was a constitution; and he is himself an evidence, that no such thing as a constitution exists in England. But it may be put as a question, not improper to be investigated, that if a constitution does not exist, how came the idea of its existence so generally established?

In order to decide this question, it is necessary to consider a constitution in both its cases: 1st, as creating a government and giving it powers: 2d, as regulating and restraining the powers so given.

If we begin with William of Normandy, we find that the government of England was originally a tyranny, founded on an invasion and conquest of the country. This being admitted, it will then appear that the exertion of the nation, at different periods, to abate that tyranny, and render it less intolerable, has been credited for a constitution.

Magna Charta, as it was called, (it is now like an almanac of the same date) was no more than compelling the government to renounce a part of its assumptions. It did not create and give powers to government in the manner a constitution does; but was, as far as it went, of the nature of a re-conquest, and not of a constitution; for, could the nation have totally expelled the usurpation, as France has done its despotism, it would then have had a constitution to form.

The history of the Edwards and the Henries, and up to the commencement of the Stuarts, exhibits as many instances of tyranny as could be acted within the limits to which the nation had restricted it. The Stuarts endeavored to pass those limits, and their fate is well known. In all those instances we see nothing of a constitution, but only of restrictions on assumed power.

After this, another William, descended from the same stock, and claiming from the same origin, gained possession; and of the two evils, James and William, the nation preferred what it thought the least; since, from the circumstances, it must take one. The act, called the Bill of Rights, comes here into view. What is it but a bargain, which the parts of the government made with each other to divide power, profit, and privileges? You shall have so much, and I will have the rest; and with respect to the nation, it said, for *your share*, you *shall have the right of petitioning*. This being the case, the bill of rights is more properly a bill of wrongs, and of insult. As to what is called the convention-parliament, it was a thing that made itself, and then made the authority by which it acted. A few persons got together, and called themselves by that name. Several of them had never been elected, and none of them for the purpose.

From the time of William, a species of government arose, issuing out of this coalition bill of rights; and more so, since the corruption introduced at the Hanover succession, by the agency of Walpole: that can be described by no other name than a despotic legislation. Though the parts may embarrass each other, the whole has no bounds; and the only right it acknowledges out of itself, is the right of petitioning. Where then is the constitution that either gives or restrains power?

It is not because a part of the government is elective, that makes it less a despotism, if the persons so elected, possess afterwards, as a parliament, unlimited powers. Election, in this case, becomes separated from representation, and the candidates are candidates for despotism.

I cannot believe that any nation, reasoning on its own rights, would have thought of calling those things a *constitution*, if the cry of constitution had not been set up by the government. It has got into circulation like the words *bore*, and *quiz*, by being chalked up in speeches of parliament, as those words were on window-shutters and door posts; but whatever the constitution may be in other respects, it has undoubtedly been *the most productive machine for taxation that was ever invented*. The taxes in France, under the new constitution, are not quite thirteen shillings per head,* and the taxes in England, under what is called its present constitution, are forty-eight shillings and sixpence per head, men, women, and children, amounting to nearly seventeen millions sterling, besides the expense of collection, which is upwards of a million more.

In a country like England, where the whole of the civil government is executed by the people of every town and county, by means of parish officers, magistrates, quarterly sessions, juries, and assize, without any trouble to what is called government, or any other expense to the revenue than the salary of the judges, it is astonishing how such a mass of taxes can be employed. Not even the internal defence of the country is paid out of the revenue. On all occasions, whether real or contrived, recourse is continually had to new loans and to new taxes. No wonder then, that a machine of government so advantageous to the advocates of a court, should be so triumphantly extolled! No wonder that St. James's or St. Stephen's should echo with the continual cry of constitution! No wonder that the French revolution should be reprobated, and the *res-publica* treated with reproach! The *red book* of England, like the red book of France, will explain the reason.†

I will now, by way of relaxation, turn a thought or two to Mr. Burke. I ask his pardon for neglecting him so long.

---

* The whole amount of the assessed taxes of France, for the present year, is three hundred millions of francs, which is twelve millions and a half sterling; and the incidental taxes are estimated at three millions, making in the whole fifteen millions and an half; which among twenty-four millions of people, is not quite thirty shillings per head. France has lessened her taxes since the revolution, nearly nine millions sterling annually. Before the revolution, the city of Paris paid a duty of upwards of thirty per cent. on all articles brought into the city. This tax was collected at the city gates. It was taken off on the first of last May, and the gates taken down.

† What was called the *livre rouge*, or the red book, in France, was not exactly similar to the court calendar in England; but it sufficiently showed how a great part of the taxes were lavished.

" America," says he, (in his speech on the Canada constitution bill) " never dreamed of such absurd doctrine as
the Rights of Man."

Mr. Burke is such a bold presumer, and advances his
assertions and premises with such a deficiency of judgment,
that, without troubling ourselves about principles of philosophy or politics, the mere logical conclusions they produce, are ridiculous. For instance :

If governments, as Mr. Burke asserts, are not founded
on the rights of *man*, and are founded on *any rights* at all,
they consequently must be founded on the rights of *something* that is *not man*. What, then, is that something?

Generally speaking, we know of no other creatures that
inhabit the earth than man and beast; and in all cases,
where only two things offer themselves, and one must be
admitted, a negation proved on any one, amounts to an af-
firmative on the other ; and therefore, Mr. Burke, by proving against the rights of *man*, proves in behalf of the *beast ;*
and consequently, proves that government is a beast: and
as difficult things sometimes explain each other, we now
see the origin of keeping wild beasts in the Tower; for
they certainly can be of no other use than to show the origin of the government. They are in the place of a constitution. O! John Bull, what honors thou hast lost by not
being a wild beast. Thou mightest, on Mr. Burke's system, have been in the Tower for life.

If Mr. Burke's arguments have not weight enough to
keep one serious, the fault is less mine than his ; and as I
am willing to make an apology to the reader for the liberty
I have taken, I hope Mr. Burke will also make his for giving
the cause.

Having thus paid Mr. Burke the compliment of remembering him, I return to the subject.

From the want of a constitution in England, to restrain
and regulate the wild impulse of power, many of the laws
are irrational and tyrannical, and the administration of
them vague and problematical.

The attention of the government of England (for I rather
choose to call it by this name, than the English government) appears, since its political connexion with Germany,
to have been so completely engrossed and absorbed by foreign affairs, and the means of raising taxes, that it seems
to exist for no other purposes. Domestic concerns are

neglected; and, with respect to regular law, there is scarcely such a thing.

Almost every case must now be determined by some precedent, be that precedent good or bad, or whether it properly applies or not; and the practice is become so general, as to suggest a suspicion, that it proceeds from a deeper policy than at first sight appears.

Since the revolution of America, and more so since that of France, this preaching up the doctrine of precedents, drawn from times and circumstances antecedent to those events, has been the studied practice of the English government. The generality of those precedents are founded on principles and opinions, the reverse of what they ought to be; and the greater distance of time they are drawn from, the more they are to be suspected. But by associating those precedents with a superstitious reverence for ancient things, as monks show relics and call them holy, the generality of mankind are deceived into the design. Governments now act as if they were afraid to awaken a single reflection in man. They are softly leading him to the sepulchre of precedents, to deaden his faculties and call his attention from the scene of revolutions. They feel that he is arriving at knowledge faster than they wish, and their policy of precedents is the barometer of their fears. This political popery, like the ecclesiastical popery of old, has had its day, and is hastening to its exit. The ragged relic and the antiquated precedent, the monk and the monarch, will moulder together.

Government by precedent, without any regard to the principle of the precedent, is one of the vilest systems that can be set up. In numerous instances, the precedent ought to operate as a warning, and not as an example, and requires to be shunned instead of imitated; but instead of this, precedents are taken in the lump and put at once for constitution and for law.

Either the doctrine of precedent is policy to keep a man in a state of ignorance, or it is a practical confession that wisdom degenerates in governments as governments increase in age, and can only hobble along by the stilts and crutches of precedents. How is it that the same persons who would proudly be thought wiser than their predecessors, appear at the same time only as the ghosts of departed wisdom? How strangely is antiquity treated! To answer some purposes it is spoken of as the times of darkness and ignorance, and to answer others it is put for the light of the world.

If the doctrine of precedents is to be followed, the expenses of government need not continue the same. Why pay men extravagantly, who have but little to do? If every thing that can happen is already in precedent, legislation is at an end, and precedent, like a dictionary, determines every case. Either, therefore, government has arrived at its dotage, and requires to be renovated, or all the occasions for exercising its wisdom have occurred.

We now see all over Europe, and particularly in England, the curious phenomenon of a nation looking one way, and a government the other; the one forward, and the other backward. If governments are to go on by precedent, while nations go on by improvement, they must at last come to a final separation, and the sooner, and the more civilly, they determine this point, the better it will be for them.*

Having thus spoken of constitutions generally, as things distinct from actual governments, let us proceed to consider the parts of which a constitution is composed.

Opinions differ more on this subject, than with respect to the whole. That a nation ought to have a constitution, as a rule for the conduct of its government, is a simple question in which all men, not directly courtiers, will agree. It is only on the component parts that questions and opinions multiply.

But this difficulty, like every other, will diminish when put into a train of being rightly understood.

The first thing is, that a nation has a right to establish a constitution.

Whether it exercises this right in the most judicious manner at first, is quite another case. It exercises it agreeably to the judgment it possesses; and by continuing to do so, all errors will at last be exploded.

---

* In England, the improvements in agriculture, useful arts, manufactures, and commerce, have been made in opposition to the genius of its government, which is that of following precedents. It is from the enterprise and industry of the individuals, and their numerous associations, in which, tritely speaking, government is neither pillow nor bolster, that these improvements have proceeded. No man thought about the government, or who was in, or who was out, when he was planning or executing those things : and all he had to hope, with respect to government, was, that it would let him alone. Three or four very silly ministerial newspapers are continually offending against the spirit of national improvement, by ascribing it to a minister.— They may with as much truth ascribe this book to a minister.

When this right is established in a nation, there is no fear that it will be employed to its own injury. A nation can have no interest in being wrong.

Though all the constitutions of America are on one general principle, yet no two of them are exactly alike in their component parts, or in the distribution of the powers which they give to the actual governments. Some are more, and others less complex.

In forming a constitution, it is first necessary to consider what are the ends for which government is necessary: secondly, what are the best means, and the least expensive, for accomplishing those ends.

Government is nothing more than a national association; and the object of this association is the good of all, as well individually as collectively. Every man wishes to pursue his occupation, and to enjoy the fruits of his labors, and the produce of his property in peace and safety, and with the least possible expense. When these things are accomplished, all the objects for which government ought to be established are answered.

It has been customary to consider government under three distinct general heads. The legislative, the executive, and the judicial.

But if we permit our judgment to act unincumbered by the habit of multiplied terms, we can perceive no more than two divisions of power, of which civil government is composed, namely, that of legislating or enacting laws, and that of executing or administering them. Every thing, therefore, appertaining to civil government, classes itself under one or other of these two divisions.

So far as regards the execution of the laws, that which is called the judicial power, is strictly and properly the executive power of every country. It is that power to which every individual has an appeal, and which causes the laws to be executed; neither have we any other clear idea with respect to the official execution of the laws. In England, and also in America and France, this power begins with the magistrate, and proceeds up through all the courts of judicature.

I leave to courtiers to explain what is meant by calling monarchy the executive power. It is merely a name in which acts of government are done; and any other, or none at all, would answer the same purpose. Laws have neither more nor less authority on this account. It must be from the justness of their principles, and the interest which a nation feels therein, that they derive support; if they require any other than this, it is a sign that something in the system of government is imperfect. Laws difficult to be executed cannot be generally good.

With respect to the organization of the *legislative power*, different modes have been adopted in different countries. In America it is generally composed of two houses. In France it consists but of one, but in both countries it is wholly by representation.

The case is, that mankind (from the long tyranny of assumed power) have had so few opportunities of making the necessary trials on modes and principles of government, in order to discover the best, *that government is but now beginning to be known*, and experience is yet wanting to determine many particulars.

The objections against two houses are, first, that there is an inconsistency in any part of a whole legislature, coming to a final determination by vote on any matter, whilst *that matter* with respect to *that whole*, is yet only in a train of deliberation, and consequently open to new illustrations.

2d, That by taking the vote on each, as a separate body, it always admits of the possibility, and is often the case in practice, that the minority governs the majority, and that, in some instances, to a great degree of inconsistency.

3d, That two houses arbitrarily checking or controlling each other, is inconsistent; because it cannot be proved, on the principles of just representation, that either should be wiser, or better than the other. They may check in the wrong as well as in the right; and therefore, to give the power where we cannot give the wisdom to use it, nor be assured of its being rightly used, renders the hazard at least equal to the precaution.*

---

* With respect to the two houses, of which the English parliament is composed, they appear to be effectually influenced into one, and, as a legislature, to have no temper of its own. The minister, whoever he at any time may be, touches it as with an opium wand, and it sleeps obedience.

But if we look at the distinct abilities of the two houses, the difference will appear so great, as to show the inconsistency of placing power where there can be no certainty of the judgment to use it. Wretched as the state of representation is in England, it is manhood compared with what is called the house of lords; and so little is this nick-named house regarded, that the people scarcely inquire at any time what it is doing. It appears also to be most under influence, and the furthest removed from the general interest of the nation. In the debate on engaging in the Russian and Turkish war, the majority in the house of peers in favor of it was upwards of ninety, when in the other house, which is more than double its numbers, the majority was sixty-three.

The objection against a single house is, that it is always in a condition of committing itself too soon. But it should at the same time be remembered that when there is a constitution which defines the power, and establishes the principles within which a legislature shall act, there is already a more effectual check provided, and more powerfully operating, than any other check can be. For example,

Were a bill to be brought into any of the American legislatures, similar to that which was passed into an act by the English parliament, at the commencement of the reign of George I. to extend the duration of the assemblies to a longer period than they now sit, the check is in the constitution, which in effect says, *thus far shalt thou go and no further.*

But in order to remove the objection against a single house (that of acting with too quick an impulse) and at the same time to avoid the inconsistencies, in some cases absurdities, arising from the two houses, the following method has been proposed as an improvement on both.

1st, To have but one representation.

2d, To divide that representation, by lot, into two or three parts.

3d. That every proposed bill shall first be debated in those parts, by succession, that they may become hearers of each other, but without taking any vote. After which the whole representation to assemble, for a general debate and determination, by vote.

To this proposed improvement has been added another, for the purpose of keeping the representation in a state of constant renovation ; which is, that one third of the representation of each county shall go out at the expiration of one year, and the number be replaced by new elections. Another third at the expiration of the second year, replaced in like manner, and every third year to be a general election.*

The proceedings on Mr. Fox's bill, respecting the rights of juries, merits also to be noticed. The persons called the peers, were not the objects of that bill. They are already in possession of more privileges than that bill gave to others. They are their own jury, and if any one of that house were prosecuted for a libel, he would not suffer, even upon conviction, for the first offence. Such inequality in laws ought not to exist in any country The French constitution says, that *the law is the same to every individual, whether to protect or to punish. All are equal in its sight.*

* As to the state of representation in England, it is too absurd to be reasoned upon. Almost all the represented parts are decreasing in population, and the unrepresented parts are increasing. A general convention of the nation is necessary to take the whole state of its government into consideration.

But in whatever manner the separate parts of a constitution may be arranged, there is one general principle that distinguishes freedom from slavery, which is, that all *hereditary government over a people is to them a species of slavery, and representative government is freedom.*

Considering government in the only light in which it should be considered, that of a NATIONAL ASSOCIATION, it ought to be so constructed as not to be disordered by any accident happening among the parts ; and therefore, no extraordinary power, capable of producing such an effect, should be lodged in the hands of any individual. The death, sickness, absence, or defection, of any one individual in a government, ought to be a matter of no more consequence, with respect to the nation, than if the same circumstance had taken place in a member of the English parliament, or the French national assembly.

Scarcely any thing presents a more degrading character of national greatness, than its being thrown into confusion by any thing happening to, or acted by an individual ; and the ridiculousness of the scene is often increased by the natural insignificance of the person by whom it is occasioned. Were a government so constructed, that it could not go on unless a goose or a gander were present in the senate, the difficulties would be just as great and as real on the flight or sickness of the goose or the gander, as if they were called a king. We laugh at individuals for the silly difficulties they make to themselves, without perceiving that the greatest of all ridiculous things are acted in governments.*

All the constitutions of America are on a plan that excludes the childish embarrassments which occur in monarchical countries. No suspension of government can there

---

* It is related, that in the canton of Berne, in Switzerland, it had been customary, from time immemorial, to keep a bear at the public expense, and the people had been taught to believe, that if they had not a bear, they should all be undone. It happened some years ago, that the bear, then in being, was taken sick, and died too suddenly to have his place immediately supplied with another. During the interregnum the people discovered, that the corn grew and the vintage flourished, and the sun and moon continued to rise and set, and every thing went on the same as before, and, taking courage from these circumstances, they resolved not to keep any more bears : for, said they, " a bear is a very voracious, expensive animal, and we were obliged to pull out his claws, lest he should hurt the citizens "

The story of the bear of Berne was related in some of the French newspapers, at the time of the flight of Louis XVI. and the application of it to monarchy could not be mistaken in France ; but it seems, that the aristocracy of Berne applied it to themselves, and have since prohibited the reading of French newspapers.

take place for a moment, from any circumstance whatever. The system of representation provides for every thing, and is the only system in which nations and governments can always appear in their proper character.

As extraordinary power ought not be lodged in the hands of any individual, so ought there to be no appropriations of public money to any person beyond what his services in a state may be worth. It signifies not whether a man be called a president, a king, an emperor, a senator, or by any other name, which propriety or folly may devise, or arrogance assume ; it is only a certain service he can perform in the state ; and the service of any such individual in the routine of office, whether such office be called monarchical, presidential, senatorial, or by another name or title, can never exceed the value of ten thousand pounds a-year. All the great services that are done in the world are performed by volunteer characters, who accept no pay for them ; but the routine of office is always regulated to such a general standard of abilities as to be within the compass of numbers in every country to perform, and therefore cannot merit very extraordinary recompense. *Government*, says Swift, *is a plain thing, and fitted to the capacity of many heads.*

It is inhuman to talk of a million sterling a-year, paid out of the public taxes of any country, for the support of any individual, whilst thousands who are forced to contribute thereto are pining with want, and struggling with misery. Government does not consist in a contrast between prisons and palaces, between poverty and pomp ; it is not instituted to rob the needy of his mite, and increase the wretchedness of the wretched.—But of this part of the subject I shall speak hereafter, and confine myself at present to political observations.

When extraordinary power and extraordinary pay are allotted to any individual in a government, he becomes the centre, round which every kind of corruption generates and forms. Give to any man a million a-year, and add thereto the power of creating and disposing of places, at the expense of a country, and the liberties of that country are no longer secure. What is called the splendor of a throne, is no other than the corruption of the state. It is made up of a band of parasites, living in luxurious indolence, out of the public taxes.

When once such a vicious system is established, it becomes the guard and protection of all inferior abuses. The man who is in the receipt of a million a-year is the last person to promote a spirit of reform, lest, in the event, it should reach to himself. It is always his interest to defend inferior abuses, as so many out-works to protect the citadel; and in this species of political fortification, all the parts have such a common dependance, that it is never to be expected they will attack each other.*

Monarchy would not have continued so many ages in the world had it not been for the abuses it protects. It is the master-fraud, which shelters all others. By admitting a participation of the spoil, it makes itself friends; and when it ceases to do this, it will cease to be the idol of courtiers.

As the principle on which constitutions are now formed, rejects all hereditary pretensions to government, it also rejects all that catalogue of assumptions known by the name of prerogatives.

If there is any government where prerogatives might with apparent safety be intrusted to any individual, it is in the federal government of America. The president of the United States of America is elected only for four years. He is not only responsible in the general sense of the word, but a particular mode is laid down in the constitution for trying him. He cannot be elected under thirty-five years of age; and he must be a native of the country.

---

* It is scarcely possible to touch on any subject, that will not suggest an allusion to some corruption in governments. The simile of "*fortifications,*" unfortunately involves with it a circumstance, which is directly in point with the matter above alluded to.

Among the numerous instances of abuse which have been acted or protected by governments, ancient or modern, there is not a greater than that of quartering a man and his heirs upon the public, to be maintained at its expense.

Humanity dictates a provision for the poor—but by what right, moral or political, does any government assume to say, that the person called the duke of Richmond, shall be maintained by the public? Yet, if common report is true, not a beggar in London can purchase his wretched pittance of coal, without paying towards the civil list of the duke of Richmond. Were the whole produce of this imposition but a shilling a-year, the iniquitous principle would be still the same—but when it amounts, as it is said to do, to not less than twenty thousand pounds per ann. the enormity is too serious to be permitted to remain.—This is one of the effects of monarchy and aristocracy.

In stating this case, I am led by no personal dislike. Though I think it mean in any man to live upon the public, the vice originates in the government: and so general is it become, that whether the parties are in the ministry or in the opposition, it makes no difference; they are sure of the guarantee of each other.

In a comparison of these cases with the government of England, the difference when applied to the latter, amounts to an absurdity. In England, the person who exercises the prerogative is often a foreigner; always half a foreigner, and always married to a foreigner. He is never in full natural or political connexion with the country, is not responsible for any thing, and becomes of age at eighteen years; yet such a person is permitted to form foreign alliances, without even the knowledge of the nation; and to make war and peace without its consent.

But this is not all. Though such a person cannot dispose of the government, in the manner of a testator, he dictates the marriage connexions, which, in effect, accomplishes a great part of the same end. He cannot directly bequeath half the government to Prussia, but he can form a marriage partnership that will produce the same effect. Under such circumstances, it is happy for England that she is not situated on the continent, or she might, like Holland, fall under the dictatorship of Prussia. Holland, by marriage, is as effectually governed by Prussia, as if the old tyranny of bequeathing the government had been the means.

The presidency in America (or, as it is sometimes called, the executive) is the only office from which a foreigner is excluded; and in England it is the only one to which he is admitted. A foreigner cannot be a member of parliament, but he may be what is called a king. If there is any reason for excluding foreigners, it ought to be from those offices where most mischief can be acted, and where, by uniting every bias of interest and attachment, the trust is best secured.

But as nations proceed in the great business of forming constitutions, they will examine with more precision into the nature and business of that department which is called the executive. What the legislative and judicial departments are, every one can see; but with respect to what, in Europe, is called the executive, as distinct from those two, it is either a political superfluity or a chaos of unknown things.

Some kind of official department, to which reports shall be made from different parts of the nation, or from abroad, to be laid before the national representatives, is all that is necessary; but there is no consistency in calling this the executive; neither can it be considered in any other light than as inferior to the legislature. The sovereign authority in any country is the power of making laws, and every thing else is an official department.

Next to the arrangement of the principles and the organization of the several parts of a constitution, is the provision to be made for the support of the persons to whom the nation shall confide the administration of the constitutional powers.

A nation can have no right to the time and services of any person at his own expense, whom it may choose to employ or intrust in any department whatever; neither can any reason be given for making provision for the support of any one part of the government and not for the other.

But, admitting that the honor of being intrusted with any part of a government, is to be considered a sufficient reward, it ought to be so to every person alike. If the members of the legislature of any country are to serve at their own expense, that which is called the executive, whether monarchical, or by any other name, ought to serve in like manner. It is inconsistent to pay the one, and accept the service of the other gratis.

In America every department in the government, is decently provided for; but no one is extravagantly paid. Every member of congress, and of the state assemblies, is allowed a sufficiency for his expenses. Whereas in England, a most prodigal provision is made for the support of one part of the government, and none for the other; the consequence of which is, that the one is furnished with the means of corruption, and the other is put into the condition of being corrupted. Less than a fourth part of such expense, applied as it is in America, would remedy a great part of the corruption,

Another reform in the American constitutions, is the exploding all oaths of personality. The oath of allegiance is to the nation only. The putting any individual as a figure for a nation is improper. The happiness of a nation is the first object, and therefore the intention of an oath of allegiance ought not to be obscured by being figuratively taken, to, or in the name of, any person. The oath, called the civic oath, in France, *viz.* the "*nation, the law, and the king,*" is improper. If taken at all, it ought to be as in America, to the nation only. The law may or may not be good; but, in this place, it can have no other meaning, than as being conducive to the happiness of the nation, and therefore is included in it. The remainder of the oath is improper, on the ground that all personal oaths ought to be abolished. They are the remains of tyranny on one part, and slavery on the other; and the name of the Creator ought not to be introduced to witness the degradation of his creation; or if taken, as is already mentioned, as figurative of the nation, it is in this place redundant. But whatever apology may be made for oaths at the first establishment of a government, they ought not to be permitted afterwards. If a government requires the support of oaths, it is a sign that it is not worth supporting, and ought not to be supported. Make government what it ought to be, and it will support itself.

To conclude this part of the subject. One of the greatest improvements that has been made for the perpetual security and progress of constitutional liberty, is the provision which the new constitutions make for occasionally revising, altering and amending them.

The principle upon which Mr. Burke formed his political creed, that " *of binding and controlling posterity to the end of time, and renouncing and abdicating the rights of all posterity for ever,*" is now become too detestable to be made a subject of debate; and, therefore, I pass it over with no other notice than exposing it.

Government is but now beginning to be known. Hitherto it has been the mere exercise of power, which forbad all effectual inquiry into rights, and grounded itself wholly on possession. While the enemy of liberty was its judge, the progress of its principles must have been small indeed.

The constitutions of America, and also that of France, have either fixed a period for their revision, or laid down the mode by which improvements shall be made. It is perhaps impossible to establish any thing that combines principles with opinions and practice, which the progress of circumstances, through a length of years, will not in some measure derange, or render inconsistent; and, therefore, to prevent inconveniences accumulating, till they discourage reformations or provoke revolutions, it is best to regulate them as they occur. The rights of man are the rights of all generations of men, and cannot be monopolized by any. That which is worth following, will be followed for the sake of its worth; and it is in this that its security lies, and not in any conditions with which it may be

incumbered. When a man leaves property to his heirs,
he does not connect it with an obligation that they shall
accept it. Why then should we do otherwise with respect
to constitutions?

The best constitution that could now be devised, consistent with the condition of the present moment, may be far
short of that excellence which a few years may afford.
There is a morning of reason rising upon man, on the subject of government, that has not appeared before. As the
barbarism of the present old governments expires, the moral
condition of nations, with respect to each other, will be
changed. Man will not be brought up with the savage
idea of considering his species as enemies, because the accident of birth gave the individuals existence in countries
distinguished by different names; and as constitutions have
always some relation to external as well as to domestic circumstances, the means of benefiting by every change,
foreign or domestic, should be a part of every constitution.

We already see an alteration in the national disposition of
England and France towards each other, which, when we
look back only a few years, is itself a revolution. Who
could have foreseen, or who would have believed, that a
French national assembly would ever have been a popular
toast in England, or that a friendly alliance of the two nations should become the wish of either? It shows, that
man, were he not corrupted by governments, is naturally
the friend of man, and that human nature is not of itself
vicious. That spirit of jealousy and ferocity, which the
governments of the two countries inspired, and which they
rendered subservient to the purpose of taxation, is now
yielding to the dictates of reason, interest, and humanity.
The trade of courts is beginning to be understood, and the
affectation of mystery, with all the artificial sorcery by
which they imposed upon mankind, is on the decline. It
has received its death wound; and though it may linger, it
will expire.

Government ought to be as much open to improvement
as any thing which appertains to man, instead of which it
has been monopolized from age to age, by the most ignorant and vicious of the human race. Need we any other
proof of their wretched management, than the excess of
debts and taxes with which every nation groans, and the
quarrels into which they have precipitated the world?

Just emerging from such a barbarous condition, it is too soon to determine to what extent of improvement government may yet be carried. For what we can foresee, all Europe may form but one great republic, and man be free of the whole.

CHAPTER V.

WAYS AND MEANS OF IMPROVING THE CONDITION OF EUROPE: INTERSPERSED WITH MISCELLANEOUS OBSERVATIONS.

In contemplating a subject that embraces with equatorial magnitude the whole region of humanity, it is impossible to confine the pursuit in any one single direction. It takes ground on every character and condition that appertains to man, and blends the individual, the nation, and the world.

From a small spark, kindled in America, a flame has arisen, not to be extinguished. Without consuming, like the *ultima ratio regum*, it winds its progress from nation to nation, and conquers by a silent operation. Man finds himself changed, he scarcely perceives how. He acquires a knowledge of his rights by attending justly to his interest, and discovers in the event that the strength and powers of despotism consist wholly in the fear of resisting it, and that, in order " *to be free, it is sufficient that he wills it.*"

Having in all the preceding parts of this work endeavored to establish a system of principles as a basis on which governments ought to be erected, I shall proceed, in this, to the ways and means of rendering them into practice. But in order to introduce this part of the subject with more propriety, and stronger effect, some preliminary observations, deducible from, or connected with, those principles, are necessary.

Whatever the form or constitution of government may be, it ought to have no other object than the general happiness. When, instead of this, it operates to create and increase wretchedness in any of the parts of society, it is on a wrong system, and reformation is necessary.

Customary language has classed the condition of man under the two descriptions of civilized and uncivilized life. To the one it has ascribed felicity and affluence; to the other, hardship and want. But however our imagination may be impressed by painting and comparison, it is nevertheless true, that a great portion of mankind, in what are called civilized countries, are in a state of poverty and wretchedness far below the condition of an Indian. I speak not of one country, but of all. It is so in England, it is so all over Europe. Let us inquire into the cause.

It lies not in any natural defect in the principles of civilization, but in preventing those principles having an universal operation; the consequence of which is, a perpetual system of war and expense, that drains the country and defeats the general felicity of which civilization is capable.

All the European governments (France now excepted,) are constructed, not on the principle of universal civilization, but on the reverse of it. So far as those governments relate to each other, they are in the same condition as we conceive of savage uncivilized life; they put themselves beyond the law as well of God as of man, and are, with respect to principle and reciprocal conduct, like so many individuals in a state of nature.

The inhabitants of every country, under the civilization of laws, easily associate together; but governments being in an uncivilized state and almost continually at war, they pervert the abundance which civilized life produces, to carry on the uncivilized part to a greater extent. By thus ingrafting the barbarism of government upon the internal civilization of a country, it draws from the latter, and more especially from the poor, a great portion of those earnings which should be applied to their own subsistence and comfort. Apart from all reflections of morality and philosophy, it is a melancholy fact, that more than one fourth of the labor of mankind is annually consumed by this barbarous system.

What has served to continue this evil, is the pecuniary advantage, which all the governments of Europe have found in keeping up this state of uncivilization. It affords to them pretences for power and revenue, for which there would be neither occasion nor apology, if the circle of civilization were rendered complete. Civil government alone, or the government of laws, is not productive of pretences for many taxes; it operates at home, directly under the eye of the country, and precludes the possibility of much imposition. But when the scene is laid in the uncivilized contention of governments, the field of pretences is enlarged, and the country, being no longer a judge, is open to every imposition which governments please to act.

Not a thirtieth, scarcely a fortieth, part of the taxes which are raised in England, are either occasioned by, or applied to, the purposes of civil government. It is not difficult to see, that the whole which the actual government does in this respect, is to enact laws, and that the country administers and executes them, at its own expense, by means of magistrates, juries sessions, and assize, over and above the taxes which it pays.

In this view of the case, we have two distinct characters of government; the one, the civil government, or the government of laws, which operates at home; the other, the court or cabinet government, which operates abroad on the rude plan of uncivilized life; the one attended with little charge, the other with boundless extravagance; and so distint are the two, that if the latter were to sink, as it were by a sudden opening of the earth, and totally disappear, the former would not be deranged. It would still proceed because it is the common interest of the nation that it should, and all the means are in practice.

Revolutions, then, have for their object, a change in the moral condition of governments, and with this change the burden of public taxes will lessen, and civilization will be left to the enjoyment of that abundance, of which it is now deprived.

In contemplating the whole of this subject, I extend my views into the department of commerce. In all my publications, where the matter would admit, I have been an advocate for commerce, because I am a friend to its effects. It is a pacific system, operating to unite mankind, by rendering nations, as well as individuals, useful to each other. As to mere theoretical reformation, I have never preached it up. The most effectual process is that of improving the condition of man by means of his interest; and it is on this ground that I take my stand.

If commerce were permitted to act to the universal extent it is capable of, it would extirpate the system of war, and produce a revolution in the uncivilized state of governments. The invention of commerce has arisen since those governments began, and is the greatest approach towards universal civilization, that has yet been made by any means not immediately flowing from moral principles.

Whatever has a tendency to promote the civil intercourse of nations, by an exchange of benefits, is a subject as worthy of philosophy as of politics. Commerce is no other than the traffic of two persons, multiplied on a scale of numbers; and by the same rule that nature intended the intercourse of two, she intended that of all. For this purpose she has distributed the materials of manufactures and commerce, in various and, distant parts of a nation and of the world; and as they cannot be procured by war so cheaply or so commodiously as by commerce, she has rendered the latter the means of extirpating the former.

As the two are nearly the opposites of each other, consequently, the uncivilized state of European governments is injurious to commerce. Every kind of destruction or embarrassment serves to lessen the quantity, and it matters but little in what part of the commercial world the reduction begins. Like blood, it cannot be taken from any of the parts, without being taken from the whole mass in circulation, and all partake of the loss. When the ability in any nation to buy is destroyed, it equally involves the seller. Could the government of England destroy the commerce of all other nations, she would most effectually ruin her own.

It is possible that a nation may be the carrier for the world, but she cannot be the merchant. She cannot be the seller and the buyer of her own merchandize. The ability to buy must reside out of herself; and, therefore, the prosperity of any commercial nation is regulated by the prosperity of the rest. If they are poor, she cannot be rich; and her condition, be it what it may, is an index of the height of the commercial tide in other nations.

That the principles of commerce, and its universal operation may be understood, without understanding the practice, is a position that reason will not deny; and it is on this ground only that I argue the subject. It is one thing in the counting-house, in the world it is another. With respect to its operation, it must necessarily be contemplated as a reciprocal thing, that only one half its powers resides within the nation, and that the whole is as effectually destroyed by destroying the half that resides without, as if the destruction had been committed on that which is within, for neither can act without the other.

When in the last, as well as in former wars, the commerce of England sunk, it was because the general quantity was lessened every where; and it now rises because commerce is in a rising state in every nation. If England at this day, imports and exports more than at any other period, the nation with which she trades must necessarily do the same ; her imports are their exports, and *vice versa*.

There can be no such thing as a nation flourishing alone in commerce; she can only participate ; and the destruction of it in any part must necessarily affect all. When, therefore, governments are at war, the attack is made upon the common stock of commerce, and the consequence is the same as if each had attacked his own.

The present increase of commerce is not to be attributed to ministers, or to any political contrivances, but to its own natural operations in consequence of peace. The regular markets had been destroyed, the channels of trade broken up, and the high road of the seas infested with robbers of every nation, and the attention of the world called to other objects. Those interruptions have ceased, and peace has restored the deranged condition of things to their proper order.*

It is worth remarking, that every nation reckons the balance of trade in its own favor; and therefore something must be irregular in the common ideas upon this subject.

The fact, however, is true, according to what is called a balance ; and it is from this cause that commerce is universally supported. Every nation feels the advantage, or it would abandon the practice : but the deception lies in the mode of making up the accounts, and in attributing what are called profits to a wrong cause.

Mr. Pitt has sometimes amused himself, by showing what he called a balance of trade from the custom-house books. This mode of calculation, not only affords no rule that is true, but one that is false.

---

* In America the increase of commerce is greater in proportion than in England It is, at this time, at least one half more than at any period prior to the revolution. The greatest number of vessels cleared out of the port of Philadelphia, before the commencement of the war, was between eight and nine hundred. In the year 1788, the number was upwards of twelve hundred. As the state of Pennsylvania is estimated as an eighth part of the United States in population, the whole number of vessels must now be nearly ten thousand.

In the first place, every cargo that departs from the custom-house, appears on the books as an export; and according to the custom-house balance, the losses at sea, and
by foreign failures, are all reckoned on the side of the
profit, because they appear as exports.

Second, Because the importation by the smuggling trade
does not appear on the custom-house books, to arrange
against the exports.

No balance, therefore, as applying to superior advantages, can be drawn from these documents; and if we examine the natural operation of commerce, the idea is fallacious; and if true, would soon be injurious. The great
support of commerce consists in the balance being a level
of benefits among all nations.

Two merchants of different nations trading together, will
both become rich, and each makes the balance in his own
favor; consequently, they do not get rich out of each
other; and it is the same with respect to the nations in
which they reside. The case must be, that each nation
must get rich out of its own means, and increase that riches
by something which it procures from another in exchange.

If a merchant in England sends an article of English
manufacture abroad, which costs him a shilling at home,
and imports something which sells for two, he makes a balance of one shilling in his own favor: but this is not gained
out of the foreign nation or the foreign merchant, for he
also does the same by the article he receives, and neither
has a balance of advantage upon the other. The original
value of the two articles in their proper countries were but
two shillings; but by changing their places, they acquire
a new idea of value, equal to double what they had at first,
and that increased value is equally divided.

There is no otherwise a balance on foreign than on domestic commerce. The merchants of London and Newcastle trade on the same principle, as if they resided in
different nations, and make their balances in the same
manner: yet London does not get rich out of Newcastle,
any more than Newcastle out of London: but coals, the
merchandize of Newcastle, have an additional value at
London, and London merchandize has the same at Newcastle.

Though the principle of all commerce is the same, the
domestic, in a national view, is the part the most beneficial; because the whole of the advantages, on both sides,

rest within the nation; whereas, in foreign commerce, it is only a participation of one half.

The most unprofitable of all commerce is that connected with foreign dominion. To a few individuals it may be beneficial, merely because it is commerce; but to the nation it is a loss. The expense of maintaining dominion more than absorbs the profits of any trade. It does not increase the general quantity in the world, but operates to lessen it; and as a greater mass would be afloat by relinquishing dominion, the participation without the expense would be more valuable than a greater quantity with it.

But it is impossible to engross commerce by dominion; and therefore it is still more fallacious. It cannot exist in confined channels, and necessarily breaks out by regular or irregular means that defeat the attempt and to succeed would be still worse. France, since the revolution, has been more than indifferent as to foreign possessions; and other nations will become the same, when they investigate the subject with respect to commerce.

To the expense of dominion is to be added that of navies, and when the amount of the two is subtracted from the profits of commerce, it will appear, that what is called the balance of trade, even admitting it to exist, is not enjoyed by the nation, but absorbed by the government.

The idea of having navies for the protection of commerce, is delusive. It is putting the means of destruction for the means of protection. Commerce needs no other protection than the reciprocal interest which every nation feels in supporting it—it is common stock—it exists by a balance of advantages to all; and the only interruption it meets, is from the present uncivilized state of governments, and which is its common interest to reform.*

Quitting this subject, I now proceed to other matters.— As it is necessary to include England in the prospect of a general reformation, it is proper to inquire into the defects of its government. It is only by each nation reforming its own, that the whole can be improved, and the full benefit

---

* When I saw Mr. Pitt's mode of estimating the balance of trade, in one of his parliamentary speeches, he appeared to me to know nothing of the nature and interest of commerce: and no man has more wantonly tortured it than himself. During a period of peace, it has been shackled with the calamities of war. Three times has it been thrown into stagnation, and the vessels unmanned by impressing, within less than four years of peace.

of reformation enjoyed.   Only partial advantages can flow
from partial reforms.

France and England are the only two countries in Europe where a reformation in government could have successfully begun.   The one secure by the ocean, and the
other by the immensity of its internal strength, could defy
the malignancy of foreign despotism.   But it is with revolutions as with commerce, the advantages increase by their
becoming general, and double to either what each would
receive alone.

As a new system is now opening to the view of the
world, the European courts are plotting to counteract it.—
Alliances, contrary to all former systems, are agitating,
and a common interest of courts is forming against the
common interest of man.   The combination draws a line
that runs throughout Europe, and presents a cause so entirely new, as to exclude all calculations from former circumstances.   While despotism warred with despotism,
man had no interest in the contest; but in a cause that
unites the soldier with the citizen, and nation with nation,
the despotism of courts, though it feels the danger, and
meditates revenge is afraid to strike.

No question has arisen within the records of history that
pressed with the importance of the present.   It is not
whether this or that party shall be in or out, or whig or
tory, or high or low shall prevail; but whether man shall
inherit his rights, and universal civilization take place?—
Whether the fruits of his labor shall be enjoyed by himself, or consumed by the profligacy of governments?—
Whether robbery shall be banished from courts, and
wretchedness from countries?

When, in countries that are called civilized, we see age
going to the work-house, and youth to the gallows, something must be wrong in the system of government.   It
would seem, by the exterior appearance of such countries,
that all was happiness; but there lies hidden from the eye
of common observation, a mass of wretchedness that has
scarcely any other chance, than to expire in poverty or
infamy.   Its entrance into life is marked with the presage
of its fate; and until this is remedied, it is in vain to punish.

Civil government does not exist by executions; but in
making that provision for the instruction of youth, and the
support of age, as to exclude, as much as possible, profli-

gacy from the one, and despair from the other. Instead
of this, the resources of a country are lavished upon kings,
upon courts, upon hirelings, impostors and prostitutes; and
even the poor themselves, with all their wants upon them,
are compelled to support the fraud that oppresses them.

Why is it, that scarcely any are executed but the poor?
The fact is a proof, among other things, of a wretchedness
in their condition. Bred up without morals, and cast upon
the world without a prospect, they are the exposed sacri-
fice of vice and legal barbarity. The millions that are su-
perfluously wasted upon governments are more than sufficient to reform those evils, and to benefit the condition of
every man in a nation, not included within the purlieus of
a court. This I hope to make appear in the progress of
this work.

It is the nature of compassion to associate with misfortune. In taking up this subject I seek no recompense—I
fear no consequences. Fortified with that proud integrity,
that disdains to triumph or to yield, I will advocate the
rights of man.

At an early period, little more than sixteen years of age,
raw and adventurous, and heated with the false heroism of
a master* who had served in a man of war, I began the
carver of my own fortune, and entered on board the privateer Terrible, captain Death. From this adventure I
was happily prevented by the affectionate and moral re-
monstrance of a good father, who, from his own habits of
life, being of the Quaker profession, must have begun to
look upon me as lost. But the impression, much as it effected at the time, began to wear away, and I entered
afterwards in the privateer, King of Prussia, captain Men-
dez, and went in her to sea. Yet, from such a beginning,
and with all the inconveniences of early life against me, I
am proud to say, that with a perseverance undismayed by
difficulties, a disinterestedness that compels respect, I have
not only contributed to raise a new empire in the world,
founded on a new system of government, but I have arrived at an eminence in political literature, the most difficult
of all lines to succeed and excel in, which aristocracy,
with all its aids, has not been able to reach or to rival.

Knowing my own heart, and feeling myself, as I now do,
superior to all the skirmish of party, the inveteracy of

* Rev. William Knowles, master of the grammar school of Thetford, in
Norfolk.

interested or mistaken opponents, I answer not to falsehood or abuse, but proceed to the defects of the English government.*

* Politics and self-interest have been so uniformly connected, that the world, from being so often deceived, has a right to be suspicious of public characters: but with regard to myself, I am perfectly easy on this head. I did not, at my first setting out in public life nearly seventeen years ago, turn my thoughts to subjects of government from motives of interest—and my conduct from that moment to this, proves the fact. I saw an opportunity in which I thought I could do some good, and I followed exactly what my heart dictated. I neither read books, nor studied other people's opinions. I thought for myself. The case was this:

During the suspension of the old governments in America, both before and at the breaking out of hostilities, I was struck with the order and decorum with which every thing was conducted; and impressed with the idea, that a little more than what society naturally performed, was all the government that was necessary, and that monarchy and aristocracy were frauds and impositions upon mankind. On these principles I published the pamphlet Common Sense. The success it met with was beyond any thing since the invention of printing. I gave a copy right to every state in the union, and the demand ran to not less than one hundred thousand copies. I continued the subject in the same manner, under the title of The Crisis, till the complete establishment of the revolution.

After the declaration of independence, congress unanimously, and unknown to me, appointed me secretary in the foreign department. This was agreeable to me, because it gave me the opportunity of seeing into the abilities of foreign courts, and their manner of doing business. But a misunderstanding arising between congress and me, respecting one of their commissioners, then in Europe, Mr. Silas Deane, I resigned the office.

When the war ended I went from Philadelphia to Bordentown, on the east bank of the Delaware, where I have a small place. Congress was at this time at Princeton, fifteen miles distant; and general Washington's head-quarters were at Rocky-hill, within the neighborhood of congress, for the purpose of resigning his commission (the object for which he accepted it being accomplished) and of retiring to private life. While he was on this business, he wrote me the letter which I here subjoin.

Rocky-Hill, Sept. 10, 1783.

I have learned since I have been at this place, that you are at Bordentown. Whether for the sake of retirement or economy, I know not. Be it for either, for both, or whatever it may, if you will come to this place, and partake with me, I shall be exceedingly happy to see you.

Your presence may remind congress of your past services to this country; and if it is in my power to impress them, command my best exertions with freedom, as they will be rendered cheerfully by one, who entertains a lively sense of the importance of your works, and who, with much pleasure, subscribes himself,

Your sincere friend,

G. WASHINGTON.

During the war, in the latter end of the year 1780, I formed to myself the design of coming over to England, and communicated it to general Greene, who was then in Philadelphia, on his route to the southward, general Washington being then at too great a distance to communicate with immediately. I was strongly impressed with the idea, that if I could get over to England, without being known, and only remain in safety till I could get out a publication, I could open the eyes of the country with respect to the madness and stupidity of its government. I saw that the parties in parliament had pitted themselves as far as they could go, and could make no new impressions on each other. General Greene entered fully into my views, but the affair

I begin with charters and corporations.

It is a perversion of terms to say, that a charter gives rights. It operates by a contrary effect, that of taking rights away. Rights are inherently in all the inhabitants; but charters, by annulling those rights in the majority, leave the right by exclusion in the hands of a few. If charters were constructed so as to express in direct terms, " *that every inhabitant, who is not a member of a corporation, shall not exercise the right of voting,*" such charters would in the face be charters, not of rights, but of exclusion. The effect is the same under the form they now stand; and the only persons on whom they operate, are the persons whom they exclude. Those whose rights are guaranteed, by not being taken away, exercise no other rights, than as members of the community they are entitled to without a charter; and therefore, all charters have no other than an indirect negative operation. They do not give rights to A, but they make a difference in favor of A, by taking away the rights of B, and consequently are instruments of injustice.

But charters and corporations have a more extensive evil effect than what relates merely to elections. They are sources of endless contention in the places where they ex-

of Arnold and Andre happening just after, he changed his mind, and, under strong apprehensions for my safety, wrote to me very pressingly from Annapolis, in Maryland, to give up the design, which, with some reluctance, I did. Soon after this I accompanied colonel Laurens (son of Mr. Laurens, who was then in the Tower) to France, on business from congress. We landed at l'Orient, and while I remained there, he being gone forward, a circumstance occurred, that renewed my former design. An English packet from Falmouth to New-York, with government despatches on board, was brought into l'Orient. That a packet should be taken, is no very extraordinary thing; but that the despatches should be taken with it will scarcely be credited, as they are always slung at the cabin window, in a bag loaded with cannon ball, and ready to be sunk in a moment. The fact, however, is as I have stated it, for the despatches came into my hands, and I read them. The capture, as I was informed, succeeded by the following stratagem :—the captain of the privateer Madame, who spoke English, on coming up with the packet, passed himself for the captain of an English frigate, and invited the captain of the packet on board, which, when done, he sent some of his hands and and secured the mail. But be the circumstances of the capture what they may, I speak with certainty as to the despatches. They were sent up to Paris, to count Vergennes, and when colonel Laurens and myself returned to America, we took the originals to congress.

By these despatches I saw further into the stupidity of the English cabinet than I otherwise could have done, and I renewed my former design. But colonel Laurens was so unwilling to return alone, more especially, as among other matters, we had a charge of upwards of two hundred thousand pounds sterling in money, that I gave into his wishes, and finally gave up my plan. But I am now certain, that if I could have executed it, it would not have been altogether unsuccessful.

ist; and they lessen the common rights of national society. A native of England, under the operation of these charters and corporations, cannot be said to be an Englishman in the full sense of the word. He is not free of the nation, in the same manner that a Frenchman is free of France, and an American of America. His rights are circumscribed to the town, and, in some cases, to the parish of his birth; and in all other parts, though in his native land, he must undergo a local naturalization by purchase, or he is forbidden or expelled the place. This species of feudality is kept up to aggrandize the corporations to the ruin of the towns; and the effect is visible.

The generality of corporation towns are in a state of solitary decay, and prevented from further ruin only by some circumstances in their situation, such as a navigable river, or a plentiful surrounding country. As population is one of the chief sources of wealth, (for without it land itself has no value) every thing which operates to prevent it must lessen the value of property; and as corporations have not only this tendency, but directly this effect, they cannot but be injurious. If any policy were to be followed, instead of that of general freedom, to every person to settle where he chose, (as in France or America) it would be more consistent to give encouragement to new comers, than to preclude their admission by exacting premiums from them.*

The persons most immediately interested in the abolition of corporations, are the inhabitants of the towns where corporations are established. The instances of Manchester, Birmingham, and Sheffield, show, by contrast, the injury which those Gothic institutions are to property and commerce. A few examples may be found, such as that of London, whose natural and commercial advantages, owing to its situation on the Thames, is capable of bearing up against the political evils of a corporation; but in almost

* It is difficult to account for the origin of charter and corporation towns, unless we suppose them to have arisen out of, or having been connected with, some species of garrison services. The times in which they began justify this idea. The generality of those towns have been garrisons and the corporations were charged with the care of the gates of the towns, when no military garrison was present. Their refusing or granting admission to strangers, which has produced the custom of giving, selling and buying freedom, has more of the nature of garrison authority than civil government. Soldiers are free of all corporations throughout the nation, by the same propriety that every soldier is free of every garrison, and no other persons are. He can follow any employment, with the permission of his officers, in any corporation town throughout the nation.

all other cases the fatality is too visible to be doubted or denied.

Though the whole nation is not so directly affected by the depression of property in corporation towns as the inhabitants themselves, it partakes of the consequences. By lessening the value of property, the quantity of national commerce is curtailed. Every man is a customer in proportion to his ability; and as all parts of a nation trade with each other, whatever affects any of the parts, must necessarily communicate to the whole.

As one of the houses of the English parliament is, in a great measure, made up by elections from these corporations; and as it is unnatural that a pure stream would flow from a foul fountain, its vices are but a continuation of the vices of its origin. A man of moral honor and good political principles, cannot submit to the mean drudgery and disgraceful arts, by which such elections are carried. To be a successful candidate, he must be destitute of the qualities that constitute a just legislator: and being thus disciplined to corruption by the mode of entering into parliament, it is not to be expected that the representative should be better than the man.

Mr. Burke, in speaking of the English representation, has advanced as bold a challenge as ever was given in the days of chivalry. "Our representation," says he, "has been found *perfectly adequate to all the purposes* for which a representation of the people can be desired or devised. I defy," continues he, "the enemies of our constitution to show the contrary." This declaration from a man, who has been in constant opposition to all the measures of parliament the whole of his political life, a year or two excepted, is most extraordinary; and comparing him with himself, admits of no other alternative, than that he acted against his judgment as a member, or has declared contrary to it as an author.

But it is not in the representation only that the defects lie, and therefore I proceed in the next place to aristocracy.

What is called the house of peers, is constituted on a ground very similar to that, against which there is a law in other cases. It amounts to a combination of persons in one common interest. No reason can be given, why an house of legislation should be composed entirely of men whose occupation consists in letting landed property, than why it should be composed of those who hire, or of brewers, or bakers, or any other separate class of men.

Mr. Burke calls this house, "*the great ground and pillar of security to the landed interest.*" Let us examine this idea.

What pillar of security does the landed interest require more than any other interest in the state, or what right has it to a distinct and separate representation from the general interest of a nation? The only use to be made of this power, (and which it has always made,) is to ward off taxes from itself, and throw the burden upon such articles of consumption by which itself would be least affected.

That this has been the consequence (and will always be the consequence of constructing governments on combinations,) is evident with respect to England, from the history of its taxes.

Notwithstanding taxes have increased and multiplied upon every article of common consumption, the land-tax, which more particularly affects this "pillar," has diminished. In 1788, the amount of the land-tax was 1,950,000*l.* which is half a million less than it produced almost an hundred years ago, notwithstanding the rentals are in many instances doubled since that period.

Before the coming of the Hanoverians, the taxes were divided in nearly equal proportions between the land and articles of consumption, the land bearing rather the largest share; but since that era, nearly thirteen millions annually of new taxes have been thrown upon consumption. The consequence of which has been a constant increase in the number and wretchedness of the poor, and in the amount of the poor-rates. Yet here again the burden does not fall in equal proportions on the aristocracy with the rest of the community. Their residences, whether in town or country, are not mixed with the habitations of the poor.— They live apart from distress, and the expense of relieving it. It is in manufacturing towns and laboring villages that those burdens press the heaviest; in many of which it is one class of poor supporting another.

Several of the most heavy and productive taxes are so contrived, as to give an exemption to this pillar, thus standing in its own defence. The tax upon beer brewed for sale does not affect the aristocracy, who brew their own beer free of this duty. It falls only on those who have not conveniency or ability to brew, and who must purchase it in small quantities. But what will mankind think of the justice of taxation, when they know, that this tax alone, from which the aristocracy are from circumstances exempt, is nearly equal to the whole of the land-tax, being in the year 1788, and it is not less now, 1,666,152*l.* and with its proportion of the taxes on malt and hops, it exceeds it. That a single article, thus partially consumed, and that chiefly by the working part, should be subject to a tax, equal to that on the whole rental of a nation, is, perhaps, a fact not to be paralleled in the history of revenues.

This is one of the consequences resulting from an house of legislation, composed on the ground of a combination of common interest; for whatever their separate politics as to parties may be, in this they are united. Whether a combination acts to raise the price of any article for sale, or the rate of wages; or whether it acts to throw taxes from itself upon another class of the community, the principle and the effect are the same: and if the one be illegal, it will be difficult to show that the other ought to exist.

It is no use to say, that taxes are first proposed in the house of commons; for as the other house has always a negative, it can always defend itself; and it would be ridiculous to suppose that its acquiescence in the measures to be proposed were not understood beforehand. Besides which, it has obtained so much influence by borough-traffic, and so many of its relations and connexions are distributed on both sides of the commons, as to give it, besides an absolute negative in the house, a preponderancy in the other, in all matters of common concern.

It is difficult to discover what is meant by the *landed interest*, if it does not mean a combination of aristocratical land-holders, opposing their own pecuniary interest to that of the farmer, and every branch of trade, commerce, and manufacture. In all other respects it is the only interest that needs no partial protection. It enjoys the general protection of the world. Every individual, high or low, is interested in the fruits of the earth; men, women, and children, of all ages and degrees, will turn out to assist the farmer, rather than a harvest should not be got in; and they will not act thus by any other property. It is the only one for which the common prayer of mankind is put up, and the only one that can never fail from the want of means. It is the interest, not of the policy, but of the existence of man, and when it ceases, he must cease to be.

No other interest in a nation stands on the same united support. Commerce, manufactures, arts, sciences, and every thing else, compared with this, are supported but in parts. Their prosperity or their decay has not the same universal influence. When the vallies laugh and sing, it is not the farmer only, but all creation that rejoices. It is a prosperity that excludes all envy; and this cannot be said of any thing else.

Why then does Mr. Burke talk of his house of peers, as the pillar of the landed interest? Were that pillar to sink into the earth, the same landed property would continue, and the same ploughing, sowing, and reaping would go on. The aristocracy are not the farmers who work the land, and raise the produce, but are the mere consumers of the rent; and when compared with the active world, are the drones, a seraglio of males, who neither collect the honey nor form the hive, but exist only for lazy enjoyment.

Mr. Burke, in his first essay, called aristocracy, " *the corinthian capital of polished society*." Towards completing the figure, he has now added the *pillar ;* but still the base is wanting; and whenever a nation chooses to act a Sampson, not blind, but bold, down go the temple of Dagon, the lords and the Philistines.

If a house of legislation is to be composed of men of one class, for the purpose of protecting a distinct interest, all the other interests should have the same. The inequality as well as the burden of taxation, arises from admitting it in one case, and not in all. Had there been a house of farmers, there had been no game laws; or a house of merchants and manufacturers, the taxes had neither been so unequal nor so excessive. It is from the power of taxation being in the hands of those who can throw so great a part of it from their own shoulders, that it has raged without a check.

Men of small or moderate estates, are more injured by the taxes being thrown on articles of consumption, than they are eased by warding it from landed property, for the following reasons :

1st, They consume more of the productive taxable articles, in proportion to their property, than those of large estates.

2d, Their residence is chiefly in towns, and their property in houses; and the increase of the poor-rates, occasioned by taxes on consumption, is in much greater proportion than the land-tax has been favored. In Birmingham, the poor-rates are not less than seven shillings in the pound. From this, as is already observed, the aristocracy are in a great measure exempt.

These are but a part of the mischiefs flowing from the wretched scheme of an house of peers.

As a combination, it can always throw a considerable portion of taxes from itself; as an hereditary house, accountable to nobody, it resembles a rotten borough, whose consent is to be courted by interest. There are but few of its members, who are not in some mode or other participators, or disposers of the public money. One turns a candle-holder, or a lord in waiting; another a lord of the bedchamber, a groom of the stole, or any insignificant nominal office, to which a salary is annexed, paid out of the public taxes, and which avoids the direct appearance of corruption. Such situations are derogatory to the character of man; and where they can be submitted to, honor cannot reside.

To all these are to be added the numerous dependants, the long list of the younger branches and distant relations, who are to be provided for at the public expense: in short were an estimation to be made of the charge of the aristocracy to a nation, it will be found nearly equal to that of supporting the poor. The duke of Richmond alone (and there are cases similar to his) takes away as much for himself, as would maintain two thousand poor and aged persons. Is it, then, any wonder, that under such a system of government taxes and rates have multiplied to their present extent?

In stating these matters, I speak an open and disinterested language, dictated by no passion but that of humanity. To me, who have not only refused offers, because I thought them improper, but have declined rewards I might with reputation have accepted, it is no wonder that meanness and imposition appear disgusting. Independence is my happiness, and I view things as they are, without regard to place or person; my country is the world, and my religion is to do good.

Mr. Burke, in speaking of the aristocratical law of primogeniture, says, "It is the standing law of our landed inheritance; and which without question, has a tendency, and I think," continues, he, "a happy tendency, to preserve a character of weight and consequence."

Mr. Burke may call this law what he pleases, but humanity and impartial reflection will pronounce it a law of brutal injustice. Were we not accustomed to the daily practice, and did we only hear of it as the law of some distant part of the world, we should conclude that the legislators of such countries had not arrived at a state of civilization.

As to preserving a character of *weight and consequence,* the case appears to me directly the reverse. It is an attaint upon character; a sort of privateering on family property. It may have weight among dependant tenants, but it gives none on a scale of national, and much less of universal character. Speaking for myself, my parents were not able to give me a shilling, beyond what they gave me in education; and to do this they distressed themselves; yet, I possess more of what is called consequence, in the world, than any one in Mr. Burke's catalogue of aristocrats.

Having thus glanced at some of the defects of the two houses of parliament, I proceed to what is called the crown, upon which I shall be very concise.

It signifies a nominal office of a million sterling a-year, the business of which consists in receiving the money. Whether the person be wise or foolish, sane or insane, a native or a foreigner, matters not. Every ministry acts upon the same idea that Mr. Burke writes, namely, that the people must be hoodwinked, and held in superstitious ignorance by some bugbear or other; and what is called the crown answers this purpose, and therefore it answers all the purposes to be expected from it. This is more than can be said of the other two branches.

The hazard to which this office is exposed in all countries, is not from any thing that can happen to the man, but from what may happen to the nation; the danger of its coming to its senses.

It has been customary to call the crown the executive power, and the custom is continued, though the reason has ceased.

It was called the *executive,* because he whom it signified, used formerly to sit in the character of a judge, in administering or executing the laws. The tribunals were then a part of the court. The power, therefore, which is now called the judicial, was what is called the executive; and, consequently, one or the other of the terms is redundant, and one of the offices useless. When we speak of the crown now, it means nothing; it signifies neither a judge nor a general: besides which it is the laws that govern, and not the man. The old terms are kept up, and give an appearance of consequence to empty forms: and the only effect they have is that of increasing expenses.

Before I proceed to the means of rendering governments more conducive to the general happiness of mankind, than they are at present, it will not be improper to take a review of the progress of taxation in England.

It is a general idea, that when taxes are once laid on, they are never taken off. However true this may have been of late, it was not always so. Either, therefore, the people of former times were more watchful over government than those of the present, or government was administered with less extravagance.

It is now seven hundred years since the Norman conquest, and the establishment of what is called the crown. Taking this portion of time in seven separate periods of one hundred years each, the amount of the annual taxes, at each period will be as follows:

Annual amount of taxes levied by William the
   conqueror, beginning in the year 1066,   400,000*l*,
Annual amount of taxes at one hundred years
   from the conquest, (1166)   - - - 200,000
Annual amount of taxes at two hundred years
   from the conquest, (1266)   - - - 150,000
Annual amount of taxes at three hundred years
   from the conquest, (1366)   - - - 130,000
Annual amount of taxes at four hundred years
   from the conquest, (1466)   - - - 100,000

These statements, and those which follow, are taken from sir John Sinclair's History of the Revenue; by which it appears, that taxes continued decreasing for four hundred years, at the expiration of which time they were reduced three-fourths, *viz.* from four hundred thousand pounds to one hundred thousand. The people of England of the present day, have a traditionary and historical idea of the bravery of their ancestors; but whatever their virtues or vices might have been, they certainly were a people who would not be imposed upon, and who kept government in awe as to taxation, if not as to principle. Though they were not able to expel the monarchical usurpation, they restricted it to a public economy of taxes.

Let us now review the remaining three hundred years.
Annual amount of taxes at five hundred years
    from the conquest, (1566) - - -   500,000*l*.
Annual amount of taxes at six hundred years
    from the conquest, (1666) . - -   1,800,000
Annual amount of taxes at the present time,
    (1791) - - - - - - 17,000,000

The difference between the first four hundred years
and the last three, is so astonishing, as to warrant an opinion, that the national character of the English has changed.
It would have been impossible to have dragooned the former English into the excess of taxation that now exists; and
when it is considered that the pay of the army, the navy,
and of all the revenue-officers, is the same now as it was
above a hundred years ago, when the taxes were not above
a tenth part of what they are at present, it appears impossible to account for the enormous increase and expenditure, on any other grounds than extravagance, corruption,
and intrigue.*

---

* Several of the court newspapers have of late made frequent mention of
Wat Tyler. That his memory should be traduced by court sycophants, and
all those who live on the spoil of a public, is not to be wondered at. He was,
however, the means of checking the rage and injustice of taxation in his time,
and the nation owed much to his valor. The history is concisely this :—in
the time of Richard II. a poll-tax was levied, of one shilling per head upon
every person in the nation, of whatever class or condition, on poor as well as
rich, above the age of fifteen years. If any favor was shown in the law, it was
to the rich rather than the poor ; as no person could be charged more than
twenty shillings for himself, family and servants, though ever so numerous—
while all other families, under the number of twenty, were charged per head.
Poll-taxes had always been odious—but this being also oppressive and unjust,
it excited, as it naturally must, universal detestation among the poor and
middle classes. The person known by the name of Wat Tyler, and whose
proper name was Walter, and a tyler by trade, lived at Deptford. The gatherer of the poll-tax, on coming to his house, demanded a tax for one of his
daughters, whom Tyler declared was under the age of fifteen. The taxgatherer insisted on satisfying himself, and began an indecent examination of
the girl, which enraging the father, he struck him with a hammer, that brought
him to the ground, and was the cause of his death.

This circumstance served to bring the discontents to an issue. The inhabitants of the neighborhood espoused the cause of Tyler, who, in a few days
was joined, according to some historians, by upwards of fifty thousand men,
and chosen their chief. With this force he marched to London, to demand
an abolition of the tax, and a redress of other grievances. The court, finding
itself in a forlorn condition, and unable to make resistance, agreed, with Richard at its head, to hold a conference with Tyler in Smithfield, making many
fair professions, courtier-like, of its disposition to redress the oppressions.
While Richard and Tyler were in conversation on these matters, each being
on horseback, Walworth, then mayor of London, and one of the creatures of
the court, watched an opportunity, and like a cowardly assassin, stabbed Tyler with a dagger—and two or three others falling upon him, he was instantly
sacrificed.

With the revolution of 1688, and more so since the Hanover succession, came the destructive system of continental intrigues, and the rage for foreign wars and foreign dominion;.systems of such secure mystery, that the expenses admit of no accounts; a single line stands for millions. To what excess taxation might have extended, had not the French revolution contributed to break up the system, and put an end to pretences, is impossible to say. Viewed, as that revolution ought to be, as the fortunate means of lessening the load of taxes of both countries, it is of as much importance to England as to France; and, if properly improved to all the advantages of which it is capable, and to which it leads, deserves as much celebration in one country as the other.

In pursuing this subject, I shall begin with the matter that first presents itself, that of lessening the burden of taxes; and shall then add such matters and propositions, respecting the three countries of England, France and America, as the present prospect of things appear to justify; I mean an alliance of the three, for the purposes that will be mentioned in their proper places.

What has happened may happen again. By the statement before shown, of the progress of taxation, it is seen, that taxes have been lessened to a fourth part of what they had formerly been. Though the present circumstances do not admit of the same reduction, yet they admit of such a beginning, as may accomplish that end in a less time, than in the former case.

The amount of taxes for the year, ending at Michaelmas, 1778, was as follows:

Land tax - - - -	1,950,000*l.*
Customs - - - -	3,789,274
Excise (including old and new malt)	6,751,727
Stamps - - - -	1,278,214
Miscellaneous taxes and incidents	1,803,755
	15,572,970*l.*

Tyler appears to have been an intrepid, disinterested man, with respect to himself. All his proposals made to Richard, were on a more just and public ground, than those which had been made to John by the barons; and notwithstanding the sycophancy of historians, and men like Mr. Burke, who seek to gloss over a base action of the court by traducing Tyler, his fame will outlive their falsehood. If the barons merited a monument to be erected in Runneymede, Tyler merits one in Smithfield.

Since the year 1788, upwards of one million, new taxes have been laid on, besides the produce of the lotteries; and as the taxes have in general been more productive since than before, the amount may be taken, in round numbers, at 17,000,000*l.*

N. B. The expense of collection and the drawbacks, which together amount to nearly two millions, are paid out of the gross amount; and the above is the net sum paid into the exchequer.

The sum of seventeen millions is applied to two different purposes; the one to pay the interest of the national debt, the other to pay the current expenses of each year. About nine millions are appropriated to the former; and the remainder, being nearly eight millions, to the latter. As to the million, said to be applied to the reduction of the debt, it is so much like paying with one hand and taking out with the other, as not to merit much notice.

It happened, fortunately for France, that she possessed national domains for paying off her debt, and thereby lessening her taxes; but as this is not the case in England, her reduction of taxes can only take place by reducing the current expenses, which may now be done to the amount of four or five millions annually, as will hereafter appear. When this is accomplished, it will more than counterbalance the enormous charge of the American war; and the saving will be from the same sources from whence the evil arose.

As to the national debt, however heavy the interest may be in taxes, yet, as it seems to keep alive a capital, useful to commerce, it balances by its effects a considerable part of its own weight; and as the quantity of gold and silver in England is, by some means or other, short of its proper proportion,* (being not more than twenty millions, whereas it should be sixty) it would, besides the injustice, be bad policy to extinguish a capital that serves to supply that defect. But with respect to the current expense, whatever is saved therefrom is gain. The excess may serve to keep corruption alive, but it has no reaction on credit and commerce, like the interest of the debt.

It is now very probable, that the English government (I do not mean the nation) is unfriendly to the French revo-

---

* Foreign intrigues, foreign wars, and foreign dominions, will in a great measure account for the deficiency.

lution. Whatever serves to expose the intrigue and lessen the influence of courts, by lessening taxation, will be un-welcome to those who feed upon the spoil. Whilst the clamor of French intrigue, arbitrary power, popery, and wooden shoes could be kept up, the nations were easily allured and alarmed into taxes. Those days are now past; deception, it is to be hoped, has reaped its last harvest, and better times are in prospect for both countries, and for the world.

Taking it for granted, that an alliance may be formed between England, France, and America, for the purposes hereafter to be mentioned, the national expenses of France and England may consequently be lessened. The same fleets and armies will no longer be necessary to either, and the reduction can be made ship for ship on each side. But to accomplish these objects, the governments must neces-sarily be fitted to a common correspondent principle. Confidence can never take place, while an hostile disposi-tion remains in either, or where mystery and secrecy on one side, is opposed to candor and openness on the other.

These matters admitted, the national expenses might be put back, *for the sake of a precedent*, to what they were at some period when France and England were not enemies. This, consequently, must be prior to the Hanover succes-sion, and also to the revolution of 1688.* The first in-stance that presents itself, antecedent to those dates, is in the very wasteful and profligate time of Charles II. at which time England and France acted as allies. If I have chosen a period of great extravagance, it will serve to show modern extravagance in a still worse light; espec-ially as the pay of the navy, the army, and the revenue-officers has not increased since that time.

* I happened to be in England at the celebration of the centenary of the revolution of 1688. The characters of William and Mary have always ap-peared to me detestable; the one seeking to destroy his uncle, and the other her father, to get possession of power themselves : yet, as the nation was dis-posed to think something of that event, I felt hurt at seeing it ascribe the whole reputation of it to a man who had undertaken it as a job, and who, be-sides what he otherwise got, charged six hundred thousand pounds for the expense of the little fleet that brought him from Holland. George I. acted the same close-fisted part as William had done, and bought the duchy of Bre-men with the money he got from England, two hundred and fifty thousand pounds over and above his pay as king ; and having thus purchased it at the expense of England, added it to his Hanoverian dominions for his own pri-vate benefit. In fact every nation that does not govern itself, is governed as a job. England has been the prey of jobs ever since the revolution.

The peace establishment was then as follows: See sir John Sinclair's History of the Revenue.

Navy	-	-	-	300,000*l.*
Army	-	-	-	212,000
Ordnance	-	-	-	40,000
Civil List	-	-	-	462,115

                            1,014,115*l.*

The parliament, however, settled the whole annual peace establishment at 1,200,000.* If we go back to the time of Elizabeth, the amount of all the taxes was but half a million, yet the nation sees nothing during that period, that reproaches it with want of consequence.

All circumstances then taken together, arising from the French revolution, from the approaching harmony and reciprocal interest of the two nations, the abolition of court intrigue on both sides, and the progress of knowledge in the science of government, the annual expenditure might be put back to one million and a half, *viz.*

Navy	-	-	-	500,000*l.*
Army	-	-	-	500,000
Expenses of government				500,000

                            1,500,000*l.*

Even this sum is six times greater than the expenses of government are in America, yet the civil internal government of England (I mean that administered by means of quarter sessions, juries, and assize, and which, in fact, is nearly the whole, and is performed by the nation,) is less expense upon the revenue, than the same species and portion of government is in America.

It is time that nations should be rational, and not be governed like animals for the pleasure of their riders. To read the history of kings, a man would be almost inclined to suppose that government consisted in stag-hunting, and that every nation paid a million a-year to the huntsman. Man ought to have pride, or shame enough to blush at being thus imposed upon, and when he feels his proper character, he will. Upon all subjects of this nature, there is often passing in the mind a train of ideas he has not yet

---

* Charles, like his predecessors and successors, finding that war was the harvest of governments, engaged in a war with the Dutch, the expense of which increased the annual expenditure to 1,800,000*l.* as stated under the date of 1666; but the peace establishment was but 1,200,000*l.*

accustomed himself to encourage and communicate. Restrained by something that puts on the character of prudence, he acts the hypocrite to himself as well as to others. It is, however, curious to observe how soon this spell can be dissolved. A single expression, boldly conceived and uttered, will sometimes put a whole company into their proper feelings, and whole nations are acted upon in the same manner.

As to the offices of which any civil government may be composed, it matters but little by what names they are described. In the routine of business, as before observed, whether a man be styled a president, a king, an emperor, a senator, or any thing else, it is impossible that any service he can perform, can merit from a nation more than ten thousand pounds a-year; and as no man should be paid beyond his services, so every man of a proper heart will not accept more. Public money ought to be touched with the most scrupulous consciousness of honor. It is not the produce of riches only, but of the hard earnings of labor and poverty. It is drawn even from the bitterness of want and misery. Not a beggar passes, or perishes in the streets, whose mite is not in that mass.

Were it possible that the congress of America, could be so lost to their duty, and to the interest of their constituents, as to offer general Washington, as president of America, a million a-year, he would not, and he could not, accept it. His sense of honor is of another kind. It has cost England almost seventy millions sterling, to maintain a family imported from abroad, of very inferior capacity to thousands in the nation ; and scarcely a year has passed that has not produced some mercenary application. Even the physicians' bills have been sent to the public to be paid. No wonder that jails are crowded, and taxes and poor-rates increased. Under such systems, nothing is to be looked for but what has already happened ; and as to reformation, whenever it comes, it must be from the nation, and not from the government.

To show that the sum of five hundred thousand pounds is more than sufficient to defray all the expenses of government, exclusive of navies and armies, the following estimate is added for any country, of the same extent as England.

In the first place three hundred representatives, fairly elected, are sufficient for all the purposes to which legislation can apply, and preferable to a larger number. They may be divided into two, or three houses, or meet in one, as in France, or in any manner a constitution shall direct.

As representation is always considered, in free countries, as the most honorable of all stations, the allowance made to it is merely to defray the expense which the representatives incur by that service, and not to it as an office.

If an allowance, at the rate of five hundred pounds per annum be made to every representative, deducting for non-attendance, the expense, if the whole number attended for six months each year would be	75,000*l*.
The official departments cannot reasonably exceed the following number, with the salaries annexed:	
Three offices, at ten thousand pounds each	30,000
Ten ditto, at five thousand pounds each	50,000
Twenty ditto, at two thousand pounds each	40,000
Forty ditto, at one thousand pounds each	40,000
Two hundred do. at five hundred pounds each	100,000
Three hundred ditto, at two hundred pounds each - - - - - -	60,000
Five hundred ditto, at one hundred pounds each - - - - - -	50,000
Seven hundred ditto, at seventy-five pounds each - - - - - -	52,500
	497,500*l*.

If a nation chooses, it can deduct four per cent. from all offices, and make one of twenty thousand per annum.

All revenue-officers are paid out of the monies they collect and therefore, are not included in this estimation.

The foregoing is not offered as an exact detail of offices, but to show the number and rate of salaries which five hundred thousand pounds will support; and it will, on experience, be found impracticable to find business sufficient to justify even this expense. As to the manner in which office-business is now performed, the chiefs, in several offices, such as the post-office, and certain offices in the exchequer, &c. do little more than sign their names three or four times a year; and the whole duty is performed by under clerks.

Taking, therefore, one million and an half as a sufficient peace establishment for all the honest purposes of government, which is three hundred thousand pounds more than the peace establishment in the profligate and prodigal times of Charles II. (notwithstanding, as has been already observed, the pay and salaries of the army, navy, and rev-nue-officers, continue the same as at that period,) there will remain a surplus of upwards of six millions out of the present current expenses. The question then will be, how to dispose of this surplus.

Whoever has observed the manner in which trade and taxes twist themselves together, must be sensible of the impossibility of separating them suddenly.

1st, Because the articles now on hand are already charged with the duty, and the reduction cannot take place on the present stock.

2d. Because, on all those articles on which the duty is charged in the gross, such as per barrel, hogshead, hundred weight, or ton, the abolition of the duty does not admit of being divided down so as fully to relieve the consumer, who purchases by the pint, or the pound. The last duty laid on strong beer and ale, was three shillings per barrel, which, if taken off, would lessen the purchase only half a farthing per pint, and consequently, would not reach to practical relief.

This being the condition of a greater part of the taxes, it will be necessary to look for such others as are free from this embarrassment, and where the relief will be direct and visible, and capable of immediate operation.

In the first place, then, the poor-rates are a direct tax which every housekeeper feels, and who knows also, to a farthing, the sum which he pays. The national amount of the whole of the poor-rates is not positively known, but can be procured. Sir John Sinclair, in his History of the Revenue, has stated it at 2,100,587*l.* A considerable part of which is expended in litigations, in which the poor, instead of being relieved, are tormented. The expense, however, is the same to the parish from whatever cause it arises.

In Birmingham, the amount of the poor-rates is fourteen thousand pounds a-year. This, though a large sum, is moderate, compared with the population. Birmingham is said to contain seventy thousand souls, and on a proportion of seventy thousand to fourteen thousand pounds poor-rates, the national amount of poor-rates, taking the population of England at seven millions, would be but one million four hundred thousand pounds. It is, therefore, most probable, that the population of Birmingham is over-rated. Fourteen thousand pounds is the proportion upon fifty thousand souls, taking two millions of poor-rates as the national amount.

Be it, however, what it may, it is no other than the consequence of the excessive burden of taxes, for, at the time when the taxes were very low, the poor were able to maintain themselves; and there were no poor-rates.* In the present state of things, a laboring man, with a wife and two or three children, does not pay less than between seven and eight pounds a year in taxes. He is not sensible of this, because it is disguised to him in the articles which he buys, and he thinks only of their dearness; but as the taxes take from him, at least, a fourth part of his yearly earnings, he is consequently disabled from providing for a family, especially if himself, or any of them, are afflicted with sickness.

The first step, therefore, of practical relief would be to abolish the poor-rates entirely, and in lieu thereof, to make a remission of taxes to the poor to double the amount of the present poor-rates, *viz.* four millions annually out of the surplus taxes. By this measure, the poor would be benefited two millions, and the housekeepers two millions. This alone would be equal to a reduction of one hundred and twenty millions of the national debt, and consequently equal to the whole expense of the American war.

It will then remain to be considered which is the most effectual mode of distributing the remission of four millions.

It is easily seen, that the poor are generally composed of large families of children, and old people unable to labor. If these two classes are provided for, the remedy will so far reach to the full extent of the case, that what remains will be incidental, and, in a great measure, fall within the compass of benefit clubs, which though of humble invention, merit to be ranked amongst the best of modern institutions.

Admitting England to contain seven millions of souls; if one fifth thereof are of that class of poor which need support, the number will be one million four hundred thousand. Of this number, one hundred and forty thousand

---

* Poor-rates began about the time of Henry VIII. when the taxes began to increase, and they have increased as the taxes increased ever since.

will be aged poor, as will be hereafter shown, and for which a distinct provision will be proposed.

There will then remain one million two hundred and sixty thousand, which, at five souls to each family, amount to two hundred and fifty-two thousand families, rendered poor from the expense of children and the weight of taxes.

The number of children under fourteen years of age, in each of those families, will be found to be five to every two families; some having two, others three; some one, and others four; some none, and others five; but it rarely happens that more than five are under fourteen years of age, and after this age they are capable of service, or of being apprenticed.

Allowing five children (under fourteen years) to every two families.

The number of children will be   630,000
The number of parents, were they all living, would be   504,000

It is certain that if the children are provided for, the parents are relieved of consequence, because it is from the expense of bringing up children that their poverty arises.

Having thus ascertained the greatest number that can be supposed to need support on account of young families, I proceed to the mode of relief, or distribution which is,

To pay as a remission of taxes to every poor family, out of the surplus taxes, and in room of poor-rates, four pounds a-year for every child under fourteen years of age ; enjoining the parents of such children to send them to school, to learn reading, writing, and common arithmetic ; the ministers of every parish, of every denomination, to certify jointly to an office, for this purpose, that the duty is performed.

The amount of this expense will be, for six hundred and thirty thousand children, at 4l. each per ann.   2,520,000l.

By adopting this method, not only the poverty of the parents will be relieved, but ignorance will be banished from the rising generation, and the number of poor will hereafter become less, because their abilities, by the aid of education, will be greater. Many a youth, with good natural genius, who is apprenticed to a mechanical trade, such as a carpenter, wheelwright, blacksmith, &c. is prevented getting forward the whole of his life, from the want of a little common education when a boy.

I now proceed to the case of the aged.

I divide age into two classes. 1st, the approach of old age, beginning at fifty: 2d, old age commencing at sixty.

At fifty, though the mental faculties of man are in full vigor, and his judgment better than at any preceding date, the bodily powers are on the decline. He cannot bear the same quantity of fatigue as at an earlier period. He begins to earn less, and is less capable of enduring the wind and weather; and in those retired employments where much sight is required, he fails apace, and feels himself like an old horse, beginning to be turned adrift.

At sixty, his labor ought to be over, at least from direct necessity. It is painful to see old age working itself to death, in what are called civilized countries, for its daily bread.

To form some judgment of the number of those above fifty years of age, I have several times counted the persons I met in the streets of London, men, women, and children, and have generally found that the average is about one in sixteen or seventeen. If it be said that aged persons do not come much into the streets, so neither do infants; and a great proportion of grown children are in schools, and in the work-shops as apprentices. Taking then sixteen for a divisor, the whole number of persons, in England, of fifty years and upwards, of both sexes, rich and poor, will be four hundred and twenty thousand.

The persons to be provided for out of this gross number will be, husbandmen, common laborers, journeymen of every trade and their wives, sailors, and disbanded soldiers, worn out servants of both sexes, and poor widows.

There will be also a considerable number of middling tradesmen, who, having lived decently in the former part of life, begin, as age approaches, to lose their business, and at last fall into decay.

Besides these, there will be constantly thrown off from the revolutions of that wheel, which no man can stop, nor regulate, a number from every class of life connected with commerce and adventure.

To provide for all those accidents, and whatever else may befal, I take the number of persons, who at one time or other of their lives, after fifty years of age, may feel it necessary or comfortable to be better supported, than they can support themselves, and that not as a matter of grace and favor, but of right, at one third of the whole number; which is one hundred and forty thousand, as stated p. 228, and for whom a distinct provision was proposed to be made. If there be more, society, notwithstanding the show and pomposity of government, is in a deplorable condition in England.

Of this one hundred and forty thousand, I take one half, seventy thousand, to be of the age of fifty and under sixty, and the other half to be sixty years and upwards.—Having thus ascertained the probable proportion of the number of aged persons, I proceed to the mode of rendering their condition comfortable, which is,

To pay to every such person of the age of fifty years, and until he shall arrive at the age of sixty, the sum of six pounds per ann. out of the surplus taxes; and ten pounds per ann. during life, after the age of sixty. The expense of which will be,

Seventy thousand persons at   6*l.* per ann.   420,000*l.*
Seventy thousand persons at 10   per ann.   700,000

                                                1,120,000*l.*

This support as already remarked, is not of the nature of charity, but of a right. Every person in England, male and female, pays on an average in taxes, two pounds eight shillings and sixpence per ann. from the day of his (or her) birth ; and if the expense of collection be added, he pays two pounds eleven shillings and sixpence ; consequently, at the end of fifty years he has paid one hundred and twenty-eight pounds fifteen shillings ; and at sixty, one hundred and fifty-four pounds ten shillings. Converting, therefore, his (or her) individual tax into a tontine, the money he shall receive after fifty years, is but little more than the legal interest of the net money he has paid ; the rest is made up from those whose circumstances do not require them to draw such support, and the capital in both cases defrays the expenses of government. It is on this ground that I have extended the probable claims to one third of the number of aged persons in the nation.—Is it then better that the lives of one hundred and forty thousand aged persons be rendered comfortable, or that a million a-year of public money be expended on any one individual and he often of the most worthless and insignificant character ? Let reason and justice, let honor and humanity, let even hypocrisy, sycophancy and Mr. Burke, let George, let Louis, Leopold, Frederic, Catherine, Cornwallis, or Tippoo Saib, answer the question.*

The sum thus remitted to the poor will be,

To two hundred and fifty-two thousand poor families, containing six hundred and thirty thousand children, - - - -	2,520,000*l.*
To one hundred and forty thousand aged persons, - - - - - -	1,120,000
	3,640,000*l.*

There will then remain three hundred and sixty thousand pounds out of the four millions, part of which may be applied as follows:

After all the above cases are provided for, there will still be a number of families who, though not properly of the class of poor, yet find it difficult to give education to their children; and such children, under such a case, would be in a worse condition than if their parents were actually poor. A nation under a well regulated government, should permit none to remain uninstructed. It is monarchical and aristocratical governments only that require ignorance for their support.

Suppose then four hundred thousand children to be in this condition, which is a greater number than ought to be supposed, after the provisions already made, the method will be,

To allow for each of those children ten shillings a-year for the expense of schooling, for six years each, which will give them six months schooling each year, and half a crown a-year for paper and spelling books.

---

* Reckoning the taxes by families, five to a family, each family pays on an average, 12*l.* 17*s.* and 6*d.* per ann. to this sum are to be added the poor-rates. Though all pay taxes in the articles they consume, all do not pay poor-rates. About two millions are exempted, some as not being housekeepers, others as not being able, and the poor themselves who receive the relief. The average, therefore of poor-rates on the remaining number, is forty shillings for every family of five persons, which makes the whole average amount of taxes and rates, 14*l.* 17*s.* 6*d.* for six persons, 17*l.* 17*s.*—for seven persons, 20*l.* 16*s.* 6*d.*

The average of taxes in America, under the new or representative system of government, including the interest of the debt contracted in the war, and taking the population at four millions of souls, which it now amounts to, and is daily increasing, is five shillings per head, men, women, and children. The difference, therefore, between the two governments, is as under,

	England.			America.		
For a family of five persons	14*l.*	17*s*	6*d.*	1*l.*	5*s.*	0*d.*
For a family of six persons	17	17	0	1	10	0
For a family of seven persons	20	16	6	1	15	0

The expense of this will be annually* 250,000*l*.

There will then remain one hundred and ten thousand pounds.

Notwithstanding the great modes of relief which the best instituted and best principled government may devise, there will still be a number of smaller cases, which it is good policy as well as beneficence in a nation to consider.

Were twenty shillings to be given to every woman immediately on the birth of a child, who should make the demand, and none will make it whose circumstances do not require it, it might relieve a great deal of instant distress.

There are about two hundred thousand births yearly in England; and if claimed by one fourth,

The amount would be   -   -   -   -   50,000*l*.

And twenty shillings to every new married couple who should claim in like manner. This would not exceed the sum of   -   -   -   -   -   -   20,000*l*.

Also twenty thousand pounds to be appropriated to defray the funeral expenses of persons, who, travelling for work, may die at a distance from their friends. By relieving parishes from this charge, the sick stranger will be better treated.

I shall finish this part of my subject with a plan adapted to the particular condition of a metropolis, such as London.

Cases are continually occurring in a metropolis different from those which occur in the country, and for which a different, or rather an additional mode, of relief is necessary. In the country, even in large towns, people have a knowledge of each other, and distress never rises to that extreme height it sometimes does in a metropolis. There is no such thing in the country as persons, in the literal sense of the word, starved to death, or dying with cold

---

* Public schools do not answer the general purpose of the poor. They are chiefly in corporation-towns, from which the country towns and villages are excluded—or if admitted the distance occasions a great loss of time. Education, to be useful to the poor, should be on the spot—and the best method, I believe, to accomplish this, is to enable the parents to pay the expense themselves. There are always persons of both sexes to be found in every village, especially when growing into years, capable of such an undertaking. Twenty children, at ten shillings each (and that not more than six months in each year,) would be as much as some livings amount to in the remote parts of England—and there are often distressed clergymen's widows to whom such an income would be acceptable. Whatever is given on this account to children answers two purposes, to them it is education, to those who educate them it is a livelihood.

from the want of a lodging. Yet such cases, and others equally as miserable, happen in London.

Many a youth comes up to London full of expectations, and little or no money, and unless he gets employment he is already half undone ; and boys bred up in London without any means of a livelihood, and as it often happens, of dissolute parents, are in a still worse condition, and servants long out of place are not much better off. In short, a world of little cases are continually arising, which busy or affluent life knows not of, to open the first door to distress. Hunger is not among the postponable wants, and a day, even a few hours, in such a condition, is often the crisis of a life of ruin.

These circumstances, which are the general cause of the little thefts and pilferings that lead to greater, may be prevented. There yet remain twenty thousand pounds out of the four millions of surplus taxes, which with another fund hereafter to be mentioned, amounting to about twenty thousand pounds more, cannot be better applied than to this purpose. The plan then will be,

1st, To erect two or more buildings, or take some already erected, capable of containing at least six thousand persons, and to have in each of these places as many kinds of employment as can be contrived, so that every person who shall come may find something which he or she can do.

2d. To receive all who shall come, without inquiring who or what they are. The only condition to be, that for so much, or so many hours work, each person shall receive so many meals of wholesome food, and a warm lodging, at least as good as a barrack. That a certain portion of what each person's work shall be worth shall be reserved, and given to him, or her, on their going away ; and that each person shall stay as long, or as short time, or come as often as he choose, on these conditions.

If each person staid three months, it would assist by rotation twenty-four thousand persons annually, though the real number, at all times, would be but six thousand. By establishing an asylum of this kind, such persons to whom temporary distresses occur, would have an opportunity to recruit themselves, and be enabled to look out for better employment.

Allowing that their labor paid but one half the expense of supporting them, after reserving a portion of their earnings for themselves, the sum of forty thousand pounds additional would defray all other charges for even a greater number than six thousand.

The fund very properly convertible to this purpose, in addition to the twenty thousand pounds, remaining of the former fund, will be the produce of the tax upon coals, and so iniquitously and wantonly applied to the support of the duke of Richmond. It is horrid that any man, more especially at the price coals now are, should live on the distresses of a community ; and any government permitting such an abuse deserves to be dissolved. This fund is said to be about twenty thousand pounds per annum.

I shall now conclude this plan with enumerating the several particulars, and then proceed to other matters.

The enumeration is as follows :

1st, Abolition of two millions poor rates.

2d, Provision for two hundred and fifty-two thousand poor families.

3d, Education for one million and thirty thousand children.

4th, Comfortable provision for one hundred and forty thousand aged persons.

5th, Donation of twenty shillings each for fifty thousand births.

6th, Donation of twenty shillings each for twenty thousand marriages.

7th, Allowance of twenty thousand pounds for the funeral expenses of persons travelling for work, and dying at a distance from their friends.

8th. Employment, at all times, for the casual poor in the cities of London and Westminster.

By the operation of this plan, the poor laws, those instruments of civil torture, will be superseded, and the wasteful expense of litigation prevented. The hearts of the humane will not be shocked by ragged and hungry children, and persons of seventy and eighty years of age begging for bread. The dying poor will not be dragged from place to place to breath their last, as a reprisal of parish upon parish. Widows will have a maintenance for their children, and not be carted away, on the death of their husbands, like culprits and criminals ; and children will no longer be considered as increasing the distresses of their parents. The haunts of the wretched will be known, because it will be to their advantage ; and the number of petty crimes, the offspring of distress and poverty, will be lessened.

The poor, as well as the rich, will then be interested in the support of government, and the cause and appre-hension of riots and tumults will cease. Ye who sit in ease, and solace yourselves in plenty, and such there are in Turkey and Russia, as well as in England, and who say to yourselves, "are we not well off," have ye thought of these things? When ye do, ye will cease to speak and feel for yourselves alone.

The plan is easy in practice. It does not embarrass trade by a sudden interruption in the order of taxes, but effects the relief by changing the application of them; and the money necessary for the purpose can be drawn from the excise collections, which are made eight times a-year in every market town in England.

Having now arranged and concluded this subject, I pro-ceed to the next.

Taking the present current expenses at seven millions and an half, which is the least amount they are now at, there will remain (after the sum of one million and an half be taken for the new current expenses, and four millions for the beforementioned service) the sum of two millions, part of which to be applied as follows:

Though fleets and armies, by an alliance with France, will, in a great measure, become useless, yet the persons who have devoted themselves to those services, and have thereby unfitted themselves for other lines of life, are not to be sufferers by the means that make others happy.—They are a different description of men to those who form or hang about a court.

A part of the army will remain at least for some years, and also of the navy, for which a provision is already made in the former part of this plan of one million, which is al-most half a million more than the peace establishment of the army and navy in the prodigal times of Charles II.

Suppose then fifteen thousand soldiers to be disbanded, and to allow to each of those men three shillings a week during life, clear of all deductions, to be paid in the same manner as the Chelsea college pensioners are paid, and for them to return to their trades and their friends; and also to add fifteen thousand sixpences per week to the pay of the soldiers who shall remain; the annual expense will be,

To the pay of fifteen thousand disbanded soldiers, at three shillings per week,   -   117,000*l.*
Additional pay to the remaining soldiers,   19,500
Suppose that the pay to the officers of the disbanded corps be of the same amount as the
sum allowed to the men   -   -   117,000
                                                          ———————
                                                          253,500*l.*
To prevent bulky estimations, admit the same
sum to the disbanded navy as to the army,
and the same increase of pay   -   253,500*l.*
                                                          ———————
                              Total,   507,000*l.*

Every year some part of this sum of half a million (I
omit the odd seven thousand pounds, for the purpose of
keeping the account unembarrassed) will fall in, and the
whole of it in time, as it is on the ground of life annuities,
except the increased pay of thirty-nine thousand pounds.
As it falls in, a part of the taxes may be taken off; for instance, when thirty thousand pounds fall in, the duty on
hops may be wholly taken off; and as other parts fall in,
the duties on candles and soap may be lessened, till at last
they will totally cease.

There now remains at least one million and an half of
surplus taxes.

The tax on houses and windows is one of those direct
taxes, which, like the poor-rates, is not confounded with
trade; and when taken off, the relief will be instantly felt.
This tax falls heavy on the middle class of people,

The amount of this tax by the returns of 1788,

	l.	*s.*	*d.*
was,			
Houses and windows by the act of 1766	385,459	11	7
do. do. by the act of 1779	130,739	14	5½
Total,	516,199	6	0½

If this tax be struck off, there will then remain about
one million of surplus taxes, and as it is always proper to
keep a sum in reserve, for incidental matters, it may be
best not to extend reductions further, in the first instance,
but to consider what may be accomplished by other modes
of reform.

Among the taxes most heavily felt is the commutation
tax. I shall, therefore, offer a plan for its abolition, by

substituting another in its place, which will effect three objects at once :

1st, That of removing the burden to where it can best be borne.

2d, Restoring justice among families by a distribution of property.

3d. Extirpating the overgrown influence arising from the unnatural law of primogeniture, and which is one of the principal sources of corruption at elections.

The amount of the commutation tax by the returns of 1788, was,   -   -   -   771,657*l.*

When taxes are proposed, the country is amused by the plausible language of taxing luxuries. One thing is called a luxury at one time, and something else at another; but the real luxury does not consist in the article, but in the means of procuring it, and this is always kept out of sight.

I know not why any plant or herb of the field should be a greater luxury in one country than another, but an overgrown estate in either is a luxury at all times, and as such is the proper object of taxation. It is, therefore, right to take those kind tax-making gentlemen up on their own word, and argue on the principle themselves have laid down, that of *taxing luxuries.* If they, or their champion, Mr. Burke, who, I fear, is growing out of date like the man in armor, can prove that an estate of twenty, thirty or forty thousand pounds a-year is not a luxury, I will give up the argument.

Admitting that any annual sum, say, for instance, one thousand pounds, is necessary or sufficient for the support of a family, consequently the second thousand is of the nature of a luxury, the third still more so, and by proceeding on, we shall at last arrive at a sum that may not improperly be called a prohibitable luxury. It would be impolitic to set bounds to property acquired by industry, and therefore it is right to place the prohibition beyond the probable acquisition to which industry can extend; but there ought to be a limit to property, or the accumulation of it by bequest. It should pass in some other line. The richest in every nation have poor relations, and those often very near in consanguinity.

The following table of progressive taxation is constructed on the above principles, and as a substitute for the commutation tax. It will reach the point of prohibition by a

regular operation, and thereby supersede the aristocratical law of primogeniture.

TABLE I.

A tax on all estates of the clear yearly value of fifty
pounds, after deducting the land tax, and up

To 500l.	-	-	-	-	0	3d.	per pound
From 500 to 1000		-	-	0	6	"	"
On the 2d thousand		-	-	0	9	"	"
On the 3d ditto	-	-	-	1s.	0	"	"
On the 4th ditto	-	-	-	1	6	"	"

And so on, adding 1s. per pound on every additional thousand.

At the twenty-third thousand the tax becomes twenty
shillings in the pound, and consequently every thousand
beyond that sum can produce no profit but by dividing the
estate. Yet formidable as this tax appears, it will not, I
believe, produce so much as the commutation tax; should
it produce more, it ought to be lowered to that amount
upon estates under two or three thousand a-year.

On small and middling estates it is lighter (as it is intended to be) than the commutation tax. It is not till after
seven or eight thousand a-year, that it begins to be heavy.
The object is not so much the produce of the tax as the
justice of the measure. The aristocracy has screened itself too much, and this serves to restore a part of the lost
equilibrium.

As an instance of its screening itself, it is only necessary
to look back to the first establishment of the excise laws,
at what is called the revolution, or the coming of Charles
II. The aristocratical interest then in power, commuted
the feudal services itself was under, by laying a tax on
beer brewed for *sale;* that is, they compounded with
Charles for an exemption from those services for themselves and their heirs, by a tax to be paid by other people.
The aristocracy do not purchase beer brewed for sale, but
brew their own beer free of the duty, and if any commutation at that time was necessary, it ought to have been at
the expense of those for whom the exemptions from those
services were intended;* instead of which it was thrown
on an entire different class of men.

* The tax on beer brewed for sale, from which the aristocracy are exempt
is almost one million more than the present commutation tax, being by the

But the chief object of this progressive tax (besides the justice of rendering taxes more equal than they are) is, as already stated, to extirpate the overgrown influence arising from the unnatural law of primogeniture, and which is one of the principle sources of corruption at elections.

It would be attended with no good consequences to inquire how such vast estates as thirty, forty, or fifty thousand a-year could commence, and that at a time when commerce and manufactures were not in a state to admit of such acquisitions. Let it be sufficient to remedy the evil by putting them in a condition of descending again to the community by the quiet means of apportioning them among all the heirs and heiresses of those families. This will be the more necessary because hitherto the aristocracy have quartered their younger children and connexions upon the public, in useless posts, places, and offices, which when abolished will leave them destitute, unless the law of primogeniture be also abolished or superseded.

A progressive tax will in a great measure, effect this object, and that as a matter of interest to the parties most immediately concerned, as will be seen by the following table; which shows the nett produce upon every estate, after subtracting the tax. By this it will appear, that after an estate exceeds thirteen or fourteen thousand a-year, the remainder produces but little profit to the holder, and consequently, will either pass to the younger children, or to other kindred.

returns of 1788, 1,666,152*l.*—and consequently they ought to take on themselves the amount of the commutation tax, as they are already exempted from one which is almost a million greater.

TABLE II.

Showing the nett produce of every estate, from one thousand to twenty-three thousand pounds a-year.

No. of thousands per ann.	Total tax subtracted.	Nett produce.
1000*l.*	21*l.*	979*l.*
2000	59	1941
3000	109	2891
4000	184	3861
5000	284	4716
6000	434	5566
7000	634	6366
8000	880	7120
9000	1180	7820
10,000	1530	8470
11,000	1930	9070
12,000	2380	9620
13,000	2880	10,120
14,000	3430	10,570
15,000	4030	10,970
16,000	4680	11,320
17,000	5380	11,620
18,000	6130	11,870
19,000	6930	12,170
20,000	7780	12,220
21,000	8680	12,320
22,000	9630	12,370
23,000	10,630	12,370

N. B. The odd shillings are dropped in this table.

According to this table, an estate cannot produce more than 12,370*l.* clear of the land tax and the progressive tax, and therefore the dividing such estates will follow as a matter of family interest. An estate of 23,000*l.* a-year divided into five estates of four thousand each and one of three, will be charged only 1129*l.* which is but five per cent. but if held by any one possessor will be charged 10,630*l.*

Although an inquiry into the origin of those estates be unnecessary, the continuation of them in their present state is another subject. It is a matter of national concern. As hereditary estates, the law has created the evil, and it ought also to provide the remedy. Primogeniture ought to be abolished, not only because it is unnatural and unjust, but because the country suffers by its operation. By cutting off (as before observed) the younger children from their proper portion of inheritance, the public is loaded with the expense of maintaining them; and the freedom of elections violated by the overbearing influence which this unjust monopoly of family property produces. Nor is this all. It occasions a waste of national property. A considerable part of the land of the country is rendered unproductive, by the great extent of parks and chases which this law serves to keep up, and this at a time when the annual production of grain is not equal to the national consumption.*—In short, the evils of the aristocratical system are so great and numerous, so inconsistent with every thing that is just, wise, natural and beneficent, that when they are considered, there ought not to be a doubt that many, who are now classed under that description, will wish to see such a system abolished.

What pleasure can they derive from contemplating the exposed condition, and almost certain beggary of their younger offspring? Every aristocratical family has an appendage of family beggars hanging round it, which in a few ages, or a few generations, are shook off, and console themselves with telling their tale in alms-houses, work-houses, and prisons. This is the natural consequence of aristocracy. The peer and the beggar are often of the same family. One extreme produces the other: to make one rich many must be made poor; neither can the system be supported by other means.

There are two classes of people to whom the laws of England are particularly hostile, and those the most helpless; younger children and the poor. Of the former I have just spoken; of the latter I shall mention one instance out of the many that might be produced, and with which I shall close this subject.

Several laws are in existence for regulating and limiting workmen's wages. Why not leave them as free to make their own bargains, as the law-makers are to let their farms and houses? Personal labor is all the property they have. Why is that little, and the little freedom they enjoy to be infringed? But the injustice will appear stronger, if we consider the operation and effect of such laws. When wages are fixed by what is called a law, the legal wages remain stationary, while every thing else is in progression:

---

* See the Reports on the Corn Trade.

and as those who make that law, still continue to lay on new taxes by other laws, they increase the expense of living by one law, and take away the means by another.

But if these gentlemen law-makers and tax-makers thought it right to limit the poor pittance which personal labor can produce, and on which a whole family is to be supported, they certainly must feel themselves happily indulged in a limitation on their own part, of not less than twelve thousand a-year, and that of property they never acquired (nor probably any of their ancestors) and of which they have made so ill a use.

Having now finished this subject, I shall bring the several particulars into one view, and then proceed to other matters.

The first eight articles are brought forward from p. 235.

1. Abolition of two millions poor-rates.

2. Provision for two hundred and fifty-two thousand poor families, at the rate of four pounds per head for each child under fourteen years of age; which, with the addition of two hundred and fifty thousand pounds, provides also education for one million and thirty thousand children.

3. Annuity of six pounds per ann. each for all poor persons, decayed tradesmen and others, supposed seventy thousand, of the age of fifty years, and until sixty.

4. Annuity of ten pounds each for life for all poor persons, decayed tradesmen, and others, supposed seventy thousand, of the age of sixty years.

5. Donation of twenty shillings each for fifty thousand births.

6. Donation of twenty shillings each for twenty thousand marriages.

7. Allowance of twenty thousand pounds for the funeral expenses of persons travelling for work, and dying at a distance from their friends.

8. Employment at all times for the casual poor in the cities of London and Westminster.

Second enumeration.

9. Abolition of the tax on houses and windows.

10. Allowance of three shillings per week for life to fifteen thousand disbanded soldiers, and a proportionate allowance to the officers of the disbanded corps.

11. Increase of pay to the remaining soldiers of 19,500*l.* annually.

12. The same allowance to the disbanded navy, and the same increase of pay, as to the army.

13. Abolition of the commutation tax.

14. Plan of a progressive tax, operating to extirpate the unjust and unnatural law of primogeniture, and the vicious influence of the aristocratical system.*

There yet remains, as already stated, one million of surplus taxes. Some part of this will be required for circumstances that do not immediately present themselves, and such part as shall not be wanted, will admit of a further reduction of taxes equal to that amount.

Among the claims that justice requires to be made, the condition of the inferior revenue-officers will merit attention. It is a reproach to any government to wave such an immensity of revenue in sinecures and nominal and unnecessary places and offices, and not allow even a decent livelihood to those on whom the labor falls. The salary of the inferior officers of the revenue has stood at the petty pittance of less than fifty pounds a-year, for upwards of one hundred years. It ought to be seventy. About one hundred and twenty thousand pounds applied to this purpose, will put all those salaries in a decent condition.

This was proposed to be done almost twenty years ago, but the treasury board then in being, startled at it, as it might lead to similar expectations from the army and navy; and the event was, that the king, or somebody for him, applied to parliament to have his own salary raised an hun-

---

* When inquiries are made into the condition of the poor, various degrees of distress will most probably be found, to render a different arrangement preferable to that which is already proposed. Widows with families will be in greater want than where there are husbands living. There is also a difference in the expense of living in different counties—and more so in fuel.

Suppose fifty thousand extraordinary cases, at the rate of ten pounds per family per ann.   -   -   -   -   500,000*l.*
100,000 families, at 8*l.* per family per ann.   -   -   -   800,000
100,000 families, at 7*l.* per   "   "   -   -   -   700,000
104,000 families, at 5*l.* per   "   "   -   -   -   520,000
And instead of ten shillings per head for the education of other
    children, to allow fifty shillings per family for that purpose
    to fifty thousand families   -   -   -   -   250,000

                                                                        2,770,000
140,000 aged persons as before,   1,120,000

                                                                        3,890,000*l.*

This arrangement amounts to the same sum as stated in p. 232. including the 250,000*l.* for education : but it provides (including the aged people) for four hundred and four thousand families, which is almost one third of all the families in England.

dred thousand pounds a-year, which, being done, every thing else was laid aside.

With respect to another class of men, the inferior clergy, I forbear to enlarge on their condition; but all partialities and prejudices for, or against, different modes and forms of religion aside, common justice will determine, whether there ought to be an income of twenty or thirty pounds a year to one man, and of ten thousand to another. I speak on this subject with the more freedom, because I am known not to be a Presbyterian; and therefore the cant cry of court sycophants, about church and meeting, kept up to amuse and bewilder the nation, cannot be raised against me.

Ye simple men on both sides the question, do you not see through this courtly craft? If ye can be kept disputing and wrangling about church and meeting, ye just answer the purpose of every courtier, who lives the while on the spoil of the taxes, and laughs at your credulity.— Every religion is good that teaches man to be good; and I know of none that instructs him to be bad.

All the beforementioned calculations, suppose only sixteen millions and an half of taxes paid into the exchequer, after the expense of collection and drawbacks at the custom-house and excise-office are deducted; whereas the sum paid into the exchequer is very nearly, if not quite, seventeen millions. The taxes raised in Scotland and Ireland are expended in those countries, and therefore their savings will come out of their own taxes; but if any part be paid into the English exchequer, it might be remitted.— This will not make one hundred thousand pounds a-year difference.

There now remains only the national debt to be considered. In the year 1789, the interest, exclusive of the tontine, was 9,150,138*l*. How much the capital has been reduced since that time the minister best knows. But after paying the interest, abolishing the tax on houses and windows, the commutation tax and the poor-rates; and making all the provisions for the poor, for the education of children, the support of the aged, the disbanded part of the army and navy, and increaring the pay of the remainder, there will be a surplus of one million.

The present scheme of paying off the national debt appears to me, speaking as an indifferent person, to be an ill concerted, if not a fallacious job. The burden of the na-

tional debt consists not in its being so many millions, or so
many hundred millions, but in the quantity of taxes collected every year to pay the interest. If this quantity continues the same, the burden of the national debt is the same
to all intents and purposes, be the capital more or less.——
The only knowledge which the public can have of the reduction of the debt, must be through the reduction of taxes
for paying the interest. The debt, therefore, is not reduced one farthing to the public by all the millions that
have been paid; and it would require more money now
to purchase up the capital, than when the scheme began.

Digressing for a moment at this point, to which I shall
return again, I look back to the appointment of Mr. Pitt,
as minister.

I was then in America. The war was over; and though
resentment had ceased, memory was still alive.

When the news of the coalition arrived, though it was a
matter of no concern to me as a citizen of America, I felt
it as a man. It had something in it which shocked, by
publicly sporting with decency, if not with principle. It
was impudence in lord North; it was a want of firmness
in Mr. Fox.

Mr. Pitt was, at that time, what may be called a maiden
character in politics. So far from being hackneyed, he
appeared not to be initiated into the first mysteries of
court intrigue. Every thing was in his favor. Resentment against the coalition served as friendship to him, and
his ignorance of vice was credited for virtue. With the
return of peace, commerce and prosperity would rise of
itself; yet even this increase was thrown to his account.

When he came to the helm, the storm was over, and he
had nothing to interrupt his course. It required even ingenuity to be wrong, and he succeeded. A little time
showed him the same sort of man as his predecessors had
been. Instead of profiting by those errors which had accumulated a burden of taxes unparalleled in the world, he
sought, I might almost say, he advertised for enemies, and
provoked means to increase taxation. Aiming at something, he knew not what, he ransacked Europe and India
for adventures, and abandoning the fair pretensions he began with, became the knight-errant of modern times.

It is unpleasant to see character throw itself away. It
is more so to see one's self deceived. Mr. Pitt had merited nothing, but he promised much. He gave symptoms

of a mind superior to the meanness and corruption of courts. His apparent candor encouraged expectations; and the public confidence, stunned, wearied, and confounded by a chaos of parties, revived and attached itself to him. But mistaking, as he has done, the disgust of the nation against the coalition, for merit in himself, he has rushed into measures, which a man less supported would not have presumed to act.

All this seems to show that change of ministers amounts to nothing. One goes out, another comes in, and still the same measures. vices, and extravagance are pursued. It signifies not who is minister. The defect lies in the system. The foundation and the superstructure of the government is bad. Prop it as you please, it continually sinks into court government, and ever will.

I return, as I promised, to the subject of the national debt, that offspring of the Dutch-Anglo revolution, and its handmaid the Hanover succession.

But it is now too late to inquire how it began. Those to whom it is due have advanced the money; and whether it was well or ill spent, or pocketed, is not their crime.— It is, however, easy to see, that as the nation proceeds in contemplating the nature and principles of government and to understand taxes, and make comparisons between those of America, France and England, it will be next to impossible to keep it in the same torpid state it has hitherto been. Some reform must, from the necessity of the case, soon begin. It is not whether these principles press with little or much force in the present moment. They are out. They are abroad in the world, and no force can stop them. Like a secret told, they are beyond recal; and he must be blind indeed that does not see that a change is already beginning.

Nine millions of dead taxes is a serious thing; and this not only for bad, but in a great measure for foreign government. By putting the power of making war into the hands of the foreigners who came for what they could get, little else was to be expected than what has happened.

Reasons are already advanced in this work, showing that whatever the reforms in the taxes may be, they ought to be made in the current expenses of government, and not in the part applied to the interest of the national debt.— By remitting the taxes of the poor, *they* will be totally relieved and all discontent will be taken away; and by striking off such of the taxes as are already mentioned, the nation will more than recover the whole expense of the mad American war.

There will then remain only the national debt as a subject of discontent, and in order to remove, or rather to prevent this, it would be good policy in the stockholders themselves to consider it as property, subject like all other property, to bear some portion of the taxes. It would give to it both popularity and security, and as a great part of its present inconvenience is balanced by the capital which it keeps alive, a measure of this kind would so far add to that balance as to silence objections.

This may be done by such gradual means as to accomplish all that is necessary with the greatest ease and convenience.

Instead of taxing the capital, the best method would be to tax the interest by some progressive ratio, and to lessen the public taxes in the same proportion as the interest diminished.

Suppose the interest was taxed one halfpenny in the pound the first year, a penny more the second, and to proceed by a certain ratio to be determined upon, always less than any other tax upon property. Such a tax would be subtracted from the interest at the time of payment, without any expense of collection.

One halfpenny in the pound would lessen the interest and consequently the taxes, twenty thousand pounds. The tax on wagons amounts to this sum, and this tax might be taken off the first year. The second year the tax on female servants, or some other of the like amount might also be taken off, and by proceeding in this manner, always applying the tax raised from the property of the debt towards its extinction, and not carrying it to the current services, it would liberate itself.

The stockholders, notwithstanding this tax, would pay less taxes than they do now. What they would save by the extinction of the poor-rates, and the tax on houses and windows, and the commutation tax, would be considerably greater than what this tax, slow, but certain in its operation, amounts to.

It appears to me to be prudence to look out for measures that may apply under any circumstance that may approach. There is, at this moment, a crisis in the affairs of Europe that requires it. Preparation now is wisdom.

If taxation be once let loose, it will be difficult to reinstate it; neither would the relief be so effectual, as if it proceeded by some certain and gradual reduction.

The fraud, hypocrisy, and imposition of governments, are now beginning to be too well understood to promise them any longer career. The farce of monarchy and aristocracy, in all countries, is following that of chivalry, and Mr. Burke is dressing for the funeral. Let it then pass quietly to the tomb of all other follies, and the mourners be comforted.

The time is not very distant when England will laugh at itself for sending to Holland, Hanover, Zell, or Brunswick for men, at the expense of a million a-year, who understood neither her laws, her language, nor her interest, and whose capacities would scarcely have fitted them for the office of a parish constable. If government could be trusted to such hands, it must be some easy and simple thing indeed, and materials fit for all the purposes may be found in every town and village in England.

When it shall be said in any country in the world, my poor are happy: neither ignorance nor distress is to be found among them; my jails are empty of prisoners, my streets of beggars; the aged are not in want, the taxes are not oppressive; the rational world is my friend, because I am the friend of its happiness: when these things can be said, then may that country boast of its constitution and its government.

Within the space of a few years we have seen two revolutions, those of America and France. In the former, the contest was long and the conflict severe; in the latter, the nation acted with such a consolidated impulse, that having no foreign enemy to contend with, the revolution was complete in power the moment it appeared. From both those instances it is evident, that the greatest forces that can be brought into the field of revolutions, are reason and common interest. Where these can have the opportunity of acting, opposition dies with fear, or crumbles away by conviction. It is a great standing which they have now universally obtained; and we may hereafter hope to see revolutions, or changes in governments, produced with the same quiet operation by which any measure, determinable by reason and discussion, is accomplished.

When a nation changes its opinion and habits of thinking, it is no longer to be governed as before; but it would not only be wrong, but bad policy, to attempt by force what ought to be accomplished by reason. Rebellion consists in forcibly opposing the general will of a nation, whether by a party or by a government. There ought, therefore, to be in every nation a method of occasionally ascertaining the state of public opinion with respect to government. On this point the old government of France was superior to the present government of England, because, on extraordinary occasions, recourse could be had to what was then called the states-general. But in England there are no such occasional bodies; and as to those who are now called representatives, a great part of them are mere machines of the court, placemen and dependants.

I presume, that though all the people of England pay taxes, not an hundredth part of them are electors, and the members of one of the houses of parliament represent nobody but themselves. There is, therefore, no power but the voluntary will of the people that has a right to act in any matter respecting a general reform; and by the same right that two persons can confer on such a subject, a thousand may. The object, in all such preliminary proceedings, is to find out what the general sense of a nation is, and to be governed by it. If it prefer a bad or defective government to a reform, or choose to pay ten times more taxes than there is any occasion for, it has a right so to do; and so long as the majority do not impose conditions on the minority, different from what they impose upon themselves, though there may be much error, there is no injustice. Neither will the error continue long. Reason and discussion will soon bring things right, however wrong they may begin. By such a process no tumult is to be apprehended. The poor, in all countries, are naturally both peaceable and grateful in all reforms in which their interest and happiness are included. It is only by neglecting and rejecting them that they become tumultuous.

The objects that now press on the public attention are, the French revolution, and the prospect of a general revolution in governments. Of all nations in Europe there is none so much interested in the French revolution as England. Enemies for ages, and that at a vast expense, and without any national object, the opportunity now presents itself of amicably closing the scene, and joining their efforts to reform the rest of Europe. By doing this they will not only prevent the further effusion of blood, and increase.

of taxes, but be in a condition of getting rid of a considerable part of their present burdens, as has been already stated. Long experience however, has shown, that reforms of this kind are not those which old governments wish to promote, and therefore, it is to nations, and not to such governments, that these matters present themselves.

In the preceding part of this work, I have spoken of an alliance between England, France, and America, for purposes that were to be afterwards mentioned. Though I have no direct authority on the part of America, I have good reason to conclude that she is disposed to enter into a consideration of such a measure, provided that the governments with which she might ally, acted as national governments, and not as courts enveloped in intrigue and mystery. That France as a nation and a national government, would prefer an alliance with England, is a matter of certainty. Nations, like individuals who have long been enemies, without knowing each other, or knowing why, become better friends when they discover the errors and impositions under which they had acted.

Admitting, therefore, the probability of such a connexion, I will state some matters by which such an alliance, together with that of Holland, might render service, not only to the parties immediately concerned, but to all parts of Europe.

It is, I think, quite certain, that if the fleets of England, France, and Holland were confederated, they could propose, with effect, a limitation to, and a general dismantling of, all the navies in Europe, to a certain proportion to be agreed upon.

1st, That no new ship of war shall be built by any power in Europe, themselves included.

2d, That all the navies now in existence shall be put back, supposed to one tenth of their present force. This will save to France and England, each, at least two millions annually, and their relative force be in the same proportion as it is now. If men will permit themselves to think, as rational beings ought to think, nothing can appear more ridiculous and absurd, exclusive of all moral reflections, than to be at the expense of building navies, filling them with men, and then hauling them into the ocean, to try which can sink each other fastest. Peace, which costs nothing, is attended with infinitely more advantage, than any victory with all its expense. But this, though it best answers the purpose of nations, does not that of court governments, whose habitual policy is pretence for taxation, places, and offices.

It is, I think, also certain, that the above confederated powers, together with that of the United States of America, can propose, with effect, to Spain, the independence of South-America, and the opening those countries of immense extent and wealth to the general commerce of the world, as North-America now is.

With how much more glory, and advantage to itself, does a nation act, when it exerts its powers to rescue the world from bondage, and to create to itself friends, than when it employs those powers to increase ruin, desolation, and misery. The horrid scene that is now acting by the English government in the East-Indies, is fit only to be told of Goths and Vandals, who, destitute of principle, robbed and tortured the world which they were incapable of enjoying.

The opening of South-America would produce an immense field for commerce, and a ready money market for manufactures, which the eastern world does not. The East is already a country of manufactures, the importation of which is not only an injury to the manufactures of England, but a drain upon its specie. The balance against England by this trade is regularly upwards of half a million annually sent out in the East-India ships in silver; and this is the reason, together with German intrigue, and German subsidies, that there is so little silver in England.

But any war is harvest to such governments, however ruinous it may be to a nation. It serves to keep up deceitful expectations, which prevent people from looking into the defects and abuses of government. It is the *lo here!* and the *lo there!* that amuses and cheats the multitude.

Never did so great an opportunity offer itself to England, and to all Europe, as is produced by the two revolutions of America and France. By the former, freedom has a national champion in the western world; and by the latter, in Europe. When another nation shall join France, despotism and bad government will scarcely dare to appear. To use a trite expression, the iron is becoming hot all over Europe. The insulted German and the enslaved Spaniard, the Russ and the Pole, are beginning to think. The present age will hereafter merit to be called the Age of Reason, and the present generation will appear to the future as the Adam of a new world.

When all the governments of Europe shall be established on the representative system, nations will become acquainted, and the animosities and prejudices fomented by the intrigues and artifice of courts, will cease. The oppressed soldier will become a freeman; and the tortured sailor, no longer dragged through the streets like a felon, will pursue his mercantile voyage in safety. It would be better that nations should continue the pay of their soldiers during their lives, and give them their discharge and restore them to freedom and their friends, and cease recruiting, than retain such multitudes at the same expense, in a condition useless to society and to themselves. As soldiers have hitherto been treated in most countries, they might be said to be without a friend. Shunned by the citizen on an apprehension of their being enemies to liberty, and too often insulted by those who commanded them, their condition was a double oppression. But where genuine principles of liberty pervade a people, every thing is restored to order; and the soldier civilly treated, returns the civility.

In contemplating revolutions, it is easy to perceive that they may arise from two distinct causes; the one, to avoid or get rid of some great calamity, the other, to obtain some great and positive good; and the two may be distinguished by the names of active and passive revolutions. In those which proceed from the former cause, the temper becomes incensed and soured; and the redress, obtained by danger, is too often sullied by revenge. But in those which proceed from the latter, the heart, rather animated than agitated, enters serenely upon the subject. Reason and discussion, persuasion and conviction, become the weapons in the contest, and it is only when those are attempted to be suppressed that recourse is had to violence. When men unite in agreeing that a *thing is good*, could it be obtained, such for instance as relief from a burden of taxes and the extinction of corruption, the object is more than half accomplished. What they approve as the end, they will promote in the means.

Will any man say in the present excess of taxation, falling so heavily on the poor, that a remission of five pounds annually of taxes to one hundred and four thousand poor families is not a *good thing?* Will he say that a remission of seven pounds annually to one hundred thousand other poor families; of eight pounds annually to another hundred thousand poor families, and of ten pounds annually to fifty thousand poor and widowed families, are not *good things ?* And, to proceed a step further in this climax, will he say, that to provide against the misfortunes to which all human life is subject, by securing six pounds annually for all poor, distressed, and reduced persons of the age of fifty and until sixty, and of ten pounds annually after sixty, is not a *good thing ?*

Will he say, that an abolition of two millions of poor-rates to the housekeepers, and of the whole of the house and window-light tax and of the commutation tax is not a *good thing ?* Or will he say, that to abolish corruption is a *bad thing ?*

If, therefore, the good to be obtained be worthy of a passive, rational, and costless revolution, it would be bad policy to prefer waiting for a calamity that should force a violent one. I have no idea, considering the reforms which are now passing and spreading throughout Europe, that England will permit herself to be the last; and where the occasion and the opportunity quietly offer, it is better than to wait for a turbulent necessity. It may be considered as an honor to the animal faculties of man to obtain redress by courage and danger, but it is far greater honor to the rational faculties to accomplish the same object by reason, accommodation and general consent.*

As reforms, or revolutions, call them which you please, extend themselves among nations, those nations will form connexions and conventions, and when a few are thus confederated, the progress will be rapid, till despotism and corrupt government be totally expelled, at least out of two

---

* I know it is the opinion of many of the most enlightened characters in France (there always will be those who see further into events than others,) not only among the general mass of citizens, but of many of the principal members of the national assembly, that the monarchical plan will not continue many years in that country. They have found out, that as wisdom cannot be hereditary, power ought not—and that for a man to merit a million sterling a-year from a nation, he ought to have a mind capable of comprehending from an atom to a universe, which, if he had he would be above receiving the pay. But they wished not to appear to lead the nation faster than its own reason and interest dictated. In all the conversations where I have been present upon this subject, the idea always was, that when such a time, from the general opinion of the nation, shall arrive, that when the honorable and liberal method would be, to make a handsome present in fee simple to the person, whoever he may be, that shall then be in the monarchical office, and for him to retire to the enjoyment of private life, possessing his share of general rights and privileges, and to be no more accountable to the public for his time and his conduct than any other citizen.

quarters of the world, Europe and America. The Algerine piracy may then be commanded to cease, for it is only by the malicious policy of old governments, against each other that it exists.

Throughout this work, various and numerous as the subjects are, which I have taken up and investigated, there is only a single paragraph upon religion, viz. "*that every religion is good that teaches man to be good.*"

I have carefully avoided to enlarge upon the subject, because I am inclined to believe, that what is called the present ministry, wish to see contentions about religion kept up to prevent the nation turning its attention to subjects of government. It is, as if they were to say, "*look that way, or any way but this.*"

But as religion is very improperly made a political machine, and the reality of it is thereby destroyed, I will conclude this work with stating in what light religion appears to me.

If we suppose a large family of children, who, on any particular day, or particular occasion, made it a custom to present to their parents some token of their affection and gratitude, each of them would make a different offering, and most probably in a different manner. Some would pay their congratulations in themes of verse and prose, by some little devices, as their genius dictated, or according to what they thought would please; and, perhaps, the least of all, not able to do any of those things, would ramble into the garden, or the field, and gather what it thought the prettiest flower it could find, though, perhaps, it might be but a simple weed. The parents would be more gratified, by such a variety, than if the whole of them had acted on a concerted plan, and each had made exactly the same offering. This would have the cold appearance of contrivance, or the harsh one of control. But of all unwelcome things, nothing would more afflict the parent than to know, that the whole of them had afterwards gotten together by the ears, boys and girls, fighting, reviling, and abusing each other about which was the best or the worst present.

Why may we not suppose, that the great Father of all is pleased with variety of devotion; and that the greatest offence we can act, is that by which we seek to torment and render each other miserable? For my own part, I am fully satisfied that what I am now doing, with an endeavor to conciliate mankind, to render their condition happy, to

unite nations that have hitherto been enemies, and to extirpate the horrid practice of war, and break the chains of
slavery and oppression, is acceptable in his sight, and being the best service I can perform, I act it cheerfully.

I do not believe that any two men, on what are called
doctrinal points, think alike who think at all. It is only
those who have not thought that appear to agree. It is in
this case as with what is called the British constitution.
It has been taken for granted to be good, and encomiums
have supplied the place of proof. But when the nation
comes to examine into principles and the abuses it admits,
it will be found to have more defects than I have pointed
out in this work and the former.

As to what are called national religions, we may, with
as much propriety, talk of national gods. It is either political craft or the remains of the pagan system, when every
nation had its separate particular deity. Among all the
writers of the English church clergy, who have treated on
the general subject of religion, the present bishop of Lan-
daff, has not been excelled, and it is with much pleasure
that I take this opportunity of expressing this token of respect. I have now gone through the whole of the subject
at least, as far as it appears to me at present. It has been
my intention for the five years I have been in Europe to
offer an address to the people of England on the subject of
government, if the opportunity presented itself before I returned to America. Mr. Burke has thrown it in my way,
and I thank him. On a certain occasion, three years ago,
I pressed him to propose a national convention, to be fairly elected, for the purpose of taking the state of the nation
into consideration ; but I found that however strongly the
parliamentary current was then setting against the party
he acted with, their policy was to keep every thing within
that field of corruption, and trust to accidents. Long experience had shown that parliaments would follow any
change of ministers, and on this they rested their hopes
and their expectations.

Formerly, when divisions arose respecting governments,
recourse was had to the sword, and a civil war ensued.
That savage custom is exploded by the new system, and
reference is had to national conventions. Discussion and
the general will arbitrates the question, and to this, private
opinion yields with a good grace, and order is preserved
uninterrupted.

Some gentlemen have affected to call the principles upon which this work and the former part of the Rights of Man are founded, "a new fangled doctrine." The question is not whether these principles are new or old, but whether they are right or wrong. Suppose the former, I will show their effect by a figure easily understood.

It is now towards the middle of February. Were I to take a turn into the country, the trees would present a leafless, wintery appearance. As people are apt to pluck twigs as they go along, I perhaps might do the same, and by chance might observe, that a *single bud* on that twig had begun to swell. I should reason very unnaturally, or rather not reason at all, to suppose *this* was the *only* bud in England which had this appearance. Instead of deciding thus I should instantly conclude, that the same appearance was beginning, or about to begin, every where; and though the vegetable sleep will continue longer on some trees and plants than on others, and though some of them may not *blossom* for two or three years, all will be in leaf in the summer, except those which are *rotten*. What pace the political summer may keep with the natural, no human foresight can determine. It is, however, not difficult to perceive that the spring is begun. Thus wishing, as I sincerely do, freedom and happiness to all nations, I close the SECOND PART.

APPENDIX.

As the publication of this work has been delayed beyond the time intended, I think it not improper, all circumstances considered, to state the causes that have occasioned that delay.

The reader will probably observe, that some parts in the plan contained in this work for reducing the taxes, and certain parts in Mr. Pitt's speech at the opening of the present session, Tuesday, January 31, are so much alike, as to induce a belief, that either the author had taken the hint from Mr. Pitt, or Mr. Pitt from the author.—I will first point out the parts that are similar, and then state such circumstances as I am acquainted with, leaving the reader to make his own conclusion.

Considering it as almost an unprecedented case, that taxes should be proposed to be taken off, it is equally extraordinary that such a measure should occur to two persons at the same time; and still more so (considering the vast variety and multiplicity of taxes) that they should hit on the same specific taxes. Mr. Pitt has mentioned, in his speech, the tax on *carts* and *wagons;* that on *female servants;* the lowering the tax on *candles,* and the taking off the tax of three shillings on *houses* having under seven windows.

Every one of those specific taxes are a part of the plan contained in this work, and proposed also to be taken off. Mr. Pitt's plan, it is true, goes no further than to a reduction of three hundred and twenty thousand pounds; and the reduction proposed in this work, to nearly six millions. I have made my calculations on only sixteen millions and an half of revenue, still asserting that it was very nearly, if not quite, seventeen millions. Mr. Pitt states it at 16,690,000*l.* I know enough of the matter to say, that he has not *over*stated it. Having thus given the particulars, which correspond in this work and his speech, I will state a chain of circumstances that may lead to some explanation.

The first hint for lessening the taxes, and that as a consequence flowing from the French revolution, is to be found in the Address and Declaration of the gentlemen who met at the Thatched-House tavern, August 20, 1791. Among many other particulars stated in that address, is the following, put as an interrogation to the government opposers of the French revolution. "*Are they sorry that the pretence for new oppressive taxes, and the occasion for continuing many old taxes will be at an end?*"

It is well known, that the persons who chiefly frequent the Thatched-House tavern, are men of court connexions, and so much did they take this address and declaration respecting the French revolution and the reduction of taxes in disgust, that the landlord was under the necessity of informing the gentlemen, who composed the meeting of the 20th of August, and who proposed holding another meeting, that he could not receive them.*

* The gentleman who signed the address and declaration as chairman of the meeting, Mr. Horne Tooke, being generally supposed to be the person

What was only hinted in the address and declaration respecting taxes and principles of government, will be found reduced to a regular system in this work. But as Mr. Pitt's speech contains some of the same things respecting taxes, I now come to give the circumstances before alluded to.

The case is this: this work was intended to be published just before the meeting of parliament, and for that purpose a considerable part of the copy was put into the printer's hands in September, and all the remaining copy, as far as page 160, which contains the part to which Mr. Pitt's speech is similar, was given to him full six weeks before the meeting of parliament, and he was informed of the time at which it was to appear. He had composed nearly the whole about a fortnight before the time of parliament's meeting, and had printed as far as page 112, and had given me a proof of the next sheet, up to page 128. It was then in sufficient forwardness to be out at the time proposed, as two other sheets were ready for striking off, I had before told him, that if he thought he should be straitened for time, I could get part of the work done at another press, which he desired me not to do. In this manner the work stood on the Tuesday fortnight, preceding the meeting of parliament, when all at once, without any previous intimation, though I had been with him the evening before, he sent me by one of his workmen, all the remaining copy, from page 112, declining to go on with the work *on any consideration.*

To account for this extraordinary conduct I was totally at a loss, as he stopped at the part where the arguments on systems and principles of government closed, and where the plan for the reduction of taxes, the education of children, and the support of the poor and the aged begins;

who drew it up, and having spoken much in commendation of it, has been jocularly accused of praising his own work. To free him from this embarrassment, and to save him the repeated trouble of mentioning the author, as he has not failed to do, I make no hesitation in saying, that as the opportunity of benefiting by the French revolution easily occurred to me, I drew up the publication in question, and showed it to him and some other gentlemen ; who, fully approving it, held a meeting for the purpose of making it public, and subscribed to the amount of fifty guineas to defray the expense of advertising. I believe there are at this time in England a greater number of men acting on disinterested principles, and determined to look into the nature and practices of government themselves, and not blindly trust, as has hitherto been the case, either to government generally, or to parliaments, or to parliamentary opposition, than at any former period. Had this been done a century ago, corruption and taxation had not arrived to the height they are now at.

and still more especially, as he had, at the time of his beginning to print, and before he had seen the whole copy,
offered a thousand pounds for the copy-right, together with
the future copy-right of the former part of the Rights of
Man.   I told the person who brought me this offer that I
should not accept it, and wished it not to be renewed, giving him as my reason, that though I believed the printer
to be an honest man, I would never put it in the power of
any printer or publisher to suppress or alter a work of
mine, by making him master of the copy, or give to him
the right of selling it to any minister, or to any other person, or to treat as a mere matter of traffic, that which I intended should operate as a principle.

His refusal to complete the work (which he could not
purchase) obliged me to seek for another printer, and this
of consequence would throw the publication back till after
the meeting of parliament, otherwise it would have appeared that Mr. Pitt had only taken up a part of the plan which
I had more fully stated.

Whether that gentleman, or any other, had seen the
work or any part of it, is more than I have authority to
say.   But the manner in which the work was returned,
and the particular time at which this was done, and that
after the offers he had made, are suspicious circumstances.
I know what the opinion of booksellers and publishers
is upon such a case, but as to my own opinion, I choose to
make no declaration.   There are many ways by which
proof sheets may be procured by other persons before a
work publicly appears ; to which I shall add a certain circumstance, which is,

A ministerial bookseller in Piccadilly who has been employed, as common report says, by a clerk of one of the
boards closely connected with the ministry (the board of
trade and plantation of which Hawkesbury is president) to
publish what he calls my Life, (I wish his own life and
those of the cabinet were as good) used to have his books
printed at the same printing-office that I employed ; but
when the former part of the Rights of Man came out, he
took his work away in dudgeon ; and about a week or ten
days before the printer returned my copy, he came to
make him an offer of his work again, which was accepted.
This would consequently give him admission into the printing-office where the sheets of this work were then lying ;
and as booksellers and printers are free with each other,

he would have the opportunity of seeing what was going on. Be the case however as it may, Mr. Pitt's plan, little and diminutive as it is, would have made a very awkward appearance, had this work appeared at the time the printer had engaged to finish it.

I have now stated the particulars which occasioned the delay, from the proposal to purchase, to the refusal to print. If all the gentlemen are innocent, it is very unfortunate for them that such a variety of suspicious circumstances should, without any design, arrange themselves together.

Having now finished this part, I will conclude with stating another circumstance.

About a fortnight or three weeks before the meeting of parliament, a small addition, amounting to about twelve shillings and sixpence a year, was made to the pay of the soldiers, or rather, their pay was docked so much less.— Some gentlemen who knew in part, that this work would contain a plan of reforms respecting the oppressed condition of soldiers, wished me to add a note to the work, signifying that the part upon that subject had been in the printer's hands some weeks before that addition of pay was proposed. I declined doing this, lest it should be interpreted into an air of vanity, or an endeavor to excite suspicion (for which perhaps there might be no grounds) that some of the government gentlemen, had, by some means or other, made out what this work would contain; and had not the printing been interrupted so as to occasion a delay beyond the time fixed for publication, nothing contained in this appendix would have appeared.

THOMAS PAINE.

END OF THE RIGHTS OF MAN.

MR. SECRETARY DUNDAS.

—•—

SIR,

As you opened the debate in the house of commons, May 25th, on the proclamation for suppressing publications, which that proclamation (without naming any) calls wicked and seditious; and as you applied those opprobious epithets to the works entitled Rights of Man, I think it unnecessary to offer any other reason for addressing this letter to you.

I begin, then, at once, by declaring, that I do not believe there are to be found in the writings of any author, ancient or modern, on the subject of government, a spirit of greater benignity, and a stronger inculcation of moral principles than in those which I have published. They come, sir, from a man, who, by having lived in different countries, and under different systems of government, and who, being intimate in the construction of them, is a better judge of the subject than it is possible that you, from the want of those opportunities can be : and besides this, they come from a heart that knows not how to beguile.

I will further say, that when that moment arrives in which the best consolation that shall be left, will be looking back on some past actions, more virtuous and more meritorious than the rest, I shall then with happiness remember, among other things, that I have written the Rights of Man. As to what proclamations, or prosecutions, or placemen, and place expectants ; those who possess, or those who are gaping for office, may say of them, it will not alter their character, either with the world or with me.

Having, sir, made this declaration, I shall proceed to remark, not particularly on your speech, but on any one to which your motion gave rise. To begin with Mr. Adam.

He accuses me of not having done the very thing that I have done.

In his speech, (see the Morning Chronicle of May 26) he says, "that he had well considered the subject of constitutional publications, and was by no means ready to say that books of science upon government though recommending a doctrine, or system different from the form of our constitution were fit objects of prosecution; that if he did, he must condemn Harrington for his Oceana, Sir Thomas More for his Utopia, and Hume for his Idea of a Perfect Commonwealth. But the publication of Mr. Paine reviled what was most sacred in the constitution, destroyed every principle of subordination, and established nothing in their room."

I readily saw that Mr. Adam had not read the second part of the Rights of Man; and I am put under the necessity either of submitting to an erroneous charge, or of justifying myself against it; and certainly shall prefer the latter. If, then, I shall prove to Mr. Adam, that in my reasoning upon systems of government, in the second part of the Rights of Man, I have shown, I think, as clearly as words can convey ideas, a certain system of government; and that not existing in theory only, but already in established practice, and systematically and practically free from all the vices and defects of the English government, and capable of producing more happiness to the people, and that also with an eightieth part of the taxes, which the present English system of government consumes; I hope he will do me the justice when he next goes to the house, to acknowledge he had been mistaken in saying, that I had established nothing, and had destroyed every principle of subordination. I now come to the point.

In the second part of the Rights of Man I have distinguished government into two classes or systems; the hereditary and the representative systems.

In the first part of the Rights of Man, I have shown, and it cannot be refuted, that there does not exist a right to establish hereditary government.

In the second part of the Rights of Man I have not repeated those arguments, because they are irrefutable, but have confined myself to show the defects of hereditary government, or hereditary succession, that it must, from the nature of it, throw government into the hands of men unworthy of it, either from want of principle or capacity.

To show the absurdity of the hereditary system still more strongly, I will now put the following case: take any fifty men promiscuously, and it will be very extraordinary, if, out of that number, more than one man should be found, whose principles and talents taken together (for some might have principles, and others have talents) would render him a person truly fitted to fill any very extraordinary office of national trust. If then such a fitness of character could not be expected to be found in more than one person out of fifty, it would happen but once in a thousand years to the eldest son of any one family, admitting each on an average, to hold the office twenty years. Mr. Adam talks of something in the constitution, which he calls most sacred; but I hope he does not mean hereditary succession, a thing which appears to me a violation of every order of nature and of common sense.

When I look into history and see the multitudes of men, otherwise virtuous, who have died and whose families have been ruined, in defence of knaves and fools, and which they would not have done had they reasoned at all upon the system; I do not know a greater good that an individual can render to mankind, than to endeavor to break the chains of political superstition. Those chains are now dissolving fast, and proclamations and prosecutions will serve but to hasten that dissolution.

Having thus spoken of the hereditary system as a bad system, and subject to every possible defect, I now come to the representative system; and this Mr. Adam will find stated in the second part of the Rights of Man, not only as the best, but as the only theory of government under which the liberties of a people can be permanently secure.

But it is needless now to talk of mere theory since there is already a government in full practice, established upon that theory; or in other words, upon the rights of man, and has been so for almost twenty years. Mr. Pitt, in a speech of his some short time since, said " That there never did, and never could exist a government established upon those rights, and that if it began at noon, it would end at night." Mr. Pitt has not yet arrived at the degree of a school boy in this species of knowledge. His practice has been confined to means of extorting the revenue, and his boast has been—how much? Whereas the boast of the system of government that I am speaking of, is not how much, but how little.

The system of government purely representative, unmixed with any thing of hereditary nonsense, began in America. I will now compare the effects of that system of government, with the system of government in England, both during and since the close of the war.

So powerful is the representative system; first, by combining and consolidating all the parts of a country together, however great the extent; and, secondly, by admitting of none but men properly qualified into the government, or dismissing them if they prove otherwise, that America was enabled thereby totally to defeat and overthrow all the schemes and projects of the hereditary government of England against her. As the establishment of the revolution and independence of America is a proof of this fact, it is needless to enlarge upon it.

I now come to the comparative effect of the two systems since the close of the war, and I request Mr. Adam to attend to it.

America had internally sustained the ravage of upwards of seven years of war, which England had not. England sustained only the expense of the war: whereas America sustained not only the expense, but the destruction of property committed by both armies. Not a house was built during that period, and many thousands were destroyed.

The farms and plantations along the coast of the country, for more than a thousand miles, were laid waste. Her commerce was annihilated. Her ships were either taken or had rotted within her own harbors. The credit of her funds had fallen upwards of ninety per cent. that is, an original hundred pounds would not sell for ten pounds. In short she was apparently put back an hundred years when the war closed; which was not the case with England.

But such was the event, that the same representative system of government, though since better organized, which enabled her to conquer, enabled her also to recover, and she now presents a more flourishing condition, and a more happy and harmonized society under that system of government, than any country in the world can boast under any other. Her towns are rebuilt much better than before; her farms and plantations are in higher improvement than ever; her commerce is spread over the world, and her funds have risen from less than ten pounds the hundred to upwards of one hundred and twenty. Mr. Pitt and his colleagues, talk of the things that have happened in his boyish administration, without knowing what greater things have happened elsewhere, and under other systems of government.

I next come to state the expense of the two systems, as they now stand in each of the countries; but it may first be proper to observe, that government in America is what it ought to be, a matter of honor and trust, and not made a trade of for the purpose of lucre.

The whole amount of nett taxes in England (exclusive of the expense of collections, of drawbacks, of seizures and condemnations, of fines and penalties, of fees of office, of litigations and informers, which are some of the blessed means of enforcing them) is seventeen millions. Of this sum, about nine millions go for the payment of the interest of the national debt, and the remainder, being about eight millions, is for the current annual expenses. Thus much for one side of the case. I now come to the other.

The expense of the several departments of the general representative government of the United States of America, extending over a space of country nearly ten times larger than England, is two hundred and ninety-four thousand five hundred and fifty-eight dollars, which at 4s. 6d. per dollar, is 66,305l. 11s. sterling, and is thus apportioned:

Expense of the Executive Department.

The office of president, for which the president receives nothing for himself - -	5,625l.	0s.
Vice-president - - - - -	1,125	0
Chief-justice - - - - - -	900	0
Five associate justices - - - -	3,937	10
Nineteen judges of districts and the attorney-general - - - - - -	6,873	15

Legislative Department.

Members of congress at 6 dolls. (1l. 7s.) per day, their secretaries, clerks, chaplains, messengers, door-keepers, &c. - -	25,515l.	0

Treasury Department.

Secretary, assistant, comptroller, auditor, treasurer, register, and loan-office keeper in each state, together with all necessary clerks, office keepers, &c. - - - -	12,825	0

Amount carried forward 56,801l. 5s.

Amount bro't forward   56,301*l.* 5*s.*

Department of State, including Foreign Affairs.

Secretary, clerks, &c.   -   -   -   -   1,406   5

Department of War.

Secretary, clerks, paymasters, commissioners,
&c.   -   -   -   -   -   -   1,462   10

Commissioners for settling old accounts.

The whole board, clerks, &c.   -   -   2,598   15

Incidental and contingent expenses.

For fire-wood, stationary, printing, &c.   -   4,036   16

66,305*l.* 11*s.*

On account of the incursions of the Indians on the back
settlements, congress is obliged at this time to keep six
thousand militia in pay, in addition to a regiment of foot,
and a battalion of artillery, which it always keeps; and this
increases the expense of the war-department to 390,000
dollars, which is 87,795*l.* sterling, but when peace shall be
concluded with the Indians, the greatest part of this expense will cease, and the total amount of the expense of
government, including that of the army, will not amount to
100,000*l.* which, as has been already stated, is but an
eightieth part of the expenses of the English government.

I request Mr. Adam and Mr. Dundas, and all those who
are talking of constitutions, and blessings, and kings, and
lords, and the Lord knows what, to look at this statement.
Here is a form and system of government, that is better
organized and better administered than any government in
the world, and that for less than one hundred thousand
pounds per annum, and yet every member of congress receives, as a compensation for his time and attendance on
public business, one pound seven shillings per day, which
is at the rate of nearly five hundred pounds a-year.

This is a government that has nothing to fear. It needs
no proclamations to deter people from writing and reading. It needs no political superstition to support it. It
was by encouraging discussion and rendering the press
free upon all subjects of government, that the principles of
government became understood in America, and the people are now enjoying the present blessings under it. You
hear of no riots, tumults and disorders in that country; because there exists no cause to produce them. Those things

are never the effect of freedom, but of restraint, oppression and excessive taxation.

In America, there is not that class of poor and wretched people that are so numerously dispersed all over England, who are to be told by a proclamation, that they are happy; and this is in a great measure to be accounted for, not by the difference of proclamations, but by the difference of governments and the difference of taxes between that country and this. What the laboring people of that country earn, they apply to their own use, and to the education of their children, and do not pay it away in taxes as fast as they earn it, to support court extravagance, and a long enormous list of placemen and pensioners; and besides this, they have learned the manly doctrine of reverencing themselves, and consequently of respecting each other; and they laugh at those imaginary beings called kings and lords, and all the fraudulent trumpery of courts.

When placemen and pensioners, or those who expect to be such, are lavish in praise of a government, it is not a sign of its being a good one. The pension-list alone in England (see sir John Sinclair's History of the Revenue, p. 6, of the Appendix) is one hundred and seven thousand four hundred and four pounds, which is more than the expenses of the whole government of America amount to; and I am now more convinced than before, that the offer that was made to me of a thousand pounds for the copyright of the second part of the Rights of Man, together with the remaining copy-right of the first part, was to have effected, by a quick suppression, what is now attempted to be done by a prosecution. The connexion which the person who made that offer has with the king's printing-office, may furnish part of the means of inquiring into this affair, when the ministry shall please to bring their prosecution to issue. But to return to my subject.

I have said, in the second part of the Rights of Man, and I repeat it here, that the service of any man, whether called king, president, senator, legislator or any thing else, cannot be worth more to any country, in the regular routine of office, than ten thousand pounds per annum. We have a better man in America, and more of a gentleman than any king I ever knew of, who does not occasion even half that expense; for though the salary is fixed at 5625l. he does not accept it, and it is only the incidental expenses that are paid out of it. The name by which a man is called, is, of itself, but an empty thing. It is worth and character alone which can render him valuable, for without this, kings and lords, and presidents, are but jingling names.

But without troubling myself about constitutions of government, I have shown in the second part of the Rights of Man, that an alliance may be formed between England, France and America, and that the expenses of government in England may be put back to one million and an half, *viz.*

Civil expense of government	500,000*l.*
Army - - -	500,000
Navy - - -	500,000
	1,500,000*l.*

And even this sum is fifteen times greater than the expenses of government are in America; and it is also greater than the whole peace establishment of England amounted to, about an hundred years ago. So much has the weight and oppression of taxes increased since the revolution, and especially since the year 1714.

To show that the sum of 500,000*l.* is sufficient to defray all the civil expenses of government, I have, in that work annexed the following estimate for any country of the same extent as England.

In the first place, three hundred representatives, fairly elected, are sufficient for all the purposes to which legislation can apply, and preferable to a larger number.

If, then, an allowance, at the rate of 500*l.* per annum be made to every representative, deducting for non-attendance, the expense, if the whole number attended six months each year, would be 75,000*l.*

The official departments could not exceed the following number, with their salaries, *viz.*

Three officers	at	10,000*l.*	each		30,000
Ten ditto	at	5,000	"		50,000
Twenty ditto	at	2,000	"		40,000
Forty ditto	at	1,000	"		40,000
Two hundred ditto	at	500	"		100,000
Three hundred ditto	at	200	"		60,000
Five hundred ditto	at	100	"		50,000
Seven hundred ditto	at	75	"		52,500
					497,500*l.*

If a nation chose, it might deduct four per cent. from all the offices, and make one of twenty thousand pounds per annum, and style the person who should fill it, king or majesty, or give him any other title.

Taking, however, this sum of one million and an half, as an abundant supply for all the expenses of government under any form whatever, there will remain a surplus of nearly six millions and an half out of the present taxes, after paying the interest of the national debt; and I have shown in the second part of the Rights of Man what appears to me, the best mode of applying the surplus money; for I am now speaking of expenses and savings, and not of systems of government.

I have in the first place, estimated the poor rates at two millions annually, and shown that the first effectual step would be to abolish the poor rates entirely (which would be a saving of two millions to the housekeepers,) and to remit four millions out of the surplus taxes to the poor, to be paid to them in money in proportion to the number of children in each family, and the number of aged persons.

I have estimated the number of persons of both sexes in England of fifty years of age and upwards at 420,000, and have taken one third of this number, viz. 140,000 to be poor people.

To save long calculations, I have taken 70,000 of them to be fifty years of age, and under sixty; and the others to be sixty years and upwards; and to allow six pounds per annum to the former class, and ten pounds per annum to the latter. The expense of which will be,

Seventy thousand persons at 6l. per annum   420,000l.

Seventy thousand persons at 10l. per annum   700,000

                                           1,120,000l.

There will then remain of the four millions, two millions eight hundred and eighty thousand pounds. I have stated two different methods of appropriating this money. The one is to pay it in proportion to the number of children in each family at the rate of three or four pounds per annum for each child; the other is to apportion it according to the expense of living in different counties: but in either of these cases it would together with the allowance to be made to the aged, completely take off taxes from one third of all the families in England, besides relieving all the other families from the burden of poor rates.

The whole number of families in England, lotting five souls to each family, is one million four hundred thou and, of which take one third, *viz.* 466,666 to be poor families, who now pay four millions of taxes, and that the poorest pays at least four guineas a-year; and that the other thirteen millions are paid by the other two-thirds. The plan, therefore, as stated in the work, is first, to remit or pay, as is already stated, this sum of four millions to the poor, because it is impossible to separate them from the others in the present mode of collecting taxes on articles of consumption: and, secondly, to abolish the poor rates, the house and window-light tax, and to change the commutation tax into a progressive tax, on large estates, the particulars of all which are set forth in the work.

I will conclude this part of my letter with an extract from the second part of the Rights of Man, which Mr. Dundas (a man rolling in luxury at the expense of the nation) has branded with the epithet of "wicked."

"By the operation of this plan, the poor laws, those instruments of civil torture, will be superseded, and the wasteful expense of litigation prevented. The hearts of the humane will not be shocked by ragged and hungry children, and persons of seventy and eighty years of age, begging for bread. The dying poor will not be dragged from place to place, to breathe their last, as a reprisal of parish upon parish. Widows will have a maintenance for their children, and not be carted away, on the death of their husbands, like culprits and criminals, and children will no longer be considered as increasing the distresses of their parents. The haunts of the wretched will be known, because it will be to their advantage, and the number of petty crimes, the offspring of poverty and distress, will be lessened. The poor, as well as the rich, will then be interested in the support of government, and the cause and apprehension of riots and tumults will cease. Ye, who sit in ease, and solace yourselves in plenty, and such there are in Turkey and Russia, as well as in England, and who say to yourselves, *are we not well off?* have ye thought of these things? when ye do, ye will cease to speak and feel for yourselves alone." Rights of Man, part ii.

After this remission of four millions be made, and the poor rates and houses and window-light tax be abolished, and the commutation tax changed, there will still remain nearly one million and an half of surplus taxes; and as by an alliance between England, France and America, armies and navies will, in a great measure, be rendered unnecessary, and as men who have either been brought up in, or long habited to, those lines of life, are still citizens of a nation in common with the rest, and have a right to participate in all plans of national benefit, it is proposed in that work (Rights of Man, part ii.) to apply annually 507,000*l.* out of the surplus taxes to this purpose, in the following manner:

To fifteen thousand disbanded soldiers, 3s. per week, clear of deductions, during life	117,000*l.*
Additional pay to the remaining soldiers per annum	19,500
To the officers of the disbanded corps, during life, the sum of	117,000
To fifteen thousand disbanded sailors, 3s. per week during life	117,000
Additional pay to the remaining sailors	19,500
To the officers of the disbanded part of the navy, during life	117,000
	507,000*l.*

The limits to which it is proper to confine this letter, will not admit of my entering into further particulars. I address it to Mr. Dundas because he took the lead in the debate, and he wishes, I suppose, to appear conspicuous; but the purport of it is to justify myself from the charge which Mr. Adam has made.

This gentleman, as has been observed in the beginning of this letter, considers the writings of Harrington, More and Hume, as justifiable and legal publications, because they reasoned by comparison, though in so doing they showed plans and systems of government, not only different from, but preferable to, that of England, and he accuses me of endeavoring to confuse, instead of producing a system in the room of that which I had reasoned by comparison of the representative system against the hereditary system; but I have gone further; for I have produced an instance of a government established entirely on the representative system, under which greater happiness is enjoyed, much fewer taxes required, and much higher credit is established, than under the system of government in England. The funds in England have arisen since the war only from 54*l.* to 97*l.* and they have been down since the proclamation, to 87*l.* whereas the funds in America rose in the mean time from 10*l.* to 120*l.*

His charge against me of " destroying every principle of subordination," is equally as groundless; which even a single paragraph from the work will prove, and which I shall here quote :

" Formerly, when divisions arose respecting government, recourse was had to the sword, and a civil war ensued. That savage custom is exploded by the new system, and recourse is had to a national convention. Discussion, and the general will, arbitrates the question, and to this private opinion yields with a good grace, and order is preserved uninterrupted." Rights of Man, part ii.

That two different charges should be brought at the same time, the one by a member of the legislature, for not doing a certain thing, and the other by the attorney-general for doing it, is a strange jumble of contradiction. I have now justified myself, or the work rather, against the first by stating the case in this letter, and the justification of the other will be undertaken in its proper place. But in any case the work will go on.

I shall now conclude this letter, with saying, that the only objection I found against the plan and principles contained in the second part of the Rights of Man when I had written the book, was, that they would beneficially interest at least ninety-nine persons out of every hundred throughout the nation, and therefore would not leave sufficient room for men to act from the direct and disinterested principles of honor; but the prosecution now commenced has fortunately removed that objection, and the approvers and protectors of that work now feel the immediate impulse of honor, added to that of national interest.

I am, Mr. Dundas,

Not your obedient humble servant,

But to the contrary,

THOMAS PAINE.

ADDRESS TO THE ADDRESSERS,

ON THE LATE PROCLAMATION.

ADDRESS TO THE ADDRESSERS.

Could I have commanded circumstances with a wish, I know not of any that would have more generally promoted the progress of knowledge, than the late proclamation, and the numerous rotten-borough and corporation addresses thereon. They have not only served as advertisements, but they have excited a spirit of inquiry into principles of government, and a desire to read the Rights of Man, in places, where that spirit and that work were before unknown.

The people of England, wearied and stunned with parties, and alternately deceived by each, had almost resigned the prerogative of thinking. Even curiosity had expired, and a universal languor had spread itself over the land. The opposition was visibly no other than a contest for power, whilst the mass of the nation stood torpidly by as the prize.

In this hopeless state of things, the first part of the Rights of Man made its appearance. It had to combat with a strange mixture of prejudice and indifference; it stood exposed to every species of newspaper abuse; and besides this, it had to remove the obstructions which Mr. Burke's rude and outrageous attack on the French revolution had artfully raised.

But how easy does even the most illiterate reader distinguish the spontaneous effusions of the heart, from the labored productions of the brain! Truth, whenever it can fully appear, is a thing so naturally familiar to the mind, that an acquaintance commences at first sight. No artificial light, yet discovered, can display all the properties of daylight; so neither can the best invented fiction fill the mind with every conviction which truth begets.

To overthrow Mr. Burke's fallacious book was scarcely the operation of a day. Even the phalanx of placemen and pensioners, who had given the tone to the multitude, by clamoring forth his political fame, became suddenly silent; and the final event to himself has been, that as he rose like a rocket, he fell like the stick.

It seldom happens, that the mind rests satisfied with the simple detection of error or imposition. Once put in motion, *that* motion soon becomes accelerated; where it had intended to stop, it discovers new reasons to proceed, and renews and continues the pursuit far beyond the limits it first prescribed to itself. Thus it has happened to the people of England. From a detection of Mr. Burke's incoherent rhapsodies, and distorted facts, they began an inquiry into the first principles of government, whilst himself, like an object left far behind, became invisible and forgotten.

Much as the first part of the Rights of Man impressed at its first appearance, the progressive mind soon discovered that it did not go far enough. It detected errors; it exposed absurdities; it shook the fabric of political superstition; it generated new ideas; but it did not produce a regular system of principles in the room of those which it displaced. And, if I may guess at the mind of the government party, they beheld it as an unexpected gale that would soon blow over, and they forbore, like sailors in threatening weather, to whistle, lest they should increase the wind. Every thing, on their part, was profound silence.

When the second part of the Rights of Man, *combining principles and practice*, was preparing to appear, they affected, for a while, to act with the same policy as before; but finding their silence had no more influence in stifling the progress of the work, than it would have in stopping the progress of time, they changed their plan, and affected to treat it with clamorous contempt. The speech-making placemen and pensioners, and place expectants, in both houses of parliament, the *outs* as well as *ins*, represented it as a silly, insignificant performance; as a work incapable of producing any effect; as something, which they were sure the good sense of the people would either despise or indignantly spurn; but such was the overstrained awkwardness with which they harangued and encouraged each other, that in the very act of declaring their confidence they betrayed their fears.

As most of the rotten-borough addressers are obscured in holes and corners throughout the country, and to whom a newspaper arrives as rarely as an almanac, they most probably have not had an opportunity of knowing how far this part of the farce (the original prelude to all the addresses) has been acted. For *their* information, I will suspend a while the more serious purpose of my letter, and entertain them with two or three speeches in the last session of parliament, which will serve them for politics till parliament meets again.

You must know, gentlemen, that the second part of the Rights of Man (the part against which you have been presenting addresses, though it is most probable that many of you did not know it) was to have come out precisely at the time that parliament last met. It happened not to be published till a few days after. But as it was well known that the book would shortly appear, the parliamentary orators entered into a very cordial coalition to cry the book down, and they began their attack by crying up the *blessings* of the constitution.

Had it been your fate to have been there, it would have been impossible not to have been moved at the heart-and-pockets-felt congratulations that passed between all the parties on this subject of *blessings;* for the *outs* enjoy places and pensions and sinecures as well as the *ins,* and are as devoutly attached to the firm of the house.

One of the most conspicuous of this motley groupe is the clerk of the court of king's bench, who calls himself lord Stormont. He is also called justice-general of Scotland, and keeper of Scoon, (an opposition man) and he draws from the public for these nominal offices, not less, as I am informed, than six thousand pounds a-year, and he is, most probably, at the trouble of counting the money, and signing a receipt, to show, perhaps, that he is qualified to be clerk as well as justice. He spoke as follows.*

" That *we* shall *all* be unanimous in expressing *our* attachment to the constitution of these realms, *I am confident.*

* See his speech in the Morning Chronicle of Feb. 1.

It is a subject upon which there can be *no* divided opinion *in this house.* I do not pretend to be deep read in the knowledge of the constitution, but I take upon me to say, that from the extent of *my* knowledge [for I have so many thousands a-year for nothing] it appears to *me* that from the period of the revolution, for it was by no means created then, it has been, both in *theory* and *practice*, the *wisest* system that ever was formed. I never was [he means he never was *till now*] a dealer in *political cant.* My life has not been occupied in *that way,* but the speculations of late years *seem to have taken a turn, for which I cannot account.* When I came into public life, the political pamphlets of the time, however they might be charged with the heat and violence of parties, were agreed in extolling the radical beauties of the constitution itself. I remember [he means he has forgotten] a most captivating eulogium on its *charms,* by lord Bolingbroke, where he recommends his readers to contemplate it in all respects, with the assurance that it would be found more estimable the more it was *seen.* I do *not recollect* his precise words, but I wish that men who write upon these subjects would take *this for their model,* instead of the political pamphlets, which, I am told, are now in circulation; [such, I suppose, as the Rights of Man] pamphlets which I have *not read,* and whose purport I know only by *report.* [he means, perhaps, by the *noise* they make] This, however, I am sure, that pamphlets tending to unsettle the public reverence for the constitution, will have very little influence. They can do very little harm; for [by the way, he is no dealer in political cant] *the English are a sober thinking people, and are more intelligent, more solid, more steady in their opinions, than any people I ever had the fortune to see.* [This is pretty well laid on, though, for a new beginner.] But if there should ever come a time when the propagation of those doctrines should agitate the public mind, I am *sure* for *every one* of your lordships, that no attack will be made on the constitution, from which it is truly said that *we* derive *all our* prosperity, without raising *every one* of your lordships to its support. It will then be found that there is no difference among *us,* but that *we* are *all* determined to *stand* or *fall* together, in defence of the inestimable system"—of places and pensions.

After Stormont, on the opposition side, sat down, up rose *another noble lord !* on the ministerial side, Grenville. This man ought to be as strong in the back as a mule, or the *sire* of a mule, or it would crack with the weight of places and offices. He rose, however, without feeling any incumbrance, full master of his weight; and thus said *this* noble lord to *t'other* noble lord!

"The *patriotic* and *manly* manner in which the noble lord has declared *his* sentiments on the subject of the constitution, demands *my cordial* approbation. The noble viscount has *proved*, that however we may differ on *particular measures*, amidst all the jars and dissonance of *parties*, we are unanimous in *principle*. There is a perfect and entire consent [between *us*] in the love and maintenance of the constitution as *happily subsisting*. It must undoubtedly give your lordships *concern*, to find that the *time is come!* [heigh ho!] when there is *propriety* in these expressions of regard to [o! o! o!] THE CONSTITUTION. And that there are men [confound—their—politics] who disseminate doctrines *hostile* to the *genuine spirit* of our *well-balanced system* [it is certainly a well-balanced system when both sides hold places and pensions at once.] I agree with the noble viscount that they have not [I hope] much success. I am convinced that there is no danger to be apprehended from their attempts: but it is *truly* important and *consolatory* [to us placemen, I suppose] to know, that if ever there should arise a serious alarm, there is but one *spirit, one sense* [and that sense I presume is not *common sense*] and *one* determination in *this house*"—which undoubtedly is to hold all their places and pensions as long as they can.

Both those speeches (except the parts enclosed in brackets, which are added for the purpose of *illustration*) are copied *verbatim* from the Morning Chronicle of the 1st of February last; and when the situation of the speakers is considered, the one in the opposition, and the other in the ministry, and both of them living at the public expense, by sinecure, or nominal places and offices, it required a very unblushing front to be able to deliver them. Can those men seriously suppose any nation to be so completely blind as not to see through them? Can Stormont imagine that the *political cant*, with which he has larded his harangue, will conceal the craft? Does he not know that there never was a cover large enough to conceal *itself*? Or can Grenville believe, that his credit with the public increases with his avarice for places?

But, if these orators will accept a service from me, in return for the allusions they have made to the Rights of

Man, I will make a speech for either of them to deliver, on the excellence of the constitution, that shall be as much to the purpose as what they have spoken, or as Bolingbroke's captivating eulogium. Here it is.

" That we shall all be unanimous in expressing our attachment to the constitution, I am confident. It is, my lords, incomprehensibly good : but the great wonder of all is the wisdom ; for it is, my lords, *the wisest system that ever was formed.*

" With respect to us, noble lords, though the world does not know it, it is very well known to us, that we have more wisdom than we know what to do with ; and what is still better, my lords, we have it all in stock. I defy your lordships to prove, that a tittle of it has been used yet ; and if we but go on, my lords, with the frugality we have hitherto done, we shall leave to our heirs and successors, when we go out of the world, the whole stock of wisdom *untouched,* that we brought in ; and there is no doubt but they will follow our example. This, my lords, is one of the blessed effects of the hereditary system ; for we can never be without wisdom so long as we keep it by us, and do not use it.

" But, my lords, as all this wisdom is hereditary property, for the sole benefit of us and our heirs, and it is necessary that the people should know where to get a supply for their own use, the excellence of our constitution has provided us a king for this very purpose, and for *no other.* But, my lords, I perceive a defect to which the constitution is subject, and which I propose to remedy by bringing a bill into parliament for that purpose.

" The constitution, my lords, out of delicacy, I presume, has left it as a matter of *choice* to a king whether he will be wise or not. It has not, I mean, my lords, insisted upon it as a constitutional point, which, I conceive it ought to have done ; for I pledge myself to your lordships to prove, and that with *true patriotic boldness,* that he has *no choice in the matter.* This bill, my lords, which I shall bring in, will be to declare, that the constitution, according to the true intent and meaning thereof, does not invest the king with this choice ; our ancestors were too wise to do that ; and, in order to prevent any doubts that might otherwise arise, I shall prepare, my lords, an enacting clause, to fix the wisdom of kings, by act of parliament ; and then, my lords, our constitution will be the wonder of the world !

" Wisdom, my lords, is the one thing needful; but that there may be no mistake in this matter, and that we may proceed consistently with the true wisdom of the constitution, I shall propose a *certain criterion* whereby the *exact quantity of wisdom* necessary for a king may be known.— [Here should be a cry of—Hear him! Hear him!]

" It is recorded, my lords, in the Statutes at large of the Jews, 'a book, my lords, which I have not read, and whose purport I know only by report,' *but perhaps the bench of bishops can recollect something about it*, that Saul gave the most convincing proofs of royal wisdom before he was made a king, *for he was sent to seek his father's asses and he could not find them.*

" Here, my lords, we have, most happily for us, a case in point: this precedent ought to be established by act of parliament; and every king, before he be crowned, should be sent to seek his father's asses, and if he cannot find them, he shall be declared wise enough to be king, according to the true meaning of our excellent constitution. All, therefore, my lords, that will be necessary to be done, by the enacting clause that I shall bring in, will be to invest the king beforehand with the quantity of wisdom necessary for this purpose, lest he should happen not to possess it; and this, my lords, we can do without making use of any of our own.

" We further read, my lords, in the said Statutes at large of the Jews, that Samuel, who certainly was as mad as any man-of-rights now-a-days, (hear him! hear him!) was displeased, and even exasperated, at the proposal of the Jews to have a king, and he warned them against it with all that assurance and impudence of which he was master. I have been, my lords, at the trouble of going all the way to Paternoster-row, to procure an extract from the printed copy. I was told that I should meet with it there, or in Amen-corner, for I was then going, my lords, to rummage for it among the curiosities of the Antiquarian society. I will read the extract to your lordships, to show how little Samuel knew of the matter.

" The extract, my lords, is from 1 Sam. chap viii.

" ' And Samuel told all the words of the Lord unto the people that asked of him a king.

" ' And he said, This will be the manner of the king that shall reign over you. He will take your sons and appoint them for himself, for his chariots, and to be his horsemen; and some shall run before his chariots.

" ' And he will appoint him captains over thousands, and captains over fifties, and will set them to ear his ground and to reap his harvest, and to make his instruments of war, and instruments of his chariots.

" ' And he will take your daughters to be confectionaries, and to be cooks, and to be bakers.

" ' And he will take your fields, and your vineyards, and your olive-yards, even the best of them, and give them to his servants.

" ' And he will take the tenth of your seed, and of your vineyards, and give to his officers, and to his servants.

" ' And he will take your men-servants, and your maid-servants, and your goodliest young men, and your asses, and put them to his work.

" ' And he will take the tenth of your sheep, and ye shall be his servants.

" ' And ye shall cry out in that day, because of your king, which ye shall have chosen you; and the lord will not hear you in that day.' "

" Now, my lords, what can we think of this man Samuel? Is there a word of truth, or any thing like truth, in all that he has said? He pretended to be a prophet, or a wise man, but has not the event proved him to be a fool, or an incendiary? Look around you, my lords, and see if any thing has happened that he pretended to foretel?— Has not the most profound peace reigned throughout the world ever since kings were in fashion? Are not, for example, the present kings of Europe the most peaceable of mankind, and the empress of Russia the very milk of human kindness? It would not be worth having kings, my lords, if it were not that they never go to war.

" If we look at home, my lords, do we not see the same things here as are seen every where else? Are our young men taken to be horsemen, or foot soldiers, any more than in Germany or in Prussia, or in Hanover or in Hesse? Are not our sailors as safe on land as at sea? Are they ever dragged from their homes, like oxen to the slaughter-house, to serve on board ships of war? When they return from the perils of a long voyage with the merchandize of distant countries, does not every man sit down under his own vine and his own fig-tree, in perfect security? Is the tenth of our seed taken by tax-gatherers, or is any part of it given to the king's servants? In short, *is not every thing as free from taxes as the light from Heaven?*

"Ah! my lords, do we not see the blessed effect of having kings in every thing we look at? Is not the G. R. or the broad R. stamped upon every thing? Even the shoes, the gloves, and the hats that we wear, are enriched with the impression, and all our candles blaze a burnt-offering.

"Besides these blessings, my lords, that cover us from the sole of the foot to the crown of the head, do we not see a race of youths growing up to be kings, who are the very paragons of virtue? There is not one of them, my lords, but might be trusted with untold gold, as safely as the other. Are they not '*more sober, intelligent, more solid, more steady,*' and withal, more learned, more wise, more every thing, than any youths '*we ever had the fortune to see.*' Ah! my lords, they are a *hopeful family.*

"The blessed prospect of succession, which the nation has at this moment before its eyes, is a most undeniable proof of the excellence of our constitution, and of the blessed hereditary system; for nothing, my lords, but a constitution founded on the truest and purest wisdom could admit such heaven-born and heaven-taught characters into the government. Permit me now, my lords, to recal your attention to the libellous chapter I have just read about kings. I mention this, my lords, because it is my intention to move for a bill to be brought into parliament to expunge that chapter from the Bible, and that the lord chancellor, with the assistance of the prince of Wales, the duke of York, and the duke of Clarence, be requested to write a chapter in the room of it; and that Mr. Burke do see that it be truly canonical, and faithfully inserted."—*Finis.*

If the clerk of the court of king's bench should choose to be the author of this luminous encomium on the constitution, I hope he will get it well by heart before he attempts to deliver it, and not have to apologize to parliament, as he did in the case of Bolingbroke's encomium, for forgetting his lesson; and, with this admonition I leave him.

Having thus informed the addressers of what passed at the meeting of parliament, I return to take up the subject at the part where I broke off in order to introduce the preceding speeches.

I was then stating, that the first policy of the government party was silence, and the next, clamorous contempt; but as people generally choose to read and judge for themselves, the work still went on, and the affectation of contempt, like the silence that preceded it, passed for nothing.

Thus foiled in their second scheme, their evil genius, like a will-with-a-wisp, led them to a third; when all at once, as if it had been unfolded to them by a fortune-teller, Mr. Dundas had discovered it by second sight, this once harmless, insignificant book, without undergoing the alteration of a single letter, became a most wicked and dangerous libel. The whole cabinet, like a ship's crew, became alarmed; all hands were piped upon deck, as if a conspiracy of elements was forming around them, and out came the proclamation and the prosecution; and addresses supplied the place of prayers.

Ye silly swains, thought I to myself, why do you torment yourselves thus? The Rights of Man is a book calmly and rationally written; why then are you so disturbed? Did you see how little or how suspicious such conduct makes you appear, even cunning alone, had you no other faculty, would hush you into prudence. The plans, principles, and arguments, contained in that work, are placed before the eyes of the nation, and of the world, in a fair, open, and manly manner, and nothing more is necessary than to refute them. Do this, and the whole is done; but if ye cannot, so neither can ye suppress the reading, nor convict the author; for the law, in the opinion of all good men, would convict itself, that should condemn what cannot be refuted.

Having now shown the addressers the several stages of the business, prior to their being called upon, like Cæsar in the Tyber, crying to Cassius, " *help, Cassius, or I sink!*" I next come to remark on the policy of the government, in promoting addresses; on the consequences naturally resulting therefrom; and on the conduct of the persons concerned.

With respect to the policy, it evidently carries with it every mark and feature of disguised fear. And it will hereafter be placed in the history of extraordinary things, that a pamphlet should be produced by an individual, unconnected with any sect or party, and not seeking to make any, and almost a stranger in the land, that should completely frighten a whole government, and that in the midst of its triumphant security. Such a circumstance cannot fail to prove, that either the pamphlet has irresistible powers, or the government very extraordinary defects, or both. The nation exhibits no signs of fear at the Rights of Man; why then should the government, unless the interest of the two are really opposite to each other, and the secret is beginning to be known? That there are two distinct classes of men in the nation, those who pay taxes, and those who receive and live upon the taxes, is evident at first sight; and when taxation is carried to excess, it cannot fail to disunite those two, and something of this kind is now beginning to appear.

It is also curious to observe, amidst all the fume and bustle about proclamations and addresses, kept up by a few noisy and interested men, how little the mass of the nation seem to care about either. They appear to me, by the indifference they show, not to believe a word the proclamation contains; and as to the addresses, they travel to London with the silence of a funeral, and having announced their arrival in the Gazette, are deposited with the ashes of their predecessors, and Mr. Dundas writes their *hic jacent.*

One of the best effects which the proclamation, and its echo the addresses have had, has been that of exciting and spreading curiosity; and it requires only a single reflection to discover, that the object of all curiosity is knowledge. When the mass of the nation saw that placemen, pensioners, and borough-mongers, were the persons that stood forward to promote addresses, it could not fail to create suspicions that the public good was not their object; that the character of the books, or writings, to which such persons obscurely alluded, not daring to mention them, was directly contrary to what they described them to be, and that it was necessary that every man, for his own satisfaction, should exercise his proper right, and read and judge for himself.

But how will the persons who have been induced to read the Rights of Man, by the clamor that has been raised against it, be surprised to find, that, instead of a wicked, inflammatory work, instead of a licentious and profligate performance, it abounds with principle of governments that are uncontrovertible—with arguments which every reader will feel, are unanswerable—with plans for the increase of commerce and manufactures—for the extinction of war—for the education of the children of the poor—for the comfortable support of the aged and decayed persons of both sexes—for the relief of the army and navy, and, in short, for the promotion of every thing that can benefit the moral, civil and political condition of man.

Why, then, some calm observer will ask, why is the work prosecuted, if these be the goodly matters it contains? I will tell thee, friend; it contains also a plan for the reduction of taxes, for lessening the immense expenses of government, for abolishing places and pensions; and it proposes applying the redundant taxes, that shall be saved by these reforms, to the purposes mentioned in the former paragraph, instead of applying them to the support of idle and profligate placemen and pensioners.

Is it, then, any wonder that placemen and pensioners, and the whole train of court expectants, should become the promoters of addresses, proclamations, and prosecutions? Or, is it any wonder, that corporations and rotten-boroughs, which are attacked and exposed, both in the first and second parts of the Rights of Man, as unjust monopolies and public nuisances, should join in the cavalcade? Yet these are the sources from which addresses have sprung. Had not such persons came forward to oppose the Rights of Man, I should have doubted the efficacy of my own writings: but those opposers have now proved to me, that the blow was well directed, and they have done it justice, by confessing the smart.

The principal deception in this business of addresses has been, that the promoters of them have not come forward in their proper characters. They have assumed to pass themselves upon the public, as a part of the public, bearing a share of the burden of taxes, and acting for the public good; whereas, they are in general that part of it that adds to the public burden, by living on the produce of the public taxes. They are to the public what the locusts are to the tree: the burden would be less, and the prosperity would be greater, if they were shaken off.

"I do not come here," said Onslow, at the Surry county meeting "as the lord lieutenant and custos rotulorum of the county, but I come here as a plain country gentleman." The fact is, that he came there as what he was, and as no other, and consequently he came as one of the class I have been describing. If it be the character of a gentleman to be fed by the public, as a pauper is by the parish, Onslow has a fair claim to the title; and the same description will suit the duke of Richmond, who led the address at the Sussex meeting. He also may set up for a gentleman.

As to the meeting in the next adjoining county (Kent) it was a scene of disgrace. About two hundred persons met, when a small part of them drew privately away from the rest, and voted an address: the consequence of which was that they got together by the ears, and produced a riot in the very act of producing an address to prevent riots.

That the proclamation and the addresses have failed of their intended effect, may be collected from the silence which the government party itself observes. The number of addresses has been weekly retailed in the Gazette; but the number of addressers has been concealed. Several of the addresses have been voted by not more than ten or twelve persons; and a considerable number of them by not more than thirty. The whole number of addresses presented at the time of writing this letter is three hundred and twenty (rotten-boroughs, and corporations included) and even admitting, on an average, one hundred addressers to each address, the whole number of addressers would be but thirty-two thousand, and nearly three months have been taken up in procuring this number. That the success of the proclamation has been less than the success of the work it was intended to discourage, is a matter within my own knowledge; for a greater number of the cheap edition of the first and second parts of the Rights of Man has been sold in the space of one month, than the whole number of addresses (admitting them to be thirty-two thousand) have amounted to in three months.

It is a dangerous attempt in any government to say to a nation, " *thou shalt not read.*" This is now done in Spain, and was formerly done under the old government of France; but it served to procure the downfal of the latter, and is subverting that of the former; and it will have the same tendency in all countries; because *thought* by some means or other, is got abroad in the world, and cannot be restrained though reading may.

If the Rights of Man were a book that deserved the vile description which the promoters of the addresses have given of it, why did not these men prove their charge, and satisfy the people, by producing it, and reading it publicly? This most certainly ought to have been done, and would also have been done, had they believed it would have answered their purpose. But the fact is, that the book contains truths, which those time-servers dreaded to hear, and dreaded that the people should know; and it is now following up the addresses in every part of the nation, and convicting them of falsehoods.

Among the unwarrantable proceedings to which the proclamation has given rise, the meetings of the justices in several of the towns and counties ought to be noticed. Those men have assumed to re-act the farce of general warrants, and to suppress by their own authority, whatever publications they please. This is an attempt at power, equalled only by the conduct of the minor despots of the most despotic governments in Europe, and yet those justices affect to call England a free country. But even this, perhaps, like the scheme for garrisoning the country, by building military barracks, is necessary to awaken the country to a sense of its rights, and, as such, it will have a good effect.

Another part of the conduct of such justices has been, that of threatening to take away the licenses from taverns and public-houses, where the inhabitants of the neighborhood associated to read and discuss the principles of government, and to inform each other thereon. This, again, is similar to what is doing in Spain and Russia; and the reflection which it cannot fail to suggest is, that the principles and conduct of any government must be bad, when that government dreads and startles at discussion, and seeks security by a prevention of knowledge.

If the government, or the constitution, or by whatever name it be called, be that miracle of perfection which the proclamation and the addresses have trumpeted it forth to be, it ought to have defied discussion and investigation, instead of dreading it. Whereas, every attempt it makes, either by proclamation, persecution, or address, to suppress investigation, is a confession that it feels itself unable to bear it. It is error only, and not truth, that shrinks from inquiry. All the numerous pamphlets, and all the newspaper falsehood and abuse, that have been published against the Rights of Man, have fallen before it like pointless arrows; and, in like manner, would any work have fallen before the constitution, had the constitution, as it is called, been founded on as good political principles as those on which the Rights of Man is written?

It is a good constitution for courtiers, placemen, pensioners, borough-holders, and the leaders of parties, and these are the men that have been the active leaders of addresses; but it is a bad constitution for at least ninety-nine parts of the nation out of an hundred, and this truth is every day making its way.

It is bad, first, because it entails upon the nation the unnecessary expense of supporting three forms and systems of government at once, namely the monarchical, the aristocratical, and the democratical.

Secondly, because it is impossible to unite such a discordant composition by any other means than perpetual corruption; and therefore the corruption so loudly and so universally complained of, is no other than the natural consequence of such an unnatural compound of governments; and in this consists that excellence which the numerous herd of placemen and pensioners so loudly extol and which at the same time, occasions that enormous load of taxes under which the rest of the nation groans.

Among the mass of national delusions calculated to amuse and impose upon the multitude, the standing one has been that of flattering them into taxes, by calling the government (or as they please to express it, the English constitution) " *the envy and admiration of the world.*" Scarcely an address has been voted in which some of the speakers have not uttered this hackneyed nonsensical falsehood.

Two revolutions have taken place, those of America and France, and both of them have rejected the unnatural compounded system of the English government; America has declared against all hereditary government, and established the representative system of government only. France has entirely rejected the aristocratical part, and is now discovering the absurdity of the monarchical, and is approaching fast to the representative system. On what ground then, do these men continue a declaration, respecting what they call the *envy and admiration of other nations,* which the voluntary practice of such nations, as have had the opportunity of establishing governments, contradicts and falsifies. Will such men never confine themselves to truth? Will they be for ever the deceivers of the people?

But I will go further, and show, that were government now to begin in England, the people could not be brought to establish the same system they now submit to.

In speaking upon this subject (or on any other) *on the pure ground of principle*, antiquity and precedent cease to be authority, and hoary-headed error loses its effect. The reasonableness and propriety of things must be examined abstractedly from custom and usage; and in this point of view, the right which grows into practice to-day is as much a right, and as old in principle and theory, as if it had the customary sanction of a thousand ages. Principles have no connexion with time, nor characters with names.

To say that the government of this country is composed of king, lords, and commons, is the mere phraseology of custom. It is composed of men; and whoever the men be to whom the government of any country is intrusted, they ought to be the best and wisest that can be found, and if they are not so, they are not fit for the station. A man derives no more excellence from the change of a name, or calling him king, or calling him lord, than I should do by changing my name from Thomas to George, or from Paine to Guelph. I should not be a whit the more able to write a book, because my name was altered; neither would any man, now called a king or a lord, have a whit the more sense than he now has, were he to call himself Thomas Paine.

As to the word "commons," applied as it is in England, it is a term of degradation and reproach, and ought to be abolished. It is a term unknown in free countries.

But to the point. Let us suppose that government was now to begin in England, and that the plan of government, offered to the nation for its approbation or rejection, consisted of the following parts:

1st, That some one individual should be taken from all the rest of the nation, and to whom all the rest should swear obedience, and never be permitted to sit down in his presence, and that they should give him one million sterling a-year. That the nation should never after have power or authority to make laws but with his express consent, and that his sons and his sons' sons, whether wise or foolish, good men or bad, fit or unfit, should have the same power, and also the same money annually paid to them for ever.

2d, That there should be two houses of legislators to assist in making laws, one of which should, in the first instance, be entirely appointed by the aforesaid person, and that their sons and their sons' sons, whether wise or foolish, good men or bad, fit or unfit, should for ever after be hereditary legislators.

3d. That the other house should be chosen in the same manner as the house now called the house of commons is chosen, and should be subject to the control of the two aforesaid hereditary powers in all things.

It would be impossible to cram such a farrago of imposition and absurdity down the throat of this or any other nation, that was capable of reasoning upon its rights and its interest.

They would ask, in the first place, on what ground of right, or on what principle, such irrational and preposterous distinctions could, or ought to be made ; and what pretensions any man could have, or what services he could render, to entitle him to a million a-year? They would go further, and revolt at the idea of consigning their children and their children's children, to the domination of persons hereafter to be born, who might, for any thing they could foresee, turn out to be knaves or fools ; and they would finally discover, that the project of hereditary governors and legislators *was a treasonable usurpation over the rights of posterity.* Not only the calm dictates of reason, and the force of natural affection, but the integrity of manly pride, would impel men to spurn such proposals.

From the grosser absurdities of such a scheme, they would extend their examination to the practical defects ; they would soon see that it would end in tyranny, accomplished by fraud. That in the operation of it, it would be two to one against them, because the two parts that were to be made hereditary, would form a common interest, and stick to each other ; and that themselves and representatives would become no better than hewers of wood and drawers of water for the other parts of the government.— Yet call one of those powers king, the other lords, and the third, the commons, and it gives the model of what is called the English government.

I have asserted, and have shown, both in the first and second parts of the Rights of Man, that there is no such thing as an English constitution, and that the people have yet a constitution to form. *A constitution is a thing antecedent to a government ; it is the act of the people creating a government and giving it powers, and defining the limits and exercise of the powers so given.* But when did the people of

England, acting in their original constituent character, by a delegation elected for that express purpose, declare and say, " *We the people of this land, do constitute and appoint this to be our system and form of government?*" The government has assumed to constitute itself, but it never was constituted by the people, in whom alone the right of constituting resides.

I will here recite the preamble to the federal constitution of the United States of America. I have shown in the second part of the Rights of Man, the manner by which the constitution was formed and afterwards ratified; and to which I refer the reader. The preamble is in the following words:

" WE, THE PEOPLE, of the United States, in order to form a more perfect union, establish justice, insure domestic tranquillity, provide for common defence, promote the general welfare, and secure the blessings of liberty to ourselves and our posterity, DO ORDAIN AND ESTABLISH THIS CONSTITUTION for the United States of America."

Then follow the several articles which appoint the manner in which the several component parts of the government, legislative and executive, shall be elected, and the period of their duration, and the powers they shall have : also, the manner by which future additions, alterations, or amendments, shall be made to the constitution. Consequently, every improvement that can be made in the science of government, follows in that country as a matter of order. It is only in governments founded on assumption and false principles, that reasoning upon, and investigating systems and principles of government, and showing their several excellencies and defects, are termed libellous and seditious. These terms were made part of the charge brought against Locke, Hampden, and Sydney, and will continue to be brought against all good men, so long as bad governments shall continue.

The government of this country has been ostentatiously giving challenges for more than an hundred years past, upon what it called its own excellence and perfection.— Scarcely a king's speech, or a parliamentary speech, has been uttered, in which this glove has not been thrown, till the world has been insulted with their challenges. But it now appears that all this was vapor and vain-boasting, or that it was intended to conceal abuses and defects, and hush the people into taxes. I have taken the challenge.

up, and in behalf of the public have shown, in a fair, open, and candid manner, both the radical and practical defects of the system; when, lo! those champions of the civil list have fled away, and sent the attorney-general to deny the challenge, by turning the acceptance of it into an attack, and defending their places and pensions by a prosecution.

I will here drop this part of the subject, and state a few particulars respecting the prosecution now pending, by which the addressers will see that they have been used as tools to the prosecuting party and their dependants. The case is as follows:

The original edition of the first and second part of the Rights of Man, having been expensively printed (in the modern style of printing pamphlets, that they might be bound up with Mr. Burke's reflections on the French revolution,) the high price precluded the generality of people from purchasing; and many applications were made to me from various parts of the country to print the work in a cheaper manner. The people of Sheffield requested leave to print two thousand copies for themselves, with which request I immediately complied. The same request came to me from Rotherham, from Leicester, from Chester, from several towns in Scotland; and Mr. James Mackintosh, author of Vindiciæ Galliciæ, brought me a request from Warwickshire, for leave to print ten thousand copies in that county. I had already sent a cheap edition to Scotland; and finding the applications increase, I concluded that the best method of complying therewith, would be to print a very numerous edition in London, under my own direction, by which means the work would be more perfect, and the price be reduced lower than it could be by printing small editions in the country, of only a few thousands each.

The cheap edition of the first part was begun about the middle of last April, and from that moment, and not before, I expected a prosecution, and the event has proved that I was not mistaken. I had then occasion to write to Mr. Thomas Walker of Manchester, and after informing him of my intention of giving up the work for the purpose of general information, I informed him of what I apprehended would be the consequence; that while the work was at a price that precluded an extensive circulation, the government party, not able to controvert the plans, arguments, and principles it contained, had chosen to remain silent;

but that I expected they would make an attempt to deprive the mass of the nation, and especially the poor, of the right of reading, by the pretence of prosecuting either the author or the publisher, or both. They chose to begin with the publisher.

Nearly a month, however, passed, before I had any information given me of their intentions. I was then at Bromley, in Kent, upon which I came immediately to town (May 14) and went to Mr. Jordan, the publisher of the original edition. He had that evening been served with a summons, to appear at the court of king's bench on the Monday following, but for what purpose was not stated. Supposing it to be on account of the work, I appointed a meeting with him on the next morning, which was accordingly had, when I provided an attorney, and took the expense of the defence on myself. But finding afterwards that he absented himself from the attorney employed, and had engaged another, and that he had been closeted with the solicitors of the treasury, I left him to follow his own choice, and he chose to plead guilty. This he might do if he pleased; and I make no objection against him for it. I believe that his idea by the word *guilty*, was no other than declaring himself to be the publisher, without any regard to the merits or demerits of the work; for were it to be construed otherwise, it would amount to the absurdity of converting a publisher into a jury, and his confession into a verdict upon the work itself. This would be the highest possible refinement upon packing of juries.

On the 21st of May, they commenced their prosecution against me as the author, by leaving a summons at my lodgings in town, to appear at the court of king's bench on the 8th of June, following; and on the same day (May 21) *they issued also their proclamation.* Thus the court of St. James and the court of king's bench, were playing into each other's hands at the same instant of time, and the farce of addresses brought up the rear; and this mode of proceeding is called by the prostituted name of law. Such a thundering rapidity, after a ministerial dormancy of almost a year and an half, can be attributed to no other cause than their having gained information of the forwardness of the cheap edition, and the dread they felt at the progressive increase of political knowledge.

I was strongly advised by several gentlemen, as well those in the practice of the law, as others, to prefer a bill of indictment against the publisher of the proclamation, as a publication tending to influence, or rather to dictate the verdict of a jury on the issue of a matter then pending; but it appeared to me much better to avail myself of the opportunity which such a precedent justified me in using, by meeting the proclamation and the addresses on their own ground, and publicly defending the work which had been thus unwarrantably attacked and traduced. And conscious as I now am, that the work entitled, Rights of Man, so far from being, as has been maliciously or erroneously represented, a false, wicked and seditious libel, is a work abounding with unanswerable truths, with principles of the purest morality and benevolence, and with arguments not to be controverted. Conscious, I say, of these things, and having no object in view but the happiness of mankind, I have now put the matter to the best proof in my power, by giving to the public a cheap edition of the first and second parts of that work. Let every man read and judge for himself, not only of the merits or demerits of the work, but of the matters therein contained, which relate to his own interest and happiness.

If, to expose the fraud and imposition of monarchy, and every species of hereditary government; to lessen the oppression of taxes; to propose plans for the education of helpless infancy, and the comfortable support of the aged and distressed; to endeavor to conciliate nations to each other; to extirpate the horrid practice of war; to promote universal peace, civilization, and commerce; and to break the chains of political superstition, and raise degraded man to his proper rank;—if these things be libellous, let me live the life of a libeller, and let the name of *libeller* be engraved on my tomb.

Of all the weak and ill-judged measures which fear, ignorance, or arrogance could suggest, the proclamation, and the project for addresses are the two worst. They served to advertise the work which the promoters of those measures wished to keep unknown; and in doing this they offered violence to the judgment of the people, by calling on them to condemn what they forbad them to know; and put the strength of their party to that hazardous issue that prudence would have avoided. The county meeting for Middlesex was attended by only one hundred and eighteen addressers. They, no doubt, expected, that thousands would flock to their standard, and clamor against the

Rights of Man. But the case most probably is, that men are not so blind to their rights and their interests, as governments believe.

Having thus shown the extraordinary manner in which the government party commenced their attack, I proceed to offer a few observations on the prosecution, and on the mode of trial by special jury.

In the first place, I have written a book; and if it cannot be refuted, it cannot be condemned. But I do not consider the prosecution as particularly levelled against me, but against the general right, or the right of every man, of investigating systems and principles of government, and showing their several excellencies or defects. If the press be free only to flatter government, as Burke has done, and to cry up and extol what certain court sycophants are pleased to call a "glorious constitution," and not free to examine into its errors or abuses, or whether a constitution really exist or not, such freedom is no other than that of Spain, Turkey or Russia; and a jury in this case, would not be a jury to try, but an inquisition to condemn.

I have asserted, and by fair and open argument maintained, the right of every nation at all times to establish such a system and form of government for itself as best accords with its disposition, interest and happiness; and to change and alter it as it sees occasion. Will any jury deny to the nation this right? If they do, they are traitors, and their verdict would be null and void. And if they admit the right, the means must be admitted also; for it would be the highest absurdity to say, that the right existed, but the means did not. The question then is, What are the means by which the possession and exercise of this national right are to be secured? The answer will be, that of maintaining, inviolably, the right of investigation; for investigation always serves to detect error, and to bring forth truth.

I have, as an individual, given my opinion upon what I believe to be not only the best, but the true system of government, which is the representative system, and I have given reasons for that opinion.

1st, Because in the representative system, no office of very extraordinary power, or extravagant pay, is attached to any individual; and consequently there is nothing to excite those national contentions and civil wars, with which countries under monarchical governments are frequently convulsed, and of which the history of England exhibits such numerous instances.

2d, Because the representative is a system of government always in maturity ; whereas monarchical government fluctuates through all the stages, from nonage to dotage.

3d, Because the representative system admits of none but men, properly qualified, into the government, or removes them if they prove to be otherwise. Whereas in the hereditary system, a nation may be encumbered with a knave or an ideot for a whole life-time, and not be benefited by a successor.

4th. Because there does not exist a right to establish hereditary government; or, in other words, hereditary successors ; because hereditary government always means a government yet to come, and the case always is, that those who are to live afterwards have the same right to establish government for themselves, as the people had who lived before them ; and, therefore, all laws attempting to establish hereditary government, are founded on assumption and political fiction.

If these positions be truths, and I challenge any man to prove the contrary ; if they tend to instruct and enlighten mankind, and to free them from error, oppression, and political superstition, which are the objects I have in view in publishing them, that jury would commit an act of injustice to their country, and to me, if not an act of perjury, that should call them *false*, *wicked*, and *malicious*.

Dragonetti, in his treatise, On Virtues and Rewards, has a paragraph worthy of being recorded in every country in the world—" The science, (says he) of the politician, consists in fixing the true point of happiness and freedom. Those men deserve the gratitude of ages, who should discover a mode of government that contained the greatest sum of *individual happiness* with the least *national expense.*" But if juries are to be made use of to prohibit inquiry, to suppress truth, and to stop the progress of knowledge, this boasted palladium of liberty becomes the most successful instrument of tyranny.

Among the arts practised at the bar, and from the bench, to impose upon the understanding of a jury, and to obtain a verdict where the consciences of men could not otherwise consent, one of the most successful has been that of calling truth a libel, and of insinuating, that the words "falsely, wickedly, and maliciously," though they are made the formidable and high sounding part of the charge, are not matters for consideration with a jury. For what purpose, then, are they retained, unless it be for that of imposition and wilful defamation?

I cannot conceive a greater violation of order, nor a more abominable insult upon morality, and upon human understanding, than to see a man sitting in the judgment seat, affecting by an antiquated foppery of dress to impress the audience with awe; then causing witnesses and jury to be sworn to truth and justice, himself having officially sworn the same; then causing to be read a prosecution against a man, charging him with having *wickedly and maliciously written and published a certain false, wicked and seditious book*; and having gone through all this with a show of solemnity, as if he saw the eye of the Almighty darting through the roof of the building like a ray of light, turn in an instant, the whole into a farce, and in order to obtain a verdict that could not otherwise be obtained, tell the jury that the charge of *falsely, wickedly, and seditiously*, meant nothing, that *truth* was out of the question; and that whether the person accused spoke truth or falsehood, or intended *virtuously or wickedly*, was the same thing; and finally conclude the wretched inquisitorial scene, by stating some antiquated precedent, equally as abominable as that which is then acting; or giving some opinion of his own, and *falsely calling the one and the other—law*. It was, most probably, to such a judge as this, that the most solemn of all reproofs was given—" *The Lord will smite thee, thou whitened wall.*"

I now proceed to offer some remarks on what is called a special jury. As to what is called a special verdict, I shall make no other remark upon it, than that it is in reality *not* a verdict. It is an attempt on the part of the jury to delegate, or of the bench to obtain, the exercise of that right, which is committed to the jury only.

With respect to special juries, I shall state such matters as I have been able to collect, for I do not find any uniform opinion concerning the mode of appointing them.

In the first place, the mode of trial is but of modern invention, and the origin of it, as I am told, is as follows:

Formerly, when disputes arose between merchants, and were brought before a court, the case was that the nature of their commerce, and the method of keeping merchants' accounts not being sufficiently understood by persons out of their own line, it became necessary to depart from the common mode of appointing juries, whose *practical knowledge* would enable them justly to decide upon the case. From this introduction, special juries became more general, but some doubts having arisen as to their legality, an act was passed in the 3d of George II. to establish them as legal, and also to extend them to all cases, not only between individuals, but in cases where *the government itself should be the prosecutor.* This most probably gave rise to the suspicion so generally entertained of packing a jury; because by this act, when the crown as it is called, is the prosecutor, the master of the crown-office, who holds his office under the crown, is the person who either wholly nominates, or has great power in nominating the jury, and therefore it has greatly the appearance of the prosecuting party selecting a jury.

The process is as follows:

On motion being made in court, by either the plaintiff or defendant, for a special jury, the court grants it or not, at its own discretion.

If it be granted, the solicitor of the party that applied for the special jury, gives notice to the solicitor of the adverse party, and a day and hour are appointed for them to meet at the office of the master of the crown-office. The master of the crown-office sends to the sheriff or his deputy, who attends with the sheriff's book of freeholders. Forty-eight names are taken, and a copy thereof given to each of the parties; and on a future day, notice is again given, and the solicitors meet a second time, and each strikes out twelve names. The list being thus reduced from forty-eight to twenty-four, the first twelve that appear in court and answer to their names, is the special jury for that cause. The first operation, that of taking the forty-eight names, is called nominating the jury; and the reducing them to twenty-four is called striking the jury.

Having thus stated the general process, I come to particulars; and the first question will be, how are the forty-eight names, out of which the jury is to be struck, obtained from the sheriff's book? For herein lies the principle ground of suspicion, with respect to what is understood by packing of juries.

Either they must be taken by some rule agreed upon between the parties, or by some common rule known and established beforehand, or at the discretion of some person, who, in such a case, ought to be perfectly disinterested in the issue, as well officially as otherwise.

In the case of merchants, and in all cases between individuals, the master of the office, called the crown-office, is officially an indifferent person, and as such may be a proper person to act between the parties, and present them with a list of forty-eight names, out of which each party is to strike twelve. But the case assumes an entire difference of character, when the government itself is the prosecutor. The master of the crown-office is then an officer holding his office under the prosecutor; and it is therefore no wonder, that the suspicion of packing juries should, in such cases, have been so prevalent.

This will apply with additional force, when the prosecution is commenced against the author or publisher of such works as treat of reforms, and of the abolition of superfluous places and offices, &c. because in such cases every person holding an office, subject to that suspicion, becomes interested as a party; and the office, called the crown-office, may, upon examination, be found to be of this description.

I have heard it asserted, that the master of the crown-office is to open the sheriff's book as it were per hazard, and take thereout forty-eight *following* names, to which the word merchant or esquire is affixed. The former of these are certainly proper, when the case is between merchants, and has reference to the origin of the custom, and to nothing else. As to the word esquire, every man is an esquire who pleases to call himself esquire; and the sensible part of mankind are leaving it off. But the matter for inquiry is, whether there be any existing law to direct the mode by which the forty-eight names shall be taken, or whether the mode be merely that of custom which the office has created; or whether the selection of the forty-eight be wholly at the discretion and choice of the master of the crown-office? One or other of the two latter appears to be the case, because the act already mentioned, of the 3d of George II. lays down no rule or mode, nor refers to any preceding law—but says only, that special juries shall hereafter be struck, " *in such manner as special juries have been and are usually struck.* "

This act appears to have been what is generally understood by a " *deep take in.* " It was fitted to the spur of the moment in which it was passed, 3d of George II. when parties ran high, and it served to throw into the hands of Walpole, who was then minister, the management of juries in crown prosecutions, by making the nomination of the forty-eight persons, from whom the jury was to be struck, follow the precedent established by custom between individuals, and by this means it slipped into practice with less suspicion. Now, the manner of obtaining special juries through the medium of an officer of the government, such, for instance, as a master of the crown-office, may be impartial in the case of merchants, or other individuals, but it becomes highly improper and suspicious in cases where the government itself is one of the parties. And it must, upon the whole, appear a strange inconsistency, that a government should keep one officer to nominate the forty-eight persons from whom the jury is to be struck, both of whom are *officers of the civil list*, and yet continue to call this by the pompous name of *the glorious right of trial by jury!*

In the case of the king against Jordan, for publishing the Rights of Man, the attorney-general moved for the appointment of a special jury, and the master of the crown-office nominated the forty-eight persons himself, and took them from such part of the sheriff's book as he pleased.

The trial did not come on, occasioned by Jordan withdrawing his plea; but if it had, it might have afforded an opportunity of discussing the subject of special juries; for though such discussion might have had no effect in the court of king's bench it would, in the present disposition for inquiry, have had a considerable effect upon the country; and in all national reforms, this is the proper point to begin at. Put a country right, and it will soon put government right. Among the improper things acted by the government in the case of special juries, on their own motion, one has been that of treating the jury with a dinner, and afterwards giving each juryman two guineas, if a verdict be found for the prosecution, and only one if otherwise; and it has been long observed, that in London and Westminster there are persons who appear to make a trade of serving, by being so frequently seen upon special juries.

Thus much for special juries. As to what is called a *common jury*, upon any government prosecution against the author or publisher of the Rights of Man, during the time of the *present sheriffry*, I have one question to offer, which is, *whether the present sheriffs of London, having publicly prejudged*

*the case, by the part they have taken in procuring an address
from the county of Middlesex, (however diminutive and insignificant the number of addressers were, being only one hundred and
eighteen) are eligible or proper persons to be intrusted with the
power of returning a jury to try the issue of any such prosecution.*

But the whole matter appears, at least to me, to be worthy of a more extensive consideration than what relates to
any jury, whether special or common; for the case is,
whether any part of a whole nation, locally selected as a
jury of twelve men always is, be competent to judge and
determine for the whole nation, on any matter that relates
to systems and principles of government, and whether it
be not applying the institution of juries to purposes for
which such institutions were not intended? For example,

I have asserted, in the work Rights of Man, that as every
man in the nation pays taxes, so has every man a right to
a share in government, and consequently that the people
of Manchester, Birmingham, Sheffield, Leeds, Halifax, &c.
have the same right as those of London. Shall then twelve
men, picked out between Temple-bar and Whitechapel, because the book happened to be first published there, decide upon the rights of the inhabitants of those towns, or
of any other town or village in the nation?

Having thus spoken of juries, I come next to offer a few
observations on the matter contained in the information or
prosecution.

The work, Rights of Man, consists of part the first, and
part the second. The first the prosecutor has thought it
most proper to let alone; and from the second part he has
selected a few short paragraphs, making in the whole not
quite two pages of the same printing as in the cheap edition. Those paragraphs relate chiefly to certain facts,
such as the revolution of 1688, and the coming of George
I. commonly called of the house of Hanover, or the
house of Brunswick, or some such house. The arguments,
plans and principles contained in the work, the prosecutor
has not ventured to attack. They are beyond his reach.

The act which the prosecutor appears to rest most upon
for the support of the prosecution, is the act, entitled "An
act, declaring the rights and liberties of the subject and
settling the succession of the crown," passed in the first
year of William and Mary, and more commonly known
by the name of the "bill of rights."

I have called this bill " *A bill of wrongs and of insult.*"
My reasons, and also my proofs, are as follow :

The method and principle which this bill takes for declaring rights and liberties, are in direct contradiction to rights and liberties ; it is an assumed attempt to take them wholly from posterity—for the declaration in the said bill is as follows :

" The lords spiritual and temporal, and commons, do, in *the name of all the people,* most humbly and faithfully *submit themselves, their heirs, and posterity forever ;*" that is, to William and Mary his wife, their heirs and successors. This is a strange way of declaring rights and liberties. But the parliament who made this declaration in the name, and on the part of the people, had no authority from them for so doing ; and with respect to *posterity for ever,* they had no right or authority whatever in the case. It was assumption and usurpation. I have reasoned very extensively against the principle of this bill, in the first part of the Rights of Man ; the prosecutor has silently admitted that reasoning, and he now commences a prosecution on the authority of the bill, after admitting the reasoning against it.

It is also to be observed, that the declaration in this bill, abject and irrational as it is, had no other intentional operation than against the family of the Stuarts, and their abettors. The idea did not then exist, that in the space of an hundred years, posterity might discover a different and much better system of government, and that every species of hereditary government might fall as popes and monks had fallen before. This, I say, was not then thought of, and therefore the application of the bill, in the present case, is a new, erroneous, and illegal application, and is the same as creating a new bill *ex post facto.*

It has ever been the craft of courtiers, for the purpose of keeping up an expensive and enormous civil list, and a mummery of useless and antiquated places and offices at the public expense, to be continually hanging England upon some individual or other, called *king,* though the man might not have capacity to be a parish constable. The folly and absurdity of this, is appearing more and more every day ; and still those men continue to act as if no alteration in the public opinion had taken place. They hear each other's nonsense, and suppose the whole nation talks the same gibberish.

Let such men cry up the house of Orange, or the house of Brunswick, if they please. They would cry up any other house if it suited their purpose, and give as good reasons for it. But what is this house, or that house, or any other house to a nation? "*For a nation to be free, it is sufficient that she wills it.*" Her freedom depends wholly upon herself, and not on any house, nor on any individual. I ask not in what light this cargo of foreign houses appears to others, but I will say in what light it appears to me. It was like the trees of the forest, saying unto the bramble, come thou and reign over us.

Thus much for both their houses. I now come to speak of two other houses, which are also put into the information, and those are the house of lords, and the house of commons. Here, I suppose, the attorney-general intends to prove me guilty of speaking either truth or falsehood; for, according to the modern interpretation of libels, it does not signify which, and the only improvement necessary to show the complete absurdity of such doctrine, would be, to prosecute a man for uttering a most *false and wicked truth.*

I will quote the part I am going to give, from the office copy, with the attorney-general's innuendoes, enclosed in parentheses, as they stand in the information, and I hope that civil list officer will caution the court not to laugh when he reads them, and also to take care not to laugh himself.

The information states, That *Thomas Paine, being a wicked, malicious, seditious, and evil disposed person, hath, with force and arms, and most wicked cunning, written and published a certain false, scandalous, malicious, and seditious libel; in one part thereof, to the tenor and effect following, that is to say :*

"With respect to the two houses, of which the English parliament (*meaning the parliament of this kingdom*) is composed, they appear to be effectually influenced into one, and, as a legislature, to have no temper of its own. The minister (*meaning the minister employed by the king of this realm, in the administration of the government thereof*) whoever he, at any time may be, touches *it* (*meaning the two houses of parliament of this kingdom*) as with an opium wand, and *it* (*meaning the two houses of parliament of this kingdom*) sleeps obedience. As I am not malicious enough to disturb their repose, though it be time they should awake, I leave the two houses and the attorney-general, to the enjoyment of their dreams, and proceed to a new subject."

The gentlemen, to whom I shall next address myself, are those who have styled themselves "*friends of the people*," holding their meeting at the Freemason's tavern, London.

One of the principal members of this society, is Mr. Grey, who, I believe, is also one of the most independent members in parliament. I collect this opinion from what Mr. Burke formerly mentioned to me, rather than from any knowledge of my own. The occasion was as follows:

I was in England at the time the bubble broke forth about Nootka Sound; and the day after the king's message, as it is called, was sent to parliament; I wrote a note to Mr. Burke, that upon the condition the French revolution should not be a subject (for he was then writing the book I have since answered) I would call on him the next day, and mention some matters I was acquainted with, respecting the affair; for it appeared to me extraordinary, that any body of men, calling themselves representatives, should commit themselves so precipitately, or, " sleep obedience," as parliament was then doing, and run a nation into expense, and, perhaps a war, without so much as inquiring into the case, or the subject, of both which I had some knowledge.

When I saw Mr. Burke, and mentioned the circumstances to him, he particularly spoke of Mr. Grey, as the fittest member to bring such matters forward; for, said Mr. Burke, "*I am not the proper person to do it, as I am in a treaty with Mr. Pitt about Mr. Hastings' trial.*" I hope the attorney-general will allow, that Mr. Burke was then *sleeping his obedience.* But to return to the society.

I cannot bring myself to believe, that the general motive of this society is any thing more than that by which every former parliamentary opposition has been governed, and by which the present is sufficiently known. Failing in their pursuit of power and place within doors, they have now (and that in not a very mannerly manner) endeavored to possess themselves of that ground out of doors, which, had it not been made by others, would not have been made by them. They appear to me to have watched, with more cunning than candor, the progress of a certain publication, and when they saw it had excited a spirit of inquiry, and was rapidly spreading, they stepped forward to profit by the opportunity, and Mr. Fox *then* called it a libel. In saying this, he libelled himself. Politicians of this cast, such, I mean, as those who trim between parties, and lie by for events, are to be found in every country, and it never yet happened that they did not do more harm than good. They embarrass business, fritter it to nothing, perplex the people, and the event to themselves generally is, that they go just far enough to make enemies of the few, without going far enough to make friends of the many.

Whoever will read the declarations of this society, of the 25th of April, and 5th of May, will find a studied reserve upon all the points that are real abuses. They speak not once of the extravagance of government, of the abominable list of unnecessary and sinecure places and pensions, of the enormity of the civil list, of the excess of taxes, nor of any one matter that substantially affects the nation; and from some conversation that has passed in that society, it does not appear to me that it is any part of their plan, to carry this class of reforms into practice. No opposition party ever did, when it gained possession.

In making these free observations, I mean not to enter into contention with this society; their incivility towards me is what I should expect from place-hunting reformers. They are welcome, however, to the ground they have advanced upon, and I wish that every individual among them may act in the same upright, uninfluenced, and public spirited manner that I have done. Whatever reforms may be obtained, and by whatever means, they will be for the benefit of others, and not of me. I have no other interest in the cause than the interest of my heart. The part I have acted has been wholly that of a volunteer, unconnected with party; and when I quit, it shall be as honorably as I began.

I consider the reform of parliament, by an application to parliament, as proposed by the society, to be a worn out hacknied subject, about which the nation is tired, and the parties are deceiving each other. It is not a subject that is cognizable before parliament, because no government has a right to alter itself, either in whole or in part. The right, and the exercise of that right, appertains to the nation only, and the proper means is by a national convention, elected for the purpose, by all the people. By this, the will of the nation whether to reform or not, or what the reform shall be, or how far it shall extend, will be known.

and it cannot be known by any other means. Partial addresses, or separate associations, are not testimonies of the general will.

It is, however, certain, that the opinions of men, with respect to systems and principles of government, are changing fast in all countries. The alteration in England, within the space of little more than a year, is far greater than could have been believed, and it is daily and hourly increasing. It moves along the country with the silence of thought. The enormous expense of government, has provoked men to think, by making them feel; and the proclamation has served to increase jealousy and disgust. To prevent, therefore, those commotions which too often and too suddenly arise from suffocated discontents, it is best that the general WILL should have the full and free opportunity of being publicly ascertained and known.

Wretched as the state of representation is in England, it is every day becoming worse, because the unrepresented parts of the nation are increasing in population and property, and the represented parts are decreasing. It is, therefore, no ill grounded estimation to say, that as not one person in seven is represented, at least fourteen millions of taxes, out of the seventeen millions, are paid by the unrepresented part; for although copyholds and leaseholds are assessed to the land tax, the holders are unrepresented. Should then a general demur take place as to the obligation of paying taxes, on the ground of not being represented, it is not the representatives of rotten-boroughs, nor special juries, that can decide the question. This is one of the possible cases that ought to be foreseen, in order to prevent the inconveniencies that might arise to numerous individuals, by provoking it.

I confess I have no idea of petitioning for rights. Whatever the rights of people are, they have a right to them, and nobody has a right either to withhold them, or to grant them. Government ought to be established on such principles of justice as to exclude the occasion of all such applications; for wherever they appear, they are virtually accusations.

I wish that Mr. Grey, since he has embarked in the business, would take the whole of it into consideration. He will then see, that the right of reforming the state of the representation does not reside in parliament, and that the only motion he could consistently make would be, that parliament should *recommend* the election of a convention of the people, because all pay taxes. But whether parliament recommended it or not, the right of the nation would neither be lessened nor increased thereby.

As to petitions from the unrepresented part, they ought not to be looked for. As well might it be expected that Manchester, Sheffield, &c. should petition the rotten-boroughs, as that they should petition the representatives of those boroughs. Those two towns alone pay far more taxes than all the rotten-boroughs put together, and it is scarcely to be expected they should pay their court either to the boroughs, or the borough-mongers.

It ought also to be observed, that what is called parliament, is composed of two houses that have always declared against the right of each other to interfere in any matter that related to the circumstances of either, particularly that of election. A reform, therefore in the representation cannot, on the ground they have individually taken, become the subject of an act of parliament, because such a mode would include the interference, against which the commons on their part have protested; but must, as well on the ground of formality, as on that of right, proceed from a national convention.

Let Mr. Grey or any other man, sit down and endeavor to put his thoughts together, for the purpose of drawing up an application to parliament for a reform of parliament, and he will soon convince himself of the folly of the attempt. He will find that he cannot get on; that he cannot make his thoughts join, so as to produce any effect; for whatever formality of words he may use, they will unavoidably include two ideas directly opposed to each other; the one in setting forth the reasons, the other in praying for relief, and the two when placed together, would stand thus : " *The representation in parliament is so very corrupt, that we can no longer confide in it,—and therefore, confiding in the justice and wisdom of parliament, we pray,*" &c.

The heavy manner in which every former proposed application to parliament has dragged, sufficiently shows, that though the nation might not exactly see the awkwardness of the measure, it could not clearly see its way, by those means. To this also may be added another remark, which is, that the worse parliament is, the less will be the inclination to petition it. This indifference, viewed as it ought to be, is one of the strongest censures the public express. It is as if they were to say to them, "Ye are not worth reforming."

Let any man examine the court-calendar of placemen in both houses, and the manner in which the civil list operates, and he will be at no loss to account for this indifference and want of confidence on one side, nor of the opposition to reforms on the other.

Who would have supposed that Mr. Burke, holding forth as he formerly did against secret influence, and corrupt majorities, should become a concealed pensioner? I will now state the case, not for the little purpose of exposing Mr. Burke, but to show the inconsistency of any application to a body of men, more than half of whom, as far as the nation can at present know, may be in the same case with himself.

Towards the end of lord North's administration, Mr. Burke brought a bill into parliament, generally known by the name of Mr. Burke's reform bill; in which, among other things, it is enacted, "That no pension exceeding the sum of three hundred pounds a-year, shall be granted to any one person, and that the whole amount of the pensions granted in one year shall not exceed six hundred thousand pounds;" a list of which, "together with the *names of the persons* to whom the same are granted, shall be laid before parliament in twenty days after the beginning of each session, until the whole pension list shall be reduced to ninety thousand pounds." A provisory clause is afterwards added, "That it shall be lawful for the first commissioner of the treasury, to return into the exchequer, any pension or annuity, *without a name*, on his making oath that such pension or annuity is not directly or indirectly for the benfit, use, or behoof of any member of the house of commons."

But soon after that administration ended, and the party Mr. Burke acted with, came into power, it appears from the circumstances I am going to relate, that Mr. Burke became himself a pensioner in disguise; in a similar manner, as if a pension had been granted in the name of John Nokes to be privately paid to and enjoyed by Tom Stiles. The name of Edmund Burke does not appear in the original transaction: but after the pension was obtained, Mr. Burke wanted to make the most of it at once, by selling or mortgaging it; and the gentleman, in whose name the pension stands, applied to one of the public offices for that purpose. This unfortunately brought forth the name of *Edmund Burke*, as the real pensioner of 1,500*l.* per annum. When men trumpet forth what they call the blessings of the constitution, it ought to be known what sort of blessings they allude to.

As to the civil list, of a million a-year, it is not to be supposed that any one man can eat, drink, or consume the whole upon himself. The case is, that above half the sum is annually apportioned among courtiers, and court members of both houses, in places and offices, altogether insignificant and perfectly useless, as to every purpose of civil, rational, and manly government. For instance,

Of what use in the science and system of government, is what is called a lord chamberlain, a master and mistress of the robes, a master of the horse, a master of the hawks, and an hundred other such things? Laws derive no additional force, nor additional excellence from such mummery.

In the disbursements of the civil list for the year 1786 (which may be seen in Sir John Sinclair's History of the Revenue) are four separate charges for this mummery office of chamberlain:

1st,	-	-	-	-	-	33,770*l.*	17*s.*	—
2d,	-	-	-	-	-	3,000	—	—
3d,	-	-	-	-	-	24,069	19	—
4th,	-	-	-	-	-	10,000	19	3*d.*

75,849*l.*	14*s.*	3*d.*

Besides 1,110*l.* charged for alms.

From this sample the rest may be guessed at. As to the master of the hawks (there are no hawks kept, and if there were, it is no reason the people should pay the expense of feeding them, many of whom are put to it to get bread for their children) his salary is 1,372*l.* 10*s.*

And besides a list of items of this kind, sufficient to fill a quire of paper, the pension lists alone are 107,404*l.* 13*s.* 4*d.* which is a greater sum than all the expenses of the federal government in America amount to.

Among the items, there are two, that I had no expectation of finding, and which, in this day of inquiry after civil list influence, ought to be exposed. The one is an annual payment of one thousand seven hundred pounds to the dissenting ministers in England, and the other, eight hundred pounds to those in Ireland.

'This is the fact, and the distribution, as I am informed, is as follows : the whole sum of 1,700*l.* is paid to one person, a dissenting minister in London, who divides it among eight others; and those eight among such others as they please. The lay-body of the dissenters, and many of their principal ministers, have long considered it as dishonorable and have endeavored to prevent it, but still it continues to be secretly paid; and as the world has sometimes seen very fulsome addresses from parts of that body, it may naturally be supposed that the receivers, like bishops and other court-clergy, are not idle in promoting them. How the money is distributed in Ireland, I know not.

To recount all the secret history of the civil list, is not the intention of this publication. It is sufficient in this place to expose its general character, and the mass of influence it keeps alive. It will necessarily become one of the objects of reform ; and therefore enough is said to show, that under its operation, no application to parliament can be expected to succeed, nor can consistently be made.

Such reforms will not be promoted by the party that is in possession of those places, nor by the opposition who are waiting for them ; and as to a *mere reform*, in the state of the representation, under the idea that another parliament, differently elected from the present, but still a component third part of the same system, and subject to the control of the other two parts, will abolish those abuses, is altogether delusion; because it is not only impracticable on the ground of formality, but is unwisely exposing another set of men to the same corruptions that have tainted the present.

Were all the objects that require a reform accomplishable by a mere reform in the state of representation, the persons who compose the present parliament might, with rather more propriety be asked to abolish all the abuses themselves, than be applied to as the mere instruments of doing it by a future parliament. If the virtue be wanting to abolish the abuse, it is also wanting to act as the means, and the nation must, from necessity, proceed by some other plan.

Having thus endeavored to show what the abject condition of parliament is, and the impropriety of going a second time over the same ground that has before miscarried, I come to the remaining part of the subject.

There ought to be, in the constitution of every country, a mode of referring back, on any extraordinary occasion, to the sovereign and original constituent power, which is the nation itself. The right of altering any part of a government, cannot, as already observed, reside in the government, or that government might make itself what it pleased.

It ought also to be taken for granted, that though a nation may feel inconveniencies, either in the excess of taxation, or in the mode of expenditure, or in any thing else, it may not at first be sufficiently assured in what part of its government the defect lies, or where the evil originates. It may be supposed to be in one part, and on inquiry be found to be in another; or partly in all. This obscurity is naturally interwoven with what are called mixed governments.

Be, however, the reform to be accomplished whatever it may, it can only follow in consequence of obtaining a full knowledge of all the causes that have rendered such reform necessary, and every thing short of this is guess-work or frivolous cunning. In this case, it cannot be supposed that any application to parliament can bring forward this knowledge. The body is itself the supposed cause, or one of the supposed causes, of the abuses in question; and cannot be expected, and ought not to be asked, to give evidence against itself. The inquiry, therefore, which is of necessity the first step in the business, cannot be trusted to parliament, but must be undertaken by a distinct body of men, separated from every suspicion of corruption or influence.

Instead, then, of referring to rotten-boroughs and absurd corporations for addresses, or hawking them about the country to be signed by a few dependant tenants, the real and effectual mode would be to come at once to the point, and to ascertain the sense of the nation by electing a national convention. By this method, as already observed, the general WILL, whether to reform or not, or what the reform shall be, or how far it shall extend, will be known, and it cannot be known by any other means. Such a body, empowered and supported by the nation, will have authority to demand information upon all matters necessary to be inquired into; and no minister, nor any person, will dare to refuse it. It will then be seen whether seventeen millions of taxes are necessary, and for what purposes they are expended. The concealed pensioners will then be obliged to unmask; and the source of influence and corruption, if any such there be, will be laid open to the nation, not for the purpose of revenge, but of redress.

By taking this public and national ground, all objections against partial addresses on the one side, or private associations on the other, will be done away, *the nation will declare its own reforms;* and the clamor about party and faction, or ins or outs, will become ridiculous.

The plan and organization of a convention is easy in practice.

In the first place, the number of inhabitants in every county can be sufficiently ascertained, from the number of houses assessed to the house and window-light tax in each county. This will give the rule for apportioning the number of members to be elected to the national convention in each of the counties.

If the total number of inhabitants in England be seven millions, and the total number of members to be elected to the convention be one thousand, the number of members to be elected in a county, containing one hundred and fifty thousand inhabitants, will be twenty-one, and in like proportion for any other county.

As the election of a convention must, in order to ascertain the general sense of the nation, go on grounds different from that of parliamentary elections, the mode that best promises this end will have no difficulties to combat with from absurd customs and pretended rights. The right of every man will be the same, whether he lives in a city, a town, or a village. The custom of attaching rights to *place,* or in other words to inanimate matter, instead of to *persons,* independently of place, is too absurd to make any part of a rational argument.

As every man in the nation, of the age of twenty-one years, pays taxes, either out of the property he possesses, or out of the product of his labor, which is property to him; and is amenable in his own person to every law of the land; so has every one the same equal right to vote, and no one part of a nation, nor any individual, has a right to dispute the right of another. The man who should do this, ought to forfeit the exercise of his *own* right for a term of years. This would render the punishment consistent with the crime.

When a qualification to vote is regulated by years, it is placed on the firmest possible ground; because the qualification is such, as nothing but dying before the time can take away; and the equality of rights, as a principle, is recognized in the act of regulating the exercise. But when rights are placed upon, or made dependant upon property, they are on the most precarious of all tenures; " Riches make themselves wings, and fly away," and the rights fly with them; and thus they become lost to the man when they would be of most value.

It is from a strange mixture of tyranny and cowardice, that exclusions have been set up and continued. The boldness to do wrong at first, changes afterwards into cowardly craft, and at last into fear. The representatives in England appear now to act as if they were afraid to do right, even in part, lest it should awaken the nation to a sense of all the wrongs it has endured. This case serves to show, that the same conduct that best constitutes the safety of an individual, namely, a strict adherence to principle, constitutes also the safety of a government, and that without it safety is but an empty name. When the rich plunder the poor of his rights, it becomes an example to the poor to plunder the rich of his property; for the rights of the one are as much property to him, as wealth is property to the other, and the *little all* is as dear as the *much.*

It is only by setting out on just principles that men are trained to be just to each other; and it will always be found, that when the rich protect the rights of the poor, the poor will protect the property of the rich. But the guarantee, to be effectual, must be parliamentarily reciprocal.

Exclusions are not only unjust, but they frequently operate as injuriously to the party who monopolizes, as to those who are excluded. When men seek to exclude others from participating in the exercise of any right, they should, at least, be assured, that they can effectually perform the whole of the business they undertake; for unless they do this, themselves will be losers by the monopoly. This has been the case with respect to the monopolized right of election. The monopolizing party has not been able to keep the parliamentary representation, to whom the power of taxation was entrusted, in the state it ought to have been, and have thereby multiplied taxes upon themselves equally with those who were excluded.

A great deal has been, and will continue to be said, about disqualifications, arising from the commission of offences; but were this subject urged to its full extent, it would disqualify a great number of the present electors, together with their representatives; for, of all offences, none are more destructive to the morals of society than bribery and corruption. It is, therefore, civility to such persons to pass this subject over, and to give them a fair opportunity of recovering, or rather of creating character.

Every thing, in the present mode of electioneering in England, is the reverse of what it ought to be, and the vulgarity that attends elections is no other than the natural consequence of inverting the order of the system.

In the first place, the candidate seeks the elector, instead of the elector seeking for a representative; and the electors are advertised as being in the interest of the candidate, instead of the candidate being in the interest of the electors. The candidate pays the elector for his vote, instead of the nation paying the representative for his time and attendance on public business. The complaint for an undue election is brought by the candidate; as if he, and not the electors, were the party aggrieved; and he takes on himself at any period of the election, to break it up, by declining, as if the election was in his right and not in theirs.

The compact that was entered into at the last Westminster election between two of the candidates (Mr. Fox and lord Hood) was an indecent violation of the principles of election. The candidates, assumed, in their own persons, the rights of the electors; for it was only in the body of the electors, and not at all in the candidates, that the right of making any such compact or compromise could exist. But the principle of election and representation is so completely done away, in every stage thereof, that inconsistency has no longer the power of surprising.

Neither from elections thus conducted, nor from rotten-borough addressers, nor from county meetings, promoted by placemen and pensioners, can the sense of the nation be known. It is still corruption appealing to itself. But a convention of a thousand persons, fairly elected, would bring every matter to a decided issue.

As to county meetings, it is only persons of leisure, or those who live near to the place of meeting, that can attend, and the number on such occasions is but like a drop in the bucket compared with the whole. The only consistent service which such meetings could render, would be that of apportioning the county into convenient districts, and when this is done, each district might, according to its number of inhabitants, elect its quota of county members to the national convention; and the vote of each elector might be taken in the parish where he resided, either by ballot or by voice, as he should choose to give it.

A national convention thus formed, would bring together the sense and opinions of every part of the nation, fairly taken. The science of government, and the interest of the public, and of the several parts thereof would then, undergo an ample and rational discussion, freed from the language of parliamentary disguise.

But in all deliberations of this kind, though men have a right to reason with, and endeavor to convince each other, upon any matter that respects their common good, yet, in point of practice, the majority of opinions, when known, forms a rule for the whole, and to this rule every good citizen practically conforms.

Mr. Burke, as if he knew (for every concealed pensioner has the opportunity of knowing) that the abuses acted under the present system, are too flagrant to be palliated, and that the majority of opinions, whenever such abuses should be made public, would be for a general and effectual reform, has endeavored to preclude the event, by sturdily denying the right of a majority of a nation to act as a whole. Let us bestow a thought upon this case.

When any matter is proposed as a subject for consultation, it necessarily implies some mode of decision. Common consent, arising from absolute necessity, has placed this in a majority of opinions; because without it there can be no decision, and consequently no order. It is perhaps the only case in which mankind however various in their ideas upon other matters, can consistently be unanimous; because it is a mode of decision derived from the primary original right of every individual concerned; *that* right being first individually exercised in giving an opinion, and whether that opinion shall arrange with the minority or the majority, is a subsequent accidental thing that neither increases nor diminishes the individual original right itself. Prior to any debate, inquiry or investigation, it is not supposed to be known on which side the majority of opinions will fall, and therefore whilst this mode of decision secures to every one the right of giving an opinion, it admits to every one an equal chance in the ultimate event.

Among the matters that will present themselves to the consideration of a national convention, there is one, wholly of a domestic nature, but so marvellously loaded with confusion, as to appear at first sight, almost impossible to be reformed. I mean the condition of what is called law.

But, if we examine into the cause from whence this confusion, now so much the subject of universal complaint, is produced, not only the remedy will immediately present itself, but with it, the means of preventing the like case hereafter.

In the first place, the confusion has generated itself from the absurdity of every parliament assuming to be eternal in power, and the laws partake in a similar manner of this assumption. They have no period of legal or natural expiration; and, however absurd in principle, or inconsistent in practice, many of them have become, they still are, if not especially repealed, considered as making a part of the general mass. By this means the body of what is called law, is spread over a space of *several hundred years*, comprehending laws obsolete, laws repugnant, laws ridiculous, and every other kind of laws forgotten or remembered; and what renders the case still worse, is, that the confusion multiplies with the progress of time.*

To bring this misshapen monster into form, and to prevent its lapsing again into a wilderness state, only two things, and those very simple, are necessary.

The first is, to review the whole mass of laws, and to bring forward such only as are worth retaining, and let all the rest drop; and to give to the laws so brought forward a new era, commencing from the time of such reform.

Secondly, that at the expiration of every twenty-one years (or any other stated period) a like review shall again be taken, and the laws, found proper to be retained, be again carried forward, commencing with that date, and the useless laws dropped and discontinued.

By this means there can be no obsolete laws, and scarcely such a thing as laws standing in direct or equivocal contradiction to each other, and every person will know the period of time to which he is to look back for all the laws in being.

* In the time of Henry IV. a law was passed, making it felony " to multiply gold or silver, or to make use of the craft of multiplication," and this law remained two hundred and eighty-five years upon the statute books. It was then repealed as being ridiculous and injurious.

It is worth remarking that whilst every other branch of science is brought within some commodious system, and the study of it simplified by easy methods, the laws take the contrary course, and become every year more complicated, entangled, confused, and obscure.

Among the paragraphs which the attorney-general has taken from the Rights of Man, and put into his information, one is, that where I have said, " that with respect to regular law, there is *scarcely such a thing.*"

As I do not know whether the attorney-general means to show this expression to be libellous, because it is *true*, or because it is *false*, I shall make no other reply to him in this place, than by remarking, that if almanac-makers had not been more judicious than law-makers, the study of almanacs would by this time have become as abstruse as the study of the law, and we should hear of a library of almanacs as we now do of statutes; but by the simple operation of letting the obsolete matter drop, and carrying forward that only which is proper to be retained, all that is necessary to be known, is found within the space of a year, and laws also admit of being kept within some given period.

I shall here close this letter, so far as it respects the addressers, the proclamation, and the prosecution; and shall offer a few observations to the society, styling itself " The Friends of the People."

That the science of government is beginning to be better understood than in former times, and that the age of fiction and political superstition, and of craft and mystery is passing away, are matters which the experience of every day proves to be true, as well in England as in other countries.

As therefore it is impossible to calculate the silent progress of opinion, and also impossible to govern a nation after it has changed its habits of thinking, by the craft or policy that it was governed by before, the only true method to prevent popular discontents and commotions is, to throw, by every fair and rational argument, all the light upon the subject that can possibly be thrown; and at the same time, to open the means of collecting the general sense of the nation; and this cannot, as already observed, be done by any plan so effectually as a national convention. Here individual opinion will quiet itself by having a centre to rest upon.

The society already mentioned (which is made up of men of various descriptions, but chiefly of those called Foxites) appears to me, either to have taken wrong grounds from want of judgment, or to have acted with cunning reserve. It is now amusing the people with a new phrase, namely, that of " a temperate and moderate reform," the interpretation of which is, *a continuance of the abuses as long as possible. If we cannot hold all let us hold some.*

Who are those that are frightened at reforms? Are the public afraid that their taxes should be lessened too much? Are they afraid that sinecure places and pensions should be abolished too fast? Are the poor afraid that their condition should be rendered too comfortable? Is the worn-out mechanic, or the aged and decayed tradesman, frightened at the prospect of receiving ten pounds a-year out of the surplus taxes? Is the soldier frightened at the thoughts of his discharge, and three shillings per week during life? Is the sailor afraid that press-warrants will be abolished? The society mistakes the fears of borough-mongers, placemen and pensioners, for the fears of the people; and the *temperate and moderate reform* it talks of, is calculated to suit the condition of the former.

Those words, " temperate and moderate," are words either of political cowardice, or of cunning, or seduction. A thing, moderately good, is not so good as it ought to be. Moderation in temper, is always a virtue; but moderation in principle, is a species of vice. But who is to be the judge of what is a temperate and moderate reform? The society is the representative of nobody; neither can the unrepresented part of the nation commit this power to those in parliament, in whose election they had no choice; and therefore, even upon the ground the society has taken, recourse must be had to a national convention.

The objection which Mr. Fox made to Mr. Grey's proposed motion for a parliamentary reform was, that it contained no plan. It certainly did not. But the plan very easily presents itself; and whilst it is fair for all parties, it prevents the dangers that might otherwise arise from private or popular discontent.

THOMAS PAINE.

This special edition of

COMMON SENSE

AND

RIGHTS OF MAN

by Thomas Paine

Film was prepared from an 1824 edition. The
book was printed and bound by Von Hoffmann Corp.